AGRARIAN SOCIALISM IN AMERICA

Agrarian Socialism in America

*Marx, Jefferson, and Jesus
in the Oklahoma Countryside, 1904–1920*

JIM BISSETT

UNIVERSITY OF OKLAHOMA PRESS : NORMAN

Library of Congress Cataloging-in-Publication Data

Bissett, Jim, 1957–
  Agrarian socialism in America: Marx, Jefferson, and Jesus in the Oklahoma countryside, 1904–1920 / Jim Bissett.
    p. cm.
  Includes bibliographical references.
  ISBN 978-0-8061-3427-7 (paper)
  1. Socialism—Oklahoma—History—20th century. 2. Oklahoma—Politics and government—20th century. 3. Socialist Party of Oklahoma. 4. Indiahoma Farmers' Union. I. Title.
  HX1.05B57   1999
  335'.009766—dc21   99-12917
                                                                  CIP

The paper in this book meets the guidelines for permanence and durability of the Committee on Production Guidelines for Book Longevity of the Council on Library Resources, Inc. ∞

Copyright © 1999 by the University of Oklahoma Press, Norman, Publishing Division of the University. Manufactured in the U.S.A. Paperback published 2002.

All rights reserved. No part of this publication may be reproduced, stored in a retrieval system, or transmitted, in any form or by any means, electronic, mechanical, photocopying, recording, or otherwise—except as permitted under Section 107 or 108 of the United States Copyright Act—without the prior written permission of the University of Oklahoma Press.

For Sheree

Contents

List of Illustrations	ix
List of Tables	xi
Preface and Acknowledgments	xiii
Introduction	3
1. Farmers and Sooners: Life in the Promised Land	9
2. Experimenting in Collective Action: The Indiahoma Farmers' Union, 1904–1906	20
3. Coercion and Co-optation: The Demise of the Indiahoma Farmers' Union, 1906–1907	40
4. The Remaking of the Socialist Party of Oklahoma, 1907–1912	58
5. "The Real Gospel of Christ": The Religion of Socialism in Oklahoma	85
6. Power and Insurgency: Democrats and the Socialist Movement, 1910–1916	105
7. The Politics of Crisis: The Destruction of the Socialist Party of Oklahoma, 1917–1920	142
8. Uncertain Legacy: Visible Failures and Hidden Achievements	174

Appendices:

A. A Comment on the Success of Crop Withholding   187

B. Selected Listing of Prominent Oklahoma Socialist Ministers   193

Notes   195

Bibliographical Essay   231

Index   245

Illustrations

PHOTOGRAPHS

1.	H. M. Sinclair	81
2–5.	Illustrations from the Socialist Party of Oklahoma's Campaign Book, 1916	110–11
6.	Patrick S. Nagle	112
7.	H. H. Stallard	117
8.	Oklahoma's First Socialist Legislative Group	128

MAPS

1.	Oklahoma and Indian Territories, 1906	19
2.	Strong Socialist Counties, 1912–1914	125

Tables

1. Tenure of Farmers in Oklahoma, 1900–1935   11
2. Tenancy Rates in Selected Oklahoma Counties, 1910   12
3. Oklahoma Election Returns, 1907 and 1908   59
4. Election Returns in Selected Counties, 1910 and 1912   123
5. Socialists Elected to County and Local Offices, 1904–1913   124
6. Election Returns in Selected Strong Socialist Precincts, Contest for Representative, 1914   127
7. Tenancy Rates and the Primary Election of 1916   138
8. Election Returns, Contest for President in Selected Counties, 1912 and 1916   140
9. Election Returns in Selected Counties, 1916 and 1918   166
10. Voter Turnout in Selected Counties, 1916 and 1918   167
11. Election Returns in Selected Counties, 1916–1920   173
12. Cotton Prices Received by Oklahoma Farmers, 1895–1920   188
13. Cotton Prices in Southern States, 1900–1910   189

Preface and Acknowledgments

The first two decades of the twentieth century stand out as the golden age of American socialism. These were years when the American socialist movement could claim as its own such respected members of society as Helen Keller, Upton Sinclair, Jack London, Sinclair Lewis, Jane Addams, and John Reed. It was a time when one of the country's most beloved figures, Eugene Debs, was the socialist standard bearer in national elections, and when hundreds of thousands of Americans subscribed to the socialist weekly, the *Appeal to Reason*. Between 1900 and 1920, socialist elected officials held the balance of political power in dozens of American cities, from Milwaukee to Schenectady, even serving in the U.S. Congress.

Through these years of socialist relevance, the state of Oklahoma supported the most vigorous, ambitious, and fascinating socialist movement of all. This book is about the surprising success of the Socialist Party in Oklahoma, where between 1907 and 1920 the organization successfully elected its candidates to a myriad of state and local offices.

Given such a level of success, it is not surprising that the story of the Socialist Party of Oklahoma has been told by other interpreters. It has been the subject of at least three books—James Green's *Grass-Roots Socialism*, Garin Burbank's *When Farmers Voted Red*, and John Thompson's *Closing the Frontier*—and at least as many dissertations.[1] I am indebted to these scholars for the careful and valuable work they have done; this book relies heavily on their efforts. Yet, as I hope will become clear in the pages that follow, my work differs from previous interpretations in significant ways.

It is striking that despite the Oklahoma socialist movement's position as one of the largest in the United States, previous studies portray Sooner socialists as fatally flawed. Ultimately, Oklahoma Party members are depicted as less legitimate, somehow less "socialist," than their comrades in the more traditional socialist strongholds of Wisconsin, New York, or Illinois. Consider, for example, Irving Howe's comments on the subject from his work on American socialism: "To many people, including some who don't identify themselves as socialists, Southwestern socialism may still seem admirable as an expression of downtrodden people asserting their humanity—a response that is surely right. But it must also be said that Southwestern socialism didn't really offer much in the way of analyzing American society or grasping the distinctive traits of American politics. The fundamentalist cast of mind, in politics as elsewhere, can rarely accommodate the problematic or the complex."[2] It is hard to miss in these words Howe's deep-seated, almost visceral suspicion that Party members from locations such as Oklahoma were not legitimate socialists.

Although scholars of Oklahoma socialism do not approach their topic with this level of antagonism, of the three mentioned above Burbank comes closest to matching Howe's distrust of the movement. Indeed, the Oklahoma Socialist Party's inherent flaws become integral to his argument in *When Farmers Voted Red*. In three crucial chapters—"The Gospel According to Local Socialists," "The Land Question," and "Local Socialists and 'Nigger' Equality"—Burbank measures Oklahoma comrades on issues central to the movement and finds them wanting. In his conclusion he calls into question the validity of the movement itself: "The absence of any strongly manifested collective memory of socialism among the people who had lived in the rural areas where the movement had flourished for a brief time suggests that that particular form of 'socialism' had indeed only been a transitory moment in the harried lives of southwestern tenant farmers."[3]

Green provides a less disparaging interpretation of the Socialist Party of Oklahoma in *Grass-Roots Socialism*, for he is willing to admit evidence of true class consciousness among the faithful. Yet this recognition comes with an important disclaimer, which in itself represents a challenge to the legitimacy of Oklahoma socialists. The comrades in Oklahoma, he implies, were successful because they were such good pupils, internalizing the wisdom brought to them by outside socialist experts and applying that wisdom to the Sooner State. Green describes in glowing terms Oklahoma socialists heeding the advice of "real" socialists from outside the state. But when they disregard the advice of these experts, he portrays them as troublesome and "individualistic." At such times, Green asserts, the farmers who supported the Party "expressed a consciousness that was more petty bourgeois than proletarian."[4] For Green the Oklahoma Socialist Party's success was a function of its willingness to adopt the values and arguments of the urban-based national socialist movement.

Herein lies a crucial difference between my work and those that have preceded it. A central premise of this book is that Oklahoma socialists were no more or less "legitimate" than their comrades in other locations. They did not have to remake themselves into the image of Party members in Milwaukee or New York in order to claim their rightful place in the American socialist movement. Whenever Oklahoma socialists took positions that were distinct from those of other American socialists, their divergence was not the result of inherent character flaws that made them poor Marxists. Rather, socialists in Oklahoma were simply demonstrating their proficiency at adapting the socialist message into a form consistent with life in the Sooner State.

At the root of many interpreters' reluctance to accept the premise that Oklahoma Party members were bona fide socialists lies a thinly veiled anti-agrarian bias. Most scholars of the Oklahoma socialist movement unconsciously bring to their subject a set of cultural preconceptions that Oklahoma socialists themselves would have found to be alien. In practice, such a bias directly affects, among other things, these scholars' interpretation of the origins of Oklahoma socialism. Both Green and Burbank assume that national socialist organizers schooled in the labor movement brought socialism to Oklahoma farmers on their southwestern organizing tours. The result is deeply ironic; this view ignores the rich tradition of agrarian insurgency that is intrinsic to the story of the Oklahoma socialist movement. Socialists in the Sooner State drew upon a deep and complex tradition of agricultural social movements—a legacy stretching back to Populism that was as rich as the labor movement, but that carried its own lessons and assumptions. This book attempts to deepen our understanding of Oklahoma socialism by grounding it in the agricultural reform movement.

The point here is hardly academic, for it has a direct bearing on the conclusions drawn by Burbank, Green, and Thompson. The tendency to question the legitimacy of the Oklahoma movement results from a failure to incorporate this rich tradition of agrarian insurgency and its resulting collective experience into the story of the Oklahoma Socialist Party. As a result, we are denied vital details, and these omissions alter the narrative in significant ways. For example, Oklahoma socialists are often portrayed as behaving in irrational or unsophisticated ways, not because they *were* irrational or unsophisticated, but because our knowledge of socialists' behavior is incomplete. Only by incorporating the agrarian tradition into the Oklahoma socialist experience and thereby considering Oklahoma farmers on their own terms will it be possible to appreciate that experience in all its complexity.

Although scholarship may seem to be a solitary enterprise, in reality it is a communal exercise, and I am pleased to acknowledge the members of the community whose contributions made this work possible.

While I disagree with some of the conclusions drawn by Burbank, Green, and Thompson, I have a deep appreciation for their achievements. I was captivated by their work early in my career, and I am grateful to them for introducing me to the story of Oklahoma socialism.

Of course, I owe a great debt of gratitude to numerous librarians and archivists for making the raw materials of history available to me. The staffs at Duke University's Perkins Library, the Western History Collections at the University of Oklahoma, the Oklahoma Historical Society, and the Oklahoma State Archives were, without exception, helpful, courteous, and professional. The interlibrary loan librarians at Elon College—especially Teresa LePors and Ruth Brown—always worked hard to find the sources I requested, no matter how obscure.

The late Mary Moran, who oversaw the newspaper collection at the Oklahoma Historical Society, deserves special mention. In addition to helping me locate and use socialist newspapers, she took me under her wing on those lonely days away from home on research trips to Oklahoma.

I still remember a small act of kindness by the staff at the Oklahoma Conference of the Pentecostal Holiness Church. On a hot, busy summer day when I arrived unannounced, they provided access to their records, gave me a place to work, and even offered me lunch.

I am grateful for financial assistance provided by Duke University, the National Endowment for the Humanities, and the Faculty Research and Development Committee at Elon College. These funds made possible three research trips to Oklahoma.

I am also grateful to the numerous friends and colleagues who read portions of this book in draft form. Among them are my fellow American historians at Elon College, Clyde Ellis, Mary Jo Festle, and Nancy Midgette; fellow travelers in graduate school, Chuck Bolton, Tracy Campbell, and Jon Sensbach; and of course my colleague and mentor, Larry Goodwyn. Their comments invariably strengthened the manuscript. I owe a special debt of gratitude to Mary Ellis for creating the maps that appear in the book. The staff at the University of Oklahoma Press—especially Randolph Lewis (now at the University of Science and Arts of Oklahoma), Ursula

Daly, and Alice Stanton—were always gracious and helpful as I worked through the complicated process of turning a manuscript into a book. Patricia Heinicke, Jr., who copyedited the manuscript, provided an especially careful reading. I greatly appreciate her efforts, which helped make this work clearer and more effective.

Throughout this process my daughters, Emily and Caroline, always helped me to see what was really important in life. Finally, I am most grateful to my wife, Sheree, without whom this book would not have been possible. I dedicate it to her with love and appreciation.

AGRARIAN SOCIALISM IN AMERICA

Introduction

It comes as something of a surprise that the strongest state expression of socialism in the United States occurred, not in the urban citadels of the American working class, but in the remote towns and hamlets of rural Oklahoma.[1] There, in the first two decades of the twentieth century, a remarkable movement emerged that successfully elected its candidates to a myriad of state and local offices. In many areas of the state, socialists surpassed Republicans as the Democratic Party's most potent challengers for political office, and between 1914 and 1917 the Socialist Party of Oklahoma was without question a major political force in the Sooner State. Although the Party's demise during the war years was rapid, for a brief and singular moment political leaders in Oklahoma confronted the prospect of sharing power with the Socialist Party.

Why was the Sooner State, of all places, more hospitable to Marxian socialism than any other state in America? Economic reasons are an indisputable factor. But, although the severe agricultural crisis that gripped the South during the early twentieth century provided the context for socialist success, it provides only part of the explanation. The twin evils of low crop prices and high credit costs consigned most Oklahoma farmers to a life of poverty and indebtedness, and many responded to this plight by turning to the Socialist Party. Yet difficult conditions prevailed throughout the South, and in no other southern state did a mature socialist movement emerge on a scale even approaching Oklahoma's. The question, therefore, must become a bit more precise. Given the economic hard times endured by millions of farmers throughout America, why did Oklahomans alone respond by mounting an organized, effective movement to fundamentally restructure the institutions of capitalist society?

The answer to this question lies in the unique qualities that Oklahoma socialists brought to their party. My task in the pages that follow is to make these qualities visible among the scores of events and developments constituting the historical phenomenon known as Oklahoma socialism. While an understanding of the complex and fascinating world in which the Oklahoma socialists operated is necessary in order to fully explain why their movement was so successful, it may be helpful here to outline briefly the principal components of that understanding.

One elemental characteristic of the movement deserves primary consideration, for it suffuses the other explanations for the Party's success. Most Oklahoma socialists had participated in other social movements prior to joining the Party, coming into the organization as experienced activists. With such experience came important lessons in movement building, and socialists in the Sooner State naturally applied these lessons to their party. As a result, the Oklahoma Socialist Party drew upon a critical mass of extraordinarily gifted social activists who understood better than most how to conduct the tactical campaigns necessary to win political battles.

This vital core of Oklahoma socialists came into the Party having internalized important lessons learned in the late nineteenth century in the Farmers Alliance, lessons refined through participation in a later agrarian movement, the Farmers' Union. Organized in 1902 as a conscious attempt to recapture the cooperative spirit of the Farmers Alliance, the Farmers' Union quickly spread northward from Texas into the Oklahoma and Indian territories, the region that in 1907 became the state of Oklahoma. Following the decline of the Farmers' Union after 1907, many of its members migrated into the Socialist Party. Clearly, these socialists were extraordinarily skilled as social activists, and their practical experience in the agrarian movement brought great vitality to the Party.

In a very real sense, then, the Oklahoma Socialist Party benefitted from two generations of activism; the insights of the Populist movement, filtered through the lessons learned in the Farmers' Union, enriched the ability of the Party to affect fundamental change in society. As a result, the rise and fall of the Farmers' Union in the territories becomes a crucial part of the Oklahoma socialist experience.

A second important ingredient in the Oklahoma socialists' success is intimately related to their experience in the Farmers Alliance and the Farmers' Union. Because of their previous efforts to reform the institutions of commercial agriculture, these activists possessed unparalleled sophistication in their understanding of that system. Indeed, the knowledge of agricultural issues among the party faithful in the Sooner State was deepened by the Jeffersonian perspective of the Alliance, eclipsing the national socialist debate on such questions. While socialists elsewhere were mired in discussion over whether those farmers who owned land could be legitimate members of the working class, Party members in Oklahoma perfected a reasoned and effective attack on the system of commercial agriculture that was dominant in early twentieth-century America. Grounded in the life experiences of its members and drawing upon Jefferson's emphasis on the farmer's "natural right" to the land, the Oklahoma Party's analysis of commercial agriculture was far more sophisticated, and far more damning, than the conventional wisdom emanating from national socialist leaders.[2] In the pages that follow, the process by which small farmers in the Oklahoma Socialist Party succeeded in redefining their organization's position on agricultural issues assumes central importance.

These ideological and tactical advances resulted from genuine dialogue between the leadership and the rank and file, pointing to yet another crucial attribute of the Oklahoma Party. Through their experience in other social movements, Oklahoma socialists developed a set of democratic principles and expectations, which they applied to their new organization. In the process, participants in the Oklahoma socialist movement attempted to create a kind of working democracy, where organizational authority was exercised according to the demands of the membership. And to an extent not generally reached by American political parties, they succeeded.

Indeed, if we are to understand the success of Oklahoma socialism, we must redefine the way we think of politics and political activism. The prevailing model, in which organizational leaders and intellectuals become responsible for the movement's successes while the rest of the membership does little more than respond to direction from above, no longer suffices.[3] Oklahoma Party members did not allow themselves to be diminished in this way, and we must search for more accurate images in describing their movement. They understood the pitfalls of movement building because they had participated in the rise and fall of previous movements.

Knowledge gained in this way brings with it a sense of urgency and a feeling of empowerment. Oklahoma socialists possessed both. As a result, in a crucial sense they created the Oklahoma Socialist Party, forcing it to conform to their expectations. In practice, the forms it took at times became cumbersome, as members insisted on participating in organizational decision making. Democratic forms are inherently disorderly, and the Oklahoma movement was no exception. But ironically, the very source of this disorder—the heightened degree to which participants claim ownership in the movement—also brings great power. And the socialist movement in Oklahoma was exceptionally powerful.

Finally, the explanation for Oklahoma activists' success includes another sort of redefinition. Party members in the Sooner State came to understand that the message of socialism would not succeed as long as it remained an alien doctrine expressed in terms unfamiliar to its intended constituency. As they searched for a way of conceptualizing the truths of Marxism that would be consistent with the life experiences of small farmers, Oklahoma socialists seized upon the deep communitarian components embedded in the evangelical Christian tradition. A dominant cultural folkway in the Oklahoma countryside, evangelical Protestantism was a tradition they knew well. Employing the powerful cultural form of Christianity to help express socialist ideas, Party members in Oklahoma transformed both the gospel of Christ and the gospel of socialism. While retaining the Marxist core of the socialist message, activists in the Sooner State presented that message in a form that was instantly recognizable to virtually all of its potential constituents.

Here are the essentials that comprise the Oklahoma socialist movement. Through their experiences in the Farmers Alliance and the Farmers' Union, many Oklahoma socialists had learned valuable lessons in conducting the campaigns necessary to change the institutions of society. They presented a clear and concise indictment of the existing agricultural system, grounded firmly in past movements and in the life experiences of small farmers. They demanded that their organization and their leaders behave in democratic ways. And they knew how to present the ideas of Marxism in a cultural form that made sense in the Oklahoma countryside.

Inherent in the experience of Oklahoma socialists, in fact, was the joining of three important political and cultural traditions: (1) the Jeffersonian emphasis on the common man, the dignity of labor, and the importance of the land, brought by the Alliance and the Farmers' Union into the twentieth century; (2) the scathing indictment of capitalism set down by Karl Marx and brought to America by his disciples; and (3) the evangelical Protestant tradition that had been central to the American experience since the Great Revival of the early nineteenth century. In the hands of Oklahoma Party members, this concoction proved to be both relevant and powerful. The Marxist message of class conflict blended easily with the Jeffersonian promise of yeoman democracy to produce an especially volatile mix that became even more compelling when instilled with the moral authority of Christianity.[4]

Yet these explanations present the Oklahoma success in terms that are almost exclusively political. As a result, they cannot completely account for its accomplishments. In the end, the energy, strength, and skill with which Oklahoma Party members built their movement was as much a cultural achievement as it was a political victory. In their party, Oklahoma socialists created a community where they could enjoy the basic privileges denied them in the larger society and through which they could work to correct the imperfections of their world.

The Oklahoma activists saw their proposed program as simply a more decent, fair, and just alternative to a world they knew to be fatally flawed. Since socialists in the Sooner State conceptualized their ideological and moral claims in a manner that fell well within accepted American boundaries, they did not think of their platform as militant or radical. Indeed, Oklahoma Party members saw the socialist program as a way of bringing their society into compliance with the democratic and moral values central to American cultural and political traditions, a goal they considered to be eminently reasonable. Even so, the core of their message remained uncompromisingly Marxist. Through their response to the European War, their stand on race, and their support for national socialist speakers and candidates, Party members in the Sooner State proved to be genuine, authentic socialists.

Here, then, was the secret to Oklahoma socialists' strength: They succeeded in presenting their views in a way that carried the power of the republican ideals expressed in the Declaration of Independence, the moral teachings of Jesus Christ, and the political theories of Karl Marx. Only if we think of the Oklahoma movement in these terms do we begin to grasp the magnitude of its achievement. Those who were part of the movement believed absolutely in the propriety of their actions. Their story represents the life experiences of thousands of citizens who learned the lessons of democracy in the schoolroom of activism. Their sense of empowerment was deep enough to force all Oklahoma politicians—Democrats, Republicans, and socialists—to conduct their discourse in terms not generally present in the American political system. Presented in this context, the story of the Socialist Party of Oklahoma promises great insight into the workings of American democracy. It is well worth our careful attention.

CHAPTER 1

Farmers and Sooners

Life in the Promised Land

"One bale of cotton is all I raised on sixty acres of land, and the bank has that tied up. And then too, I am sixty years old with this prospect before me. The worms destroyed my cotton this year but whenever I have had money the legal thieves have robbed me out of it so I am about where I have always been and where thousands of my brother farmers are."[1] So wrote an Oklahoma cotton farmer in 1905, in words that put a human face on the historical phenomenon known as "the agricultural crisis." The depth of this crisis among Oklahoma farmers, coupled with the state's legacy as a haven for displaced American Indians, created a particularly volatile political and social climate in the Sooner State. It was in this charged environment that agrarian activists built their movement.

I

By the beginning of the twentieth century there was no longer any doubt about the crisis on the land, especially in the American South. In the midst of the unparalleled expansion of the nation's industrial economy, Southern farmers remained, in the words of the leading experts on the subject, "the poorest, least educated, and most deprived of all Americans."[2] By 1900, per capita income had fallen below pre–Civil War levels in the cotton-producing states of

Louisiana, Arkansas, Mississippi, and Georgia, and had increased during the same period in the rest of the South at a pace well below the national average of 75 percent.[3] The immediate cause of such widespread poverty was the precipitous drop in the prices farmers received for cotton, corn, and wheat, the leading commodities produced by American farmers. By 1890 these crops sold at prices below the cost of production, and farmers, who could not even recover their investments in supplies and equipment, fell deeper into debt.[4]

The personal economic crises of tens of thousands of farmers were revealed most clearly in a sharp increase in tenancy rates. The statistics were starkly ominous: By 1910 fully half of all farmers in the South worked land they did not own.[5] That tenants did not own land proved to be a crucial defect, for it worked on two levels to deny them a reasonable return on their effort. First, landlords required their tenants to raise a cash crop, most often cotton, subjecting tenant farmers to the low agricultural prices that plagued all Southern farmers. Even worse, tenants surrendered one-fourth to one-half of their crop to the landlord upon harvest as rent. Thus, their income—which, given the agricultural crisis, would have been minimal even if they had been able to keep all they produced—was automatically reduced by at least 25 percent. As a result, tenant farmers lived in what can only be described as abject poverty.

Farmers in Oklahoma proved especially vulnerable to these conditions. In fact, one estimate placed the average yearly income of tenant farmers in the state at 200 dollars in 1913.[6] Even a veteran organizer like Oscar Ameringer, who as a socialist activist had considerable experience working among the poor in other regions of the United States, expressed shock at the conditions endured by Oklahoma tenants. In his autobiography, Ameringer recorded his first impressions of the state's rural population, remembering "toothless old women with sucking infants on their withered breasts." "I found a hospitable old hostess, around thirty or less," he continued, "her hands covered with rags and eczema, offering me a biscuit with those hands, apologizing that her biscuits were not as good as she used to make because with her sore hands she could no longer knead the dough as it ought to be. I saw youngsters emaciated by hookworm, malnutrition, and pellagra, who had lost their second teeth before they were twenty years old." Such experiences led Ameringer to an inescapable conclusion: "The Oklahoma farmers' standard of living was so far below that of the sweatshop workers of the New York east side that comparison could not be thought of."⁷ Ameringer's subsequent experience in Oklahoma convinced him that the depth of poverty there was unparalleled. Farmers in the state were, in his words, "as wretched a set of abject slaves as ever walked the face of the earth, anywhere or any time."⁸

Lest it be assumed that Ameringer encountered only a small and unrepresentative portion of the state's farmers in his travels, it should be noted that in terms of the total rural population, tenants had already reached majority status in Oklahoma by 1910. By 1935, tenants would outnumber owners by a margin of over two to one (see table 1). Yet these statistics, damning as they are, actually understate the depth of the problem in much of Oklahoma. Although the overall tenancy rate in the state was 55 percent in 1910, table 2 demonstrates that in twenty-seven counties, over 70 percent of the farmers were tenants, with the proportion reaching 89 percent in one county.

To this majority of Oklahoma farmers, the crisis on the land was made all the more objectionable by the exalted position farmers were

TABLE 1. *Tenure of Farmers in Oklahoma, 1900–1935*

YEAR	FULL OWNERS		TENANTS	
	NUMBER	%	NUMBER	%
1900	53,619	49.6	47,250	43.7
1910	64,884	34.1	104,137	54.8
1920	69,786	36.3	97,836	51.0
1925	60,764	30.8	115,498	58.6
1930	53,647	26.3	125,329	61.5
1935	58,796	27.6	130,661	61.2

Source: John H. Southern, "Farm Tenancy in Oklahoma," *Agricultural Experiment Station Bulletin* No. 239 (December 1939): 7.

TABLE 2. *Tenancy Rates in Selected Oklahoma Counties, 1910*

COUNTY	TENANCY RATE
Osage	89.2
Okfuskee	83.6
Murray	82.7
Seminole	82.6
Love	82.3
Haskell	81.4
Johnston	80.5
Marshall	80.5
Hughes	80.0
Creek	79.7
Coal	79.1
Le Flore	78.8
Okmulgee	78.8
McClain	78.7
Garvin	78.5
Pontotoc	78.5
Bryan	78.1
Wagoner	78.0
McIntosh	76.7
Carter	75.3
Jefferson	75.1
Latimer	74.6
Tulsa	74.3
Pittsburg	74.2
Atoka	74.0
Seqyoyah	71.8
Stephens	70.0

Source: Bureau of the Census, *Thirteenth Census of the United States Taken in the Year 1910* (Washington, D.C.: Government Printing Office, 1912, 372–378.

purported to occupy in American society. All farmers, even the most impoverished tenants, had internalized the Jeffersonian notion that yeoman farmers represented the bedrock of American democracy. Yet the dream of yeoman democracy, portrayed in glowing terms by countless politicians attempting to invoke Jefferson's memory, conflicted with the life experiences of those involved in the labor of farming. In fact, for the majority of Oklahoma farmers between 1900 and 1935, economic mobility existed only in moving from land ownership to tenancy, in exactly the opposite direction from that celebrated in the folkway known as the American Dream and its agrarian component, the Agricultural Ladder.

The intellectual explanations offered for the crisis on the land were numerous and varied, but all farmers who felt its effects knew that the problem was related to the erosion of their position relative to the larger industrial society. At every turn, agricultural producers dealt with the commercial classes from a distinct disadvantage. First, all farmers in a given region harvested and sold their crops at essentially the same time, during a period when the market was temporarily glutted with their product. If we add to this the fact that most farmers operated in an oligopsony, a market condition characterized by few buyers and many sellers, it becomes clear that agricultural producers found themselves trapped in commercial relationships that brought them artificially low prices for their crops.

A farmer from the Oklahoma Territory described this rather theoretical concept in the most concrete terms when he told the story of how he sold his cotton crop in 1905. Upon arriving in town with his harvest, he first looked for a buyer who would pay a reasonable price for his cotton. The streets of most Oklahoma towns were crowded at harvest time with farmers in wagons loaded with cotton, and it fell to a class of men referred to as "street buyers" to bring together buyers and sellers. Hardly independent agents, these street buyers were under the employ of local merchants, and they completed their transactions in the most cursory fashion, walking from wagon to wagon and naming the price each farmer would receive for his crop. Of course, street buyers had no interest in offering farmers a fair price; their major function was to benefit their employers by driving the price of cotton as low as possible. Most farmers who rejected the buyers' early offers quickly learned how limited their options were, and subsequent negotiations inevitably resulted in even lower prices.[9]

After selling his cotton, the farmer continued, he then had to purchase supplies, generally from the same merchant who employed the street buyers. Here, the farmer's inferior position in his dealings with the merchant class became most clear. "Do I meet the merchants on the streets [as they did me] asking me to come and buy and what will I give?" the writer asked rhetorically. His answer, seeped in irony, rang true to the experience of Oklahoma's rural population: "Oh, no, they give me high prices (especially on cotton goods which they say have 'gone up'—surely since I sold mine an hour ago) which I being an 'independent farmer' can pay or let alone."[10] This farmer understood clearly that he bought and sold in an environment far removed from the "free market." As he quickly learned, the logistics of the commercial agricultural system were explicitly designed to give full advantage to the merchant at the expense of the farmer.

At the heart of this commercial agony was the matter of credit, a prerequisite for agrarian producers in a cash economy. Since farmers did not receive payment for their crops until harvest, many months after they began working their fields, they were forced to purchase staples and agricultural supplies on credit from local furnishing merchants under an arrangement known as the *crop lien*. Under this system the farmers' greatest vulnerability in their dealings with the commercial class, their constant need for credit, was parlayed by merchants into a brutally exploitive system that worked with devastating simplicity. To gain access to this credit, farmers had to offer their crops as collateral, thus mortgaging their harvest while it was still in the ground. Once this had been done, farmers again became inferior partners in their relations with the furnishing merchant, forfeiting their right to patronize establishments of their choosing based on such free market factors as price and convenience.

The objectionable nature of this condition became especially clear when the farmer sold his crops. Pending the final settlement of his account with the merchant, the proceeds from the crop, which the farmer had worked, nurtured, and prayed over, did not legally belong to him. Instead, the farmer received only the portion that remained after the merchant deducted the amount necessary to satisfy the lien. The situation had so deteriorated by the twentieth century, in fact, that most farmers considered themselves fortunate if their harvest yielded enough to repay the merchant and they could begin the new season free of debt.[11]

Such hardships indicate that the merchant's relationship with the farmer was particularly exploitive. Farmers in Pittsburg County in southeastern Oklahoma, for example, paid annual interest rates in excess of 75 percent on the necessities they purchased from merchants. This tribute was exacted in a creative, yet brutally effective manner. Only a portion of this charge, an amount averaging 20 percent annually, came in the form of outright interest. The remainder resulted from the merchant's practice of employing a dual pricing system, under which the credit price, which farmers had no choice but to pay, was considerably higher than the price of the same products purchased with cash.[12] This amounted to a charge that Roger Ransom and Richard Sutch refer to as "implicit interest," which averaged more than 50 percent per year on purchases from the furnishing merchant.[13]

In practical terms, then, farmers in the early twentieth century faced a strategic disadvantage at both ends of the selling relationship. At the same time that they received artificially low prices for their products, they paid inflated prices for the commodities they needed to survive. As a result, farmers were trapped in a cycle of perpetual indebtedness.[14] Smallholders in this condition lived in constant fear of being confronted by their merchant with the fact that their debt had exceeded the expected value of the coming harvest and that, before further purchases could be made, additional collateral would be required. Under such circumstances, farmers had little choice but to mortgage their land. It was then simply a matter of time and perhaps only a single crisis—a season of drought, the loss of a mule, the onset of sickness or injury—before their land was taken and they became tenants. This, in fact, represented the grim reality of the crop lien: It provided the mechanism by which many farmers moved from ownership into tenancy.

As they fell victim to these forces, Oklahoma farmers reacted in a variety of ways. Some expressed with a hint of desperation the powerlessness they felt in the new world of commercial agriculture: "I work my children in the field, the same as everybody else has to. For the past two years I have not sent them to school at all because I couldn't afford it. We eat as little as possible—corn bread, biscuit, sorghum, an egg now and then. Mighty little meat. Except for a squirrel once in a while, we try to make cotton seed oil do in the place of meat. Last year I butchered a hog, but this year I couldn't afford a hog. I have done my best—and this is what I have come to."[15] This legacy of shared hardship provided fertile soil for the agrarian activists who nurtured Oklahoma socialism into a mature social movement.

II

For Oklahomans, the disastrous effects of the crisis on the land were worsened by the state's involvement in the bitter process contemporary observers referred to as the "Indian problem." Oklahoma achieved statehood in 1907 by repeating the process of displacing American Indians from land they had been solemnly promised would be theirs forever. It was a problem that went to the center of the American experience, dating from the first contact between Europeans and American Indians.

From the moment Europeans arrived in the New World, their relations with American Indians were shaped by one crucial reality: the land white settlers were determined to occupy in America was already inhabited by numerous tribes of indigenous people. From the outset, Europeans responded by seizing the land they wanted and killing or displacing its previous occupants. As more European settlers arrived in America this process was repeated endlessly; gradually, the plight of displaced American Indians became a significant logistical, economic, social, and—for some—moral problem. Then, as white explorers began to survey the vast expanse west of the Mississippi River, they discovered what seemed to be the perfect solution: since much of this land was seen as a barren wasteland unfit for "civilized" habitation, little more than a "Great American Desert," it seemed perfectly logical for the U.S. government to relocate tribes from the East—where demand for land was acute— to this unusable land west of the Mississippi.

Government officials had cause to regret this policy, however, when agricultural and technological innovations made portions of the Great American Desert suitable for white settlement. As a result, parts of this land were gradually made available to whites, and Indians saw their vast preserve shrink steadily. Still, officials assured American Indians that their rights would be protected. There remained a significant territory just across the northern border of Texas, federal bureaucrats promised, that would be reserved in perpetuity for American Indian tribes. That land, of course, was the area that in 1907 became the state of Oklahoma, making its pattern of white settlement unlike any other in America.[16]

The first step in Oklahoma's unique history of settlement came in 1866, when the United States government used some tribes' support for the Confederacy during the Civil War as a pretext for seizing roughly half of the territory set aside for American Indians. Land-hungry white settlers, excited by the prospect of the opening of millions of acres of "unused" territory, began pressuring government officials to make this available for settlement. In 1889 their efforts bore fruit with the opening of some two million acres of "Unassigned Lands" in what is now central Oklahoma, sparking the legendary land run by "Sooners" who crossed into the territory before its official opening. The following year, Congress authorized the establishment of a territorial government for the roughly sixty thousand inhabitants of these lands, and the Oklahoma Territory was formed.

Yet large portions of land in the region still remained under the province of American Indians. To the dismay of many whites, the Five Civilized Tribes (the Creek, Cherokee, Choctaw, Chickasaw, and Seminole tribes) retained control of more than 15 million acres called the Indian Territory, located in what is now southeastern

Oklahoma. As had been the case on countless previous occasions, the federal government responded to political pressure brought by potential white landowners and began to open this region for outside settlement. In 1893 the government achieved a breakthrough in this effort by amending the Dawes General Allotment Act to apply to the Five Civilized Tribes. Now, land in the Indian Territory formerly held communally by the tribes was allotted to individual American Indians in plots ranging from 60 to 320 acres. The implications of this change were immediately obvious: While tribal units had proved unwilling to sell or lease land to white settlers, individual American Indian landowners would be more likely to do so. Although much of this land was classified as "inalienable," not to be sold for twenty-one years, the regulations were loose enough to allow significant acreage to come under white control. Through such methods as fraud, intimidation, and outright thievery—a process euphemistically known among Oklahomans as *grafting*—a few whites became owners of huge tracts of land in the Indian Territory, standing to make enormous profits should the region be opened to unlimited white settlement. This is precisely what happened in 1907. The governments of the Five Civilized Tribes were formally dissolved, paving the way for the joining of the Oklahoma and Indian Territories, both now comfortably settled by whites, into the state of Oklahoma (see map 1).

This unique past had enormous implications for the new state of Oklahoma. Most importantly, the legacies of the two separate territories survived statehood, creating two distinct and often disparate traditions in the state.[17] Northern and western Oklahoma, the portion that had been the Oklahoma Territory, possessed many of the characteristics of the Midwestern farm states. Farmers there, although burdened by the crop lien and the twin evils of costly credit and low crop prices, tended to be smallholders who raised wheat or corn, often supplemented by livestock. In the southeast, on the other hand, a small number of white speculators took advantage of the peculiar process of tribal government dissolution to gain control of most of the land. As a result, tenancy was dominant in the old Indian Territory,

Oklahoma and Indian Territories, 1906

Map 1

with most farmers raising cotton under conditions almost identical to those found in the Old South east of the Mississippi River.

Despite these regional differences, however, the most important legacy of the government's treatment of American Indians affected all Oklahomans. In a sense, Oklahoma's unique history represents the distillation of more than two centuries of exploitation of American Indians. The steady removal of land in the Oklahoma and Indian Territories is the ultimate example of the lies and treachery that underlay American Manifest Destiny. In light of this, it is no small irony that most of the state's white farmers, who came to Oklahoma "hoping to claim their birthright of independence," were by their very presence undermining the Indians' same birthright.[18]

To complete the irony, the promise of economic self-sufficiency through land ownership proved for many white Oklahomans to be as empty as it had been for the American Indians who came before them. Just as the U.S. government had pursued a policy that undermined the Indians' claim to the land, the agricultural crisis imperiled white farmers' dream of economic self-sufficiency. If whites failed to appreciate the fullness of this irony, the legacy of unfulfilled promise nevertheless pervaded Oklahoma.

CHAPTER 2

Experimenting in Collective Action

The Indiahoma Farmers' Union, 1904–1906

By the turn of the twentieth century virtually all American activists drew inspiration from the Populist movement, the most ambitious of all attempts to effect substantive change in the institutions of agrarian capitalism. The Populists broke new ground, establishing a network of cooperative enterprises through an institutional formation known as the Farmers Alliance and creating a dramatically different political organization, the People's Party.[1] Building on the ideological and cultural resources available to them—including, in the words of one scholar, "their rural Southern experience, their evangelical Protestant heritage, and their Jeffersonian-Jacksonian tradition"—the Populists began to experiment with ways of remaking society into a more equitable form. In the process, they achieved a rare sophistication in their understanding of how agrarian capitalism worked and deepened their sense of entitlement to the promise of democracy.[2]

For all of the promise of these creative and democratic responses to the crisis on the land, however, the Populists were ultimately unsuccessful in their challenge. The end came with the disastrous presidential election of 1896, when Populists had to choose whether to temporarily cooperate with a Democratic Party candidate who seemed sympathetic to at least some of their ideals (the option known as *fusion*), or to remain true to the principles of the People's Party and nominate their own candidate (referred to as the *mid-road* option). There was no easy answer, and after intense and often acrimonious debate, the People's Party decided to support the Democratic Party's nominee, William Jennings Bryan. In retrospect this was a disastrous mistake. Bryan was defeated, deeply traumatizing both the Farmers Alliance and the People's Party. By the dawning of the twentieth century, the Populist movement had all but vanished from the American landscape.

I

The spirit of the movement outlived its institutions, however, and after 1896 alienated ex-Populists throughout the South waited expectantly for the opportunity to rekindle the old Alliance.[3] One such group took action in Rains County, Texas, in 1902, forming a new organization known as the Farmers' Educational and Cooperative Union. In spirit as well as in form, the Farmers' Union explicitly revived the Jeffersonian traditions of the old Farmers Alliance. The principal organizer was an ex-Populist named Newt Gresham who relied heavily on the ideas and tactics of the Alliance in building the new organization. Texas farmers received the revived message of cooperation enthusiastically, joining the Farmers' Union by the thousands.[4]

Texans supported the organization so aggressively, in fact, that its leaders soon turned their attention to expanding the movement beyond the Lone Star State. The Indian and Oklahoma Territories just across the state's northern border seemed particularly fertile ground, and in 1903 R. D. King, Gresham's office assistant, agreed to spearhead the expansion. On King's initial foray into the territories, he had a particularly fortuitous meeting with an alienated radical and veteran organizer named Sam Hampton, who was anxious to put his considerable skills to work for the Farmers' Union. Hampton took charge of the recruiting effort in the cotton regions of the Indian Territory, building a thriving organization within a year.[5] As in Texas, farmers in the Oklahoma and Indian Territories were hungry for the message of cooperation brought by Hampton and other organizers, and they eagerly embraced the opportunity to rekindle the spirit of Populism. Farmers like G. Ligan from Holdenville in the Indian Territory still felt the almost mystical pull of the Farmers Alliance: "I was a member of the Alliance in Texas and the Indian Territory as long as it remained in existence here. I love to write the name, Alliance. Much labor I did in that order." Looking expectantly to the Farmers' Union, Ligan pledged "to do all that I can for the Union, considering my age and white head."[6]

Fueled by sentiments like this, the Union was so successful in the territories that the Texas Farmers' Union granted territorial members organizational autonomy at its annual convention in February of 1905.[7] The following month, farmers from the Oklahoma and Indian Territories gathered in Shawnee to officially organize their new autonomous unit, combining members from the two territories into a single organization called the Indiahoma Farmers' Union. Delegates of the new organization then turned to the business at hand, adopting a constitution modeled after that of the Texas Union and electing state officers.[8]

If there were any doubts that the spirit of the Farmers Alliance lived on through the Union, they were dispelled in the person of S. O. Daws, the newly elected president of the Indiahoma Farmers' Union. Daws's achievements in the agrarian movement were legendary. Known to many in the movement as "the first Populist," Daws had helped revitalize the ailing Texas Farmers Alliance in 1883, and as the movement's original "travelling lecturer," he was the first to spread the gospel of cooperation to other states. Daws went on to become one of the most active of the original Alliance organizers and remained a committed Populist to the end.[9] After his Alliance days, Daws moved to Cordell in the Oklahoma Territory, where he operated a modest farm. He had lost none of his vigor in the transition from movement leader to small farmer, consistently presenting Union members with a clear diagnosis of the crisis on the land.

In his 1906 presidential address, Daws challenged the American commercial agricultural system in terms that called upon the Jeffersonian traditions of the Alliance while simultaneously foreshadowing the Marxist analysis of the Socialist Party. For Daws, the current system represented a threat to the democratic social order that was the birthright of every American citizen. At the heart of the problem was the self-interest of the "captains of industry and leaders of finance," whose only commitment was to "getting dollars." Where Jefferson had counted on the yeoman farmer to counteract the destructive influence of self-interest, Daws looked to the Farmers' Union, which he said had "come into the world to inspire better impulses and nobler purposes than simply buying and selling for profit."

While he refrained from using the language of Marxism, Daws's analysis nevertheless challenged the institutions of commercial agriculture just as directly. The root cause of the problems farmers faced was the "destructive madness for getting dollars," which pervaded the status quo and therefore must be permanently abolished. Radical surgery was needed to cut to the very marrow of the capitalist system.[10] Union organizer Sam Hampton was even more direct: "The mission of the farmers union is to completely overthrow the system of robbery, and to inaugurate the new and up-to-date methods."[11]

II

The real problem, of course, was how to correct the injustices described by Daws and other Union members. As the experience of the Farmers Alliance and the People's Party in the late nineteenth century demonstrates, addressing the problems faced by farmers in an emerging industrial-capitalist society was a daunting task. Farmers in the Oklahoma and Indian Territories were hardly strangers to the difficulties of movement building. Having come to the territories from states like Kansas and Texas where the agrarian reform movement reached full flower, many had themselves participated in the Alliance and People's Party. Indeed, both organizations were present in the Oklahoma Territory, paving the way for the burgeoning Farmers' Union.[12]

As in every other location where the Populist movement existed, debate over strategic issues in the Oklahoma Territory coalesced around the choice between fusion and midroad strategies. Territorial Populists experimented with both options, achieving a measure of success with each. After initially uniting with various groups in the name of political expediency, the Oklahoma People's Party officially embraced the midroad, third party strategy at their convention in 1892. The high point of midroad activism came two years later, when the People's Party congressional candidate received 33 percent of the vote, outpolling the Democratic candidate. Then in 1896, in keeping with the trend toward fusion among Populists elsewhere in the nation, Oklahoma Populists joined forces with the Democratic Party. The result was a politically powerful People's Party–Democratic Party coalition that lasted into the twentieth century.[13]

When Farmers' Union organizers moved into the territories in the early years of the twentieth century, therefore, they encountered a populace comfortable with a variety of ideological and strategic positions. As a result, the charter members of the Indiahoma Farmers' Union represented a broad base, a fact reflected in the men chosen to lead the organization at its first convention in 1905. Some had deep roots in the Populist tradition of third party activism. Among these were Daws, elected as president; veteran activist A. J. Carter—described by one Union member as "the first to champion the cause" in the territories—elected state organizer; state conductor J. H. Keltner, who had joined the Alliance shortly after moving to the Indian Territory; and J. S. Moore, a tenant farmer from Hess in the Indian Territory, elected to the office of secretary-treasurer.[14] Others were comfortable with fusion, coming into the Union with ties to the Democratic Party as well as the agrarian reform movement. Those elected to the executive committee came from this latter group, including J. W. Harrison, who had been one of the organizers of the Kiowa County Democratic Party; Robert J. Ward, who had held a variety of political offices in the territories, ranging from sheriff to Speaker of the House; and a large landowner named Campbell Russell, who operated a "river plantation" complete with numerous tenants and over five hundred cattle.[15]

In practical terms, then, the legacy of the Populist movement in the territories meant that the Indiahoma Farmers' Union was destined to continue the debate over tactics that had raged in the Alliance and People's Party. As a result, crucial questions remained unresolved. Would the organization reflect the assumptions of those, like Daws, who had personally felt the sting of capitalism's injustices and whose experience with the Democratic Party were scarred by the trauma of 1896? Or would the competing agenda of people like Campbell Russell, who had prospered under capitalism and who felt at home in the Democratic Party, prevail? To address these questions, a remarkable dialogue emerged between organizational leaders and the rank and file. The stakes were high and the tenor of the debate was often harsh, for in the balance hung the very nature and purpose of the Indiahoma Farmers' Union.

III

The opening salvo in the battle over strategy was fired during the Indiahoma Union's organizing convention, when some in the Union asserted that in the larger society, businessmen—not workers—were farmers' natural allies. To formalize this position, the executive committee included in the Indiahoma Farmers' Union constitution a clause forbidding members from aiding or participating in strikes.[16] This institutional separation of farmers and workers had been the subject of a protracted debate within the Farmers Alliance, first capturing the attention of Alliance members as they considered how to respond to the Great Southwestern Strike in 1886.[17] It proved to be just as interesting to Union members in the territories, many of whom realized that their personal experience conflicted with the measure in question. Indeed, the debate quickly expanded beyond the proscription on supporting strikes. Daws, for one, made it clear that his experience led him to classify the Union as a workers' organization rather than a businessmen's club: "If [the Farmers' Union] is not a labor or industrial organization then I have been caught in the wrong crowd. For I have been forced to labor on the farm with my own hands and helped pick the production of cotton in the snow last winter."[18]

Daws was not alone. As a local rural spokesman argued, "Some say that we are not miners, we are not railroad men, our interests are entirely different, but such surely look at this matter in a false light." For this farmer, the conclusion was inescapable: "Are we not laborers as surely as they? Are we not as cruelly robbed of the fruits of our toil as they?"[19] The Farmers' Union local in Mayberry agreed, calling for affiliation with "all other labor organizations, to be united under one head." Lest there be any doubt about what these farmers had in mind for their new organization, they announced that it should be "something like the 'Industrial Workers of the World.'"[20]

The terms of this debate were fundamentally altered by the remarks of J. S. Moore, the secretary-treasurer of the Indiahoma Farmers' Union. Noting that those who opposed the cooperation of urban and rural producers were most often "men that did not till the soil," he charged that large landowners in the Farmers' Union were attempting "to side-track the membership and open up the way for others than actual farmers to fill the offices of the institution and become the leaders thereof."[21] Moore's analysis helped make sense of internal organizational debates by conceptualizing ideological differences in terms of the socioeconomic divisions present within the Union. For Moore, large landowners like Campbell Russell, William H. Murray, J. B. Connors, and J. W. Harrison did not actually engage in the labor of farming and as a result held interests that were generally at odds with those of the working farmers who made up the Union's rank and file. Even so, representatives of both groups—large, prosperous landowners as well as smallholders and tenants—considered themselves farmers and thus were eligible for membership in the Farmers' Union. Such a dichotomy made it necessary for the Union to become more precise in defining the rural inhabitants who represented its potential constituency.

With the phrase, "men that did not till the soil," Moore created an ingenious objective test that did just that. The tenants and smallholders who actually performed the labor of farming had a very different agenda than that of large landowners, who also considered themselves farmers but who relied upon the labor of others to cultivate their crops. The implication of Moore's distinction was obvious: Since it was impossible for the Union to serve the needs of all farmers, the organization should devote itself to tenants and smallholders, who were in the majority.[22]

Moore's advice made perfect sense to most Union members. As one farmer put it, the large landowners farmed "by proxy" and were not qualified to give voice to the Union's purposes.[23] For more than two thousand farmers at a Union picnic, the best solution was to agree "That None but Tillers of the Soil should be Members of the Union."[24] It was thus with a sense of urgency that a working farmer offered his advice:

> Now, let's wake up, and get the right man in front, that is, the farmer, not the man that owns hundreds of acres of land and never works a foot of it himself. His interest is not our interest, for he is keeping the poor man oppressed to death.
>
> All of you [of the professional class] can tell what college you graduated in. We want men to tell what field they learned to plow in. I remember well where and when I learned to plow. It was in the mountains of North Carolina. Where did all you professional men learn? We want to know.[25]

The message was clear. One understood the oppression that beset ploughmen only by being behind the plow. There was no other way to get the dynamics of that oppression straight.

IV

Once established, the theory that large landowners and working farmers held opposing interests became a touchstone for the internal debate over numerous strategic issues. This was especially true of the most basic question of all: How could the Union bring relief to farmers suffering the ill effects of the crisis on the land? As they considered the alternatives, Indiahoma Union members gradually reached a consensus—that their first concern should be the problem of low crop prices and that their principal strategy should be a tactic known as *collective marketing.*

Collective marketing was an attempt to address a principal reason for low crop prices—the temporary glut of agricultural commodities created around harvest time. Daws and other Indiahoma Farmers' Union leaders proposed that farmers in the territories agree upon an acceptable minimum price and that they pledge to withhold their crops from the market until buyers were willing to pay this predetermined price. In this way, farmers collectively would refrain from selling until the market stabilized, receiving significantly higher prices as a result. Union members were persuaded by this analysis, and crop withholding became the central weapon of the Indiahoma Farmers' Union, especially among cotton farmers, beginning in 1903. The tactic seemed successful from the outset; cotton prices in the territories hovered around ten cents per pound from 1903 to 1907, a significant improvement over the 6.7 cents received in 1902.[26]

Of course, crop withholding was only a first step. Most Union members realized that the tactic was in reality quite limited in its attack on the institutions of the existing agricultural system. In the face of significant disadvantages in all phases of the farmers' relations with the commercial class, collective marketing addressed only their disadvantaged role in the selling of crops, completely ignoring the central problem of usurious interest and inflationary prices paid to furnishing merchants for staples and agricultural supplies. In addition, it was ironic that tenants and heavily indebted smallholders, who needed relief most desperately, were by the very nature of their impoverishment prevented from participating in the Union's withholding plan. The democratic space in which these farmers operated was so limited that they no longer had control over how and when to sell their cotton. Their crop was pledged to the landlord and furnishing merchant while still in the ground, and they had no choice but to accede to their creditors' demand that it be liquidated immediately upon harvest at the prevailing low price.

At this point in the debate, an object lesson in the differences between working farmers and large landowners appeared for those who took the time to notice. For those engaged directly in the labor of farming, a consensus of sorts was soon reached as to the relative merits of withholding; it was a tactic rather than a goal, merely a useful starting point for what would some day become a more serious challenge to the institutions of commercial agriculture. Large landowners, on the other hand, had the opposite concerns about crop withholding. To them, withholding was "too aggressive" and was unnecessarily "combative." There were far more appropriate ways to make life better for farmers, representatives of this group asserted.

So began the effort within the Union to defeat the crop withholding plan. Overproduction, cried the large landowners, not any significant inequity in the selling process, was to blame for low prices. Instead of attempting to alter the dynamics of the selling relationship through complicated and risky schemes like crop withholding, farmers needed only to curtail their production to effect a rise in prices. The easiest way to reach this goal, they maintained, was for Union members to participate in a voluntary plan of acreage reduction, thereby reducing the surplus of cotton and raising the price.

Thus began an elaborate debate. The stakes were high; at issue was nothing less than the soul of the farmers' movement. The debate began as a matter of theory and analysis of prevailing economic conditions and escalated into a fierce internal dispute over the future politics of the farmers' movement. In the beginning, the issue seemed to be yet another episode of the so-called overproduction debate, an exchange with which agrarian activists had become all too familiar. Proponents of collective marketing responded by dusting off the old arguments, pointing out that such a simplistic explanation as overproduction could hardly be accurate in a world where hundreds of thousands of consumers were unable to partake of the farmers' products.[27] As one farmer remarked in a devastating rebuttal of the overproduction argument, "When men, women and children go hungry and poorly clad in a country where overproduction is the cry half the time, there must be something out of joint somewhere."[28] The simplicity of this logic was compelling, and the Indiahoma Farmers' Union refused to entertain acreage reduction as a plausible alternative to crop withholding.[29]

With their acreage reduction plan in disarray, those opposed to crop withholding turned to scientific farming, yet another familiar diversionary tactic. Backed by the scientific pronouncements of self-appointed agricultural experts, advocates of this approach favored crop diversification, the use of fertilizers, and the application of the scientific method as ways of improving farmers' income. One proponent of crop diversification, the cornerstone of the scientific approach to farming, was eloquent in his praise of the tactic: "The silly farmer who has to buy the things that ought to be raised on the farm is in the middle of a bad fix, but the diversifier—ah, he is on the top of the heap now."[30] Like acreage reduction, however, scientific agriculture was purely cosmetic in its effect, leaving the essential dynamics of the commercial agricultural system untouched.[31]

The scientific farmers chose the first annual convention of the Indiahoma Farmers' Union, held in Tishomingo in the Indian Territory in July of 1905, to put their plan before the membership. William Murray, chairman of the planning committee for the convention, made the necessary arrangements. As a lawyer and large landowner who had attained great wealth representing Indian tribes in their claims against the federal government, Murray provided living proof of Moore's charge that large landowners had an agenda for the organization that was not in the best interests of working farmers. Clearly, Murray's support for scientific farming was related to his position as a wealthy landowner who did not depend directly upon his own labor for his livelihood. It was also clear to many working farmers within the Union that scientific farming offered little hope, since it did not address their fundamentally disadvantaged place in the economic system. Those who had been active in the Populist movement were not surprised by Murray's stand; he had been a leading supporter of accommodation with the Democrats in the Texas Alliance.[32]

Murray drew upon all of his experience and considerable political skills in the attempt to turn the Indiahoma Farmers' Union away from its commitment to crop withholding. Using his authority as chairman of the committee on arrangements, Murray made sure that the Tishomingo convention would be long on scientific farming and short on agricultural cooperation. In place of discussions on crop withholding, Murray scheduled a series of lectures given by "agricultural experts" on topics such as "Grape Culture," "Practical Hog Growing in the Territories," "Nut Growing and Home Adornment," "The Physics of the Soil," and "The Paper Shell Pecan Industry."[33] Executive committee member Campbell Russell, another large landowner, vigorously defended the convention program, asserting that a legitimate part of the mission of the Farmers' Union was the education of its members. After all, he argued, the organization was not formed "ENTIRELY for the purpose of giving the 16-hour-a-day laborer an opportunity to meet and cuss existing conditions."[34]

Russell's language left little doubt that he considered himself to be superior to the working farmer, and with this pronouncement, Moore's charge that large landowners did not represent the interests of most farmers again exploded onto the scene. Incorporating a heavy dose of condescension into a strangely twisted sense of logic, Russell concluded that small farmers were in trouble because they worked too hard. These farmers, he predicted, "will never amount to anything until they can get enough common sense pounded into their 'labor benumbed brains' (that is the correct expression) to know that it is not proper for any man, or woman, to work more than eight or ten hours a day, except in special emergency."[35]

To the editor of the *Indiahoma Union Signal*, Russell's discourse was objectionable in the extreme. In prose dripping with sarcasm, the editor admonished his readers to study Russell's argument carefully: "Brother Russell does not wish to be misunderstood and we apprehend that not even the dullest and most obtuse 16-hour-a-day laborer will fail to thoroughly comprehend his meaning." The editor made it clear that class differences accounted for Russell's condescending attitude, and that 90 percent of Union members in the Indian Territory belonged in the latter's "16-hour-a-day" category. The proposed Tishomingo program, the editor concluded, was a perfect example of why farmers could not allow the minority in the "educated and prosperous class to control the affairs of the Farmers' Union."[36] "We are of the opinion that if the laity, the one gallused, genuine and real farmer had arranged this program," he wrote, it would have been a very different event and "would have provided for the promulgation of some thought along the line of price making."[37]

The opponents of the Tishomingo program were explicit about the reason for their objections: scientific farming, like acreage reduction, was a diversionary tactic that failed to strike at the real causes of low farm prices. Characterizing the tactic as "theoretical dissertations upon the sciences" offered by the "professional and hot-air wind-jammer," one editor dismissed it as organically tangential to the interests of the working farmer. The members of the Farmers' Union local in Atlas agreed, making it clear in a resolution denouncing the upcoming Tishomingo convention that discussions on scientific agriculture were not uppermost in their minds: "We want to go [to the convention] to attend to the business that is so much in need of being attended to, in the interest of the farmer."[38]

Most members of the Indiahoma Farmers' Union were in agreement with these sentiments, expressing their disgust with Murray and the planning committee by staying away from Tishomingo during the week of the convention. Even though the town was located in the heart of the cotton region that contained the highest concentration of Union members in the territories, attendance at the convention was minimal. Less than half of the eligible delegates showed up in Tishomingo at the appointed time, and those who did attend were successful in subverting Murray's detailed itinerary.[39] The *Durant Independent Farmer* reported the defeat at Tishomingo in one simple sentence: "The very elaborate program arranged by the committee was not carried out."[40]

V

With acreage reduction and scientific farming formally repudiated, the Farmers' Union turned to crop withholding with renewed vigor in the summer of 1905. Under Daws's leadership, farmers agreed to hold their cotton for eleven cents per pound that year, and members were optimistic about future victories to be achieved through cooperation. Indeed, some members expressed hope that the Farmers' Union would become more aggressive in 1906 in attacking the evils of the agricultural system. After all, these working farmers argued, they had limited their attack to the farmers' disadvantaged role in the selling relationship for two years; it was now time to address the thorny problem of their need for credit and the resulting disadvantages farmers experienced in their dealings with the banker and the furnishing merchant.

Such calls for more comprehensive action against the commercial agricultural system sparked earnest debate among Union members over future tactics. As the membership began discussing this proposition, the resulting dialogue revealed much about the Indiahoma Farmers' Union, not the least of which was the clarity of analysis and sophistication with which members addressed matters of strategy and tactics. Farmers in the territories were not mystified about the causes of their impoverishment, nor did they hesitate to offer possible solutions. One farmer's analysis, offered in a letter printed in a Union newspaper, demonstrated again that at least some within the Union saw clearly the limitations of withholding: "The farmer has confined himself to production alone and has accordingly left distribution to the commercialist wolves whose religion is the 'Golden Standard Rule' i.e., 'Do thy neighbor and do him first.' The farmer got done and done brown.... The remedy is to own our own machinery of production, transportation and distribution, and, then we shall be free as our patriotic fathers were free."[41]

Another farmer concurred, suggesting that the organization establish its own system of banks in the territories to lend money to farmers at 3 percent interest.[42] Other Union members recommended establishing cooperative cotton gins, cooperative coal yards, and even a cooperative insurance company.[43] At the base of each of these suggestions was the memory of the cooperative stores established by the Farmers Alliance. The Alliance cooperative, it seemed to working farmers, had served their interests better than did crop withholding.

Although sympathetic to the interests of working farmers, Farmers' Union leaders resisted these proposals and called for the members to continue to rely on crop withholding as their principal tactic. To organizational leaders, this was a question of tactics, not ideology. The dilemma the Union faced was whether it should continue to pursue a strategy of successful yet limited action or adopt a more risky policy of directly attacking other objectionable aspects of the commercial agricultural system. While Daws, among others, was hesitant to endorse the more militant proposals offered by some members, he was at pains to point out that his reticence did not reflect a lack of commitment to fundamental reform.

As a result, when Daws and other Union leaders made public their opposition to suggestions that the organization begin a more aggressive strategy, they did so in terms that set them apart from men like Russell and Murray. Daws himself was a working farmer, and his stand resulted from his considerable experience in the Farmers' Alliance, not a lack of commitment to significant change in the agricultural system. Drawing upon the lessons of Populism, Daws felt strongly that the Union must resist the temptation to become more aggressive—at least temporarily. Farmers needed a stronger organization to effectively adopt a more aggressive strategy.

Daws was convinced that at a similar juncture in its development, the Farmers Alliance had made a critical mistake by establishing cooperative stores—which made considerable demands on the organization and its membership—as its initial strategy. Cooperatives immediately alienated merchants, creating almost instantly a well-organized and powerful enemy. In addition, cooperatives depended upon affordable credit, a commodity Alliance leaders often were unable to produce. The painful memories of the fall of the Texas Exchange highlighted the vulnerability of the cooperative enterprise. Bankers, under pressure from merchants (who, after all, were important customers), had refused to lend money to the cooperatives. Factories refused to fill orders without full payment, and the cooperative stores failed. Now, in retrospect, Daws realized that only organizations that had achieved a level of maturity sufficient to withstand these challenges should attempt to create cooperative stores.[44]

Crop withholding, by contrast, was much better suited as an opening strategy. It required no such initial investment, freeing farmers from the reliance on credit that had made the Alliance cooperatives so vulnerable, and had the added advantage of not alienating merchants at a time when the Union could ill afford to make more enemies. The Union had been in existence in the territories for only four years, the leaders pointed out, and was not yet capable of withstanding the challenges that would accompany more ambitious strategies.

Indiahoma Farmers' Union leaders shared these concerns with the membership, employing all of their persuasive powers in a remarkable dialogue with the rank and file. As the debate unfolded, supporters of crop withholding argued it was only a matter of time before more comprehensive measures would be adopted. Thus, the debate concerned *when* the Farmers' Union would be ready to fundamentally challenge the system of commercial agriculture, not *whether* such a challenge was warranted.

The contribution of one farmer to the discussion made this distinction clear: "I want to say to the brethren that it seems to me that we are expecting to shoot a big gun in the near future. I think we had better wait until we get the ammunition. We are only recruits yet and it requires twelve months drill after you enlist in the army before you are capable of doing the enemy any harm. We want to think what a powerful army the commercial world is. . . . Please brothren [sic] don't get in such a rush."[45] The editor of the *Durant Independent Farmer* made the assertion even more pointedly: "This is all; don't try to do more—not now. Wait until we get used to being organized; wait until we learn to stand without being hitched, then watch the fur fly from the back of 'the system'; we'll rub it the wrong way, then, sure!"[46] Daws himself explained that his reason for discouraging more ambitious plans was only to prevent farmers from repeating the mistakes of the Alliance. It was essential, he warned, that the Union "do one thing at a time and do that well before . . . . attempt[ing] something else."[47]

Despite the logic of this position, demands for a more aggressive strategy were becoming increasingly emphatic, and Farmers' Union leaders found themselves in an uncomfortable dilemma. They were all too familiar with the economic hardships at the root of the urgency of the farmers' pleas, but, remembering clearly the pain of the Alliance's demise, they also felt keenly the need for caution. Taking these competing impulses into account, Daws presented the Indiahoma Farmers' Union with a solution to this strategic impasse. All the locals in the territories were to meet on 22 February 1906, Washington's birthday, to celebrate "Farmer's Independence Day" and to endorse the minimum cotton price of eleven cents per pound for the 1906 crop as agreed upon at the most recent National Farmers' Union convention.[48]

Daws then unveiled a new tactic, a strategy of collective selling anchored by a network of storage and marketing facilities known as Farmers' Union Clearing Houses, which would take the Union beyond crop withholding. The system as explained by the leadership was disarmingly simple: Union members would establish local clearing houses, through which they would pledge to sell all they produced. Each town in the territories with a population of at least two hundred was to establish its own clearing house, and Union locals were encouraged to have these in place by the first of May so that the system would be ready to market the 1906 crops.[49]

Once the Farmers' Union clearing houses were in place, the entire dynamic of the selling relationship would be transformed. Instead of sitting idly in their wagons waiting for street buyers to make their offers, farmers would offer their crops for sale in a setting over which they had more control. Those interested in acquiring farm products would now do so in a central location—the local Farmers' Union Clearing House—where a wide variety of products would be readily available. As a result, it would be more difficult for a few agents to dominate the local market, and farmers would receive higher prices for their products. Thus, the clearing houses complemented crop withholding to end the oligopsony that farmers in the territories faced when they marketed their crops.

Daws's plan included specific instructions on how to establish and maintain local clearing houses. It was essential, he cautioned, that they be directly associated with the Farmers' Union and that only Union members in good standing be allowed to participate in the clearing house system. The idea was, in many respects, a model of democratic institution building. Each clearing house was to be incorporated, with the stock divided into shares worth approximately five dollars each.[50] To ensure that the clearing houses would be democratically operated, the Union encouraged each member to purchase a share in the venture, but would allow no single member to accumulate more than one share. Those who could not afford to buy a share outright would be given the option of paying in installments. In this way, all members of the Union would have a say in the operation of their local clearing house. The cost of operation would be paid by the members in the form of a commission of 1 to 3 percent of the amount received for their crops.

In terms of the narrow options facing small farmers in an increasingly commercialized and centralized economy, and given the relatively tenuous position of the Indiahoma Farmers' Union, the clearing house plan was a particularly adroit compromise. It can legitimately be said that the clearing house system moved beyond crop withholding by more directly attacking the unequal selling relationship farmers faced as they marketed their crops. At the same time, the tactic limited itself to the selling relationship, stopping short of challenging the inequities farmers endured at the hands of merchants. As a result, Daws was convinced that the clearing house would not be perceived as a direct threat by merchants, as the cooperative stores had been, allowing the Union to temporarily escape the retaliation suffered by the Alliance.[51] His explanation to the membership—one grounded in sophisticated knowledge derived from prior social experience—was explicit about this feature of the clearing house system: "Co-operation of any kind is good, but first co-operate in seizing your local market. That is, establish a clearing house in all your good towns and put in a manager. . . . When you have the clearing house in good working order so that you are getting good prices for your products you are then ready to take up canning factories, etc."[52]

Even so, Daws had no illusions that this strategy would go unopposed, and he offered practical suggestions for surviving in a hostile environment. Those members who insisted on establishing cooperative stores must under no circumstances do so through Union clearing houses. "The day you make a store out of your clearing house," he warned, "you destroy its power for good because you stir up competition against you."[53] In addition, Daws, again drawing directly from the Alliance cooperative experience, emphasized that the clearing houses must be operated with scrupulous honesty; any member found guilty of financial or other impropriety must be "promptly and peremptorily" dismissed. "This is important," he stressed, "because if any man in the business world can find any thing against your manager he will tell it to every acquaintance in the hope of poisoning the confidence of the members and killing the business."[54] As Daws knew in his bones, the politics of economic cooperation were arduous.

VI

Union members were persuaded by this analysis. By May of 1906, over one hundred Farmers' Union locals in the territories had established clearing houses, and farmers were expectant about the prices they would receive through the twin strategies of collective marketing and Union clearing houses.[55] They had reason to be optimistic, for the dialogue between the leadership and the rank and file demonstrated a sophisticated understanding of their movement and of the hostile environment in which it operated. Union members had taken the first step toward successful movement building by seeing clearly that their poverty was rooted in the institutions of commercial agriculture, a system that enriched the commercial classes at the expense of the working farmer. The closely related Jeffersonian ideals of the dignity of labor and the importance of yeoman farmers to the democratic health of the nation, nurtured in the Farmers Alliance, also informed the discussion.

In addition, most Union members had learned that not all those who called themselves farmers were qualified to speak for the majority. Large landowners, who did not participate directly in the labor of farming, had an agenda that was often at odds with the interests of working farmers, and it was agreed that they must not be allowed to direct the affairs of the Indiahoma Farmers' Union. Finally, the debate over possible tactical alternatives pointed to a deep understanding of both insurgent movements and of the existing agricultural system.

These insights had not come cheaply. They resulted from the long and often bitter experience of the Farmers Alliance, and the Union borrowed freely from this collective wisdom to create a sophisticated analysis of the workings of American agricultural society and the proper role of the working farmer. Armed with these insights and emboldened by the knowledge that their authority rested on the republican ideals of the American revolutionary tradition, members of the Indiahoma Farmers' Union were poised to do battle, with every hope of success.

CHAPTER 3

Coercion and Co-optation

*The Demise of the
Indiahoma Farmers' Union, 1906–1907*

Despite the euphoria Union members felt after the introduction of the clearing house system, not all were blindly optimistic about the future. Those with experience as activists understood that the Indiahoma Farmers' Union faced serious challenges in its effort to fundamentally restructure the system of commercial agriculture. It seemed obvious to many, for example, that defenders of the existing system would hardly allow the Union's agenda to go unopposed. After all, the merchants, bankers, lawyers, and politicians who were the principal champions of the prevailing order reaped considerable economic benefits from it and would surely work to preserve these advantages. Thus, as men like Daws well knew, a counterattack against the Union similar to that experienced by the Farmers Alliance would inevitably be forthcoming.

In addition to this disturbing reality, the Farmers' Union in the territories had not yet completely resolved the issue of which class of farmers legitimately represented the majority of the organization's members. Although the rejection of acreage reduction and scientific farming in favor of crop withholding and the clearing house system represented the defeat of the large landowners' agenda, this was by no means a permanent victory for working farmers. Russell and Murray still held important Union offices, and they could be expected to continue their attempts to mold the Indiahoma Farmers' Union into a form more amenable to the interests of large landowners.

So in the midst of the optimism following the formation of the Farmers' Union clearing houses, two great dangers emerged: direct opposition on the part of commercial interests that were threatened by farmers' activism and co-optation by large landowners within the movement whose conservative vision for the Union would alienate tenants and smallholders. Both threatened the organization's very survival. Not even the most prescient Union members, however, were prepared for the ferocity with which these hazards would threaten their organization. In 1906 and 1907, the Indiahoma Farmers' Union endured both coercion and co-optation through a disastrous series of events that ultimately left the organization weak and ineffective.

I

Union members quickly felt the sting they had expected as defenders of the status quo mounted their coercive counterattack. The first instance of direct opposition came in response to a rather modest Union plan to purchase coal cooperatively for its members in the winter of 1905–1906. Under the plan, farmers in the territories would place their orders for the winter supply of coal through the Union's business agent, who would then purchase coal by the carload directly from mines in the Indian Territory. By skirting local merchants in this way, Union members could get their coal at wholesale prices, a significant savings over prices charged in local stores. Remembering the lessons of the Alliance cooperatives, which failed because of their inability to acquire credit in sufficient quantity, the Farmers' Union business agent specified that participating members must pay in advance for their purchases. In this way, Union officials could offer cash to the mining companies at the time they placed their orders. Farmers responded enthusiastically, and by the end of

December 1905, more than seven thousand dollars had been sent to Union headquarters for coal purchases.

Despite these precautions, the business agent quickly discovered that his orders for coal were not being filled. Upon investigation, Union officials learned that mine owners in the territories flatly refused to do business with the Farmers' Union. One mine owner, when queried about this refusal, stated unequivocally that he "absolutely would not sell the Farmers' Union coal because they were not legitimate dealers."[1]

Those Union members who had been active Populists recognized immediately that such rhetoric hid more ominous meanings. Just as merchants had conspired with banks to deprive the Texas Exchange of the credit it needed to survive, Union leaders suspected that a similar alliance within the capitalist class led to the mine owners' refusal to sell to the Union. In fact, they saw this as a perfect example of the corruption of the current economic system. Farmers could not hope to participate in the market place on an equal basis. To Daws, the mine owners' fixation on trading with only "legitimate dealers" represented nothing more than a transparent attempt to keep the price of coal artificially high. After all, he argued, the only buyers recognized as legitimate were those affiliated with the coal men's association, an organization whose central, if unstated, purpose was "to make the consumer pay the highest price that the middle man may choose to exact." Based on this analysis, Daws's conclusion was self-evident: Under the present system, the "citizen, the man who feeds the world by his daily toil, cannot buy except he submit to the extortion of a lot of organized bandits who demand a princely profit for placing an order that can as well be placed by the farmers themselves."[2]

The mine owners had not expected such a forthright diagnosis of the situation and, in the face of Daws's blistering rhetoric, quickly offered a slightly less self-serving explanation for their actions. Even if they did sell coal to the organization, they argued, the railroads would refuse to deliver it. Once Union leaders defused this reasoning by eliciting a promise from the railroads to handle any coal purchased, the mine operators claimed they had sold all their coal and had none left to fill the organization's orders.[3]

After undertaking a series of strategies, including delivering a petition to President Roosevelt and initiating legal action against mining companies, the Farmers' Union forced the mine operators to sell. Significantly, however, this victory did not come until March of 1906, after the onset of warmer weather made coal less of a necessity.[4] For Union members who participated in the direct purchasing plan, the episode represented an expensive lesson in the workings of the American economic system and the dangers of challenging that system. Having sent money for their winter fuel supply to Union headquarters, participating farmers had to do without coal for the entire season.

Before these lessons could be fully internalized, Farmers' Union members encountered a second, even more sobering instance of the power of the opposition, this time involving the government of the United States. This conflict was sparked when Daws, as editor, decided to move the *Indiahoma Union Signal*, an important organ of the Union, to a new location in Shawnee. Upon arriving in Shawnee, Daws took the routine step of applying to postal officials for continuation of the right to distribute the paper at second-class mailing rates.[5] The Post Office Department rejected the application, however, forcing the publishers of the *Signal* to pay first-class postage rates on every copy sent to subscribers. This was a financial burden the paper could not long endure.

The decision to revoke the *Signal*'s second-class mailing privileges was outlined by Third Assistant Postmaster General Edward C. Madden in a ruling based on two charges. First, Madden alleged that the *Indiahoma Union Signal* failed to fulfill the department's requirement that second-class material be "published for the dissemination of information of a public character." Instead of being a publication that presented information of interest to the general populace, Madden charged that the *Signal* was "merely the organ of The Farmers' Educational and Co-Operative Union of America, and is conducted as an auxiliary to and essentially in the interests of that association. It appears to be published by the officers of said association as a means of communicating with the members thereof. It consists almost entirely of matter relating to the association."[6] Madden also charged that not all persons who received the paper were legitimate subscribers. When the editors asked the Post Office Department what specific changes in the *Signal* would render it eligible for second-class rates, Madden replied tersely that it was "not within the province of this office nor can it undertake to advise publishers of the changes necessary to render their publications admissible as second-class matter."[7]

In February of 1906, the *Indiahoma Union Signal* published a special "Protest Supplement" to respond to the charges. After dismissing both charges as irrelevant and inaccurate, the editor concluded that the government's action amounted to outright censorship:

> This does not mean that the Signal is not entitled to be carried at the second-class rate, for it is, as much as any paper in the United States. It means that Edward C. Maddden has singled out The Indiahoma Union Signal with a view to killing it.
>
> He has detected in the Signal a note of warning to the farmers that they must do their own thinking; that they must save themselves if they would become independent of the grafter, market manipulator and bucket shop traders and he has decided that it must not be allowed to enter the mails at the 1 cent a pound rate if there is any way possible to keep it out.[8]

The Post Office had, in fact, taken previous action against the organization, denying second-class rates to two other Union publications.[9]

In response to numerous protests, the Post Office Department sent an inspector to Shawnee on 23 April 1906 to review the evidence in the *Signal* case. During this visit, the editors of the *Indiahoma Union Signal* attempted to prove that they received no direct financial support from the Farmers' Union and that the paper possessed an active, legitimate subscription list. Despite the editor's confident prediction that the problem had been resolved during the visit, the paper received notification the following month that its appeal had been denied.[10]

As a result, the publishers of the *Indiahoma Union Signal* were forced to wrap each copy of the paper separately and post each with a one-cent stamp.[11] Only with considerable expenditure of labor and financial resources, made possible by donations from subscribers, did the *Signal* continue regular publication following the Post Office's action.[12]

Finally, in late June of 1906, the Post Office Department notified the *Indiahoma Union Signal* that its second-class mailing privileges were being restored. No money would be repaid, however, to offset the extra expenditures caused by the six-month period of paying first-class rates.[13]

The demise of the coal-buying effort and the denial of second-class rates to the *Signal* both occurred in 1906, straining the Union's resources. Pressure on the organization intensified the following year because of an economic crisis of national proportions, the Panic of 1907. Essentially a currency crisis caused by the restriction of specie by New York banks, the Panic resulted in conditions under which local and regional banks were themselves denied the loans that enabled them to meet their depositors' currency demands. In agricultural regions, where the need for currency was most acute, local banks had to limit the cash withdrawals of their depositors and found themselves unable to make loans they would otherwise have approved.[14]

Unfortunately, 1907 was also the year that the Farmers' Union opted to push its tactic of crop withholding to a new level of intensity. Encouraged by several years of successfully holding cotton for eleven cents per pound, the National Farmers' Union voted to set fifteen cents as the minimum price for the 1907 crop. Farmers in Oklahoma enthusiastically agreed.[15] Unfortunately, this significant increase in the minimum price would have presented a challenge for the Union in the best of economic times; it was a hopeless proposition in the context of the financial trauma of 1907, and farmers were forced to sell their cotton at prices well below the fifteen-cent minimum.

Faced with this pressure, the editor of the *Farmers' Union Advocate* fairly begged his readers to stand firm on the agreed-upon minimum price: "This is the critical moment. Our course now will shape our destinies. Now, more than ever, we must stand firm. Every bale of cotton now offered for sale invites failure. Every member of the Farmers' Union must stand firm like a soldier in battle. Victories are won this way."[16] This encouragement was not enough, however. Like farmers in other locations, Oklahoma Union members found the credit crisis brought on by the Panic of 1907 too great an obstacle to overcome. Without credit they could not delay selling their cotton, and the plan to hold for fifteen cents was doomed. In fact, some farmers who tried unsuccessfully to hold their crops were forced to sell at a price below the prevailing minimum at the time of harvest.

As farmers considered this turn of events, they detected in their defeat the guiding hand of the "monied interests." As one Union official explained, the panic enabled the "big banks [to] squeeze the little banks," which in turn "put pressure on the farmers" and forced them to sell their cotton at artificially low prices. The official's conclusion was succinct and unambiguous: "Thus, the monied interests had their way and broke the power of the Union."[17] Whatever the cause of the crisis, the events of 1907 plunged the Indiahoma Farmers' Union into a state of organizational crisis.[18]

II

As the Farmers' Union struggled to recover from the effects of the failed coal purchasing plan, the revoking of mail privileges for the *Indiahoma Union Signal*, and the Panic of 1907, the old debate over the place of large landowners in the organization again began to compete for the attention of the membership. Issues once thought settled resurfaced as large landowners, sensing a new opportunity, again pushed to remake the Union in their image. This time they would not be so easily defeated, and after a long and complicated struggle large landowners succeeded in gaining control of the organization.

The origins of the renewed struggle date from the 1904 decision to unite farmers from both territories into one organization. Striking material differences between farmers in the two territories—most in the Indian Territory were tenant farmers who raised cotton, while the majority in the Oklahoma Territory were smallholders more likely to grow corn or wheat—strained the Union from the beginning. Into this state of affairs stepped William H. Murray. Fresh from his defeat at the Tishomingo convention, Murray again entered the fray in December of 1905 by calling for the formation of a separate Union organization for farmers in the Indian Territory. Announcing that a meeting would be held for this purpose in South McAlester on 17 January 1906, Murray argued that the differences between farmers in the two territories were so fundamental that separate organizations were warranted. Furthermore, he charged, even though Indian Territory farmers represented a majority within the Indiahoma Farmers' Union, members from the Oklahoma Territory filled most of the leadership positions in the organization.[19]

Murray was critical of the Union leaders' recent decision to move the organization's headquarters from Durant, in the Indian Territory, to Shawnee, located in the Oklahoma Territory. This action had been taken in August of 1905, in response to an offer of free office space made by the Shawnee Chamber of Commerce.[20] Having moved to the Oklahoma Territory, the officers then took it upon themselves to file for a new charter for the Indiahoma Farmers' Union, listing Shawnee as its headquarters.[21] To many Union members, especially those living in the Indian Territory, this action set a dangerous precedent. While the move itself represented something of a disturbance, the fact that Union leaders failed to consult the membership before making such an important decision was much more serious. Murray's published grievance served to alert Indian Territory farmers to the danger, causing them to publicly chastise Indiahoma Farmers' Union officials.

Of course, Murray's performance at the Tishomingo convention hardly qualified him to lead the charge against a potentially autocratic leadership, and the more astute Union members must have wondered about his newfound commitment to democracy. Indeed, circumstances surrounding the incident indicate that Murray had other reasons to work toward the creation of a separate Indian Territory organization. By 1905 it was clear that the territories would soon achieve statehood, but it was much less clear whether they would enter the United States as one state or two. A powerful leader in the Indian Territory, Murray understood that separate statehood for that region would be much better politically, allowing him to emerge from the process without having to share power with leaders from other parts of the territories. As a result, he worked judiciously during these years toward the goal of statehood for the Indian Territory distinct from the Oklahoma Territory. His efforts to establish a separate Farmers' Union organization fit neatly into this plan.[22]

For their part, Indiahoma Union officials responded carefully to Murray's charges. Their decision to move had been strictly a financial one, they assured the membership, and was unrelated to any desire to isolate those from the Indian Territory. Of course, Union leaders continued, those members who felt the move had been a mistake could always overturn the action at the next annual convention of the Indiahoma Farmers' Union.[23] They urged each local that was sending delegates to the South McAlester convention, where Murray was to advance his proposal for a separate Indian Territory Farmers' Union, to poll its members in the meantime on the question and to instruct delegates to honor the opinion of the majority at the convention. Daws expressed confidence that Union members in the Indian Territory would "do the right thing" at South McAlester by choosing to remain in the Indiahoma Farmers' Union.[24] He had reason to be optimistic. In a referendum vote of all locals in the Indian Territory taken late in 1905, only 131 favored the formation of a separate organization, while 2,855 locals voted to oppose such action.[25]

Murray observed with interest the dynamic between locals in the Indian Territory and officials of the Indiahoma organization. The results of the referendum pointed plainly to widespread sentiment against the separate organization, and Murray made plans to use his authority as a convention organizer to combat this majority sentiment. It was a tactic reminiscent of his earlier performance at Tishomingo. When prospective delegates arrived at the convention, they discovered that support for the creation of an autonomous Indian Territory Farmers' Union was a prerequisite for receiving credentials to the meeting. Most had been instructed by their locals to oppose a separate organization, however, and they flatly refused to commit themselves to a contrary position before the proceedings began. Through the sheer strength of their numbers, they forced convention officials to recognize them. The delegates expressed their outrage at this blatant attempt to manipulate them by decisively rejecting the creation of a separate organization; following the South McAlester convention, the newly formed Indian Territory Farmers' Union was left with only 130 members.[26]

Murray responded to this defeat with another strategy for circumventing the will of the majority. Publishing in a sympathetic newspaper the opinion of a Dallas attorney that the Indiahoma Farmers' Union charter was invalid in the territories, Murray instructed secretaries of locals affiliated with the Indiahoma organization in the Indian Territory to renounce that affiliation by refusing to send dues to the Shawnee headquarters. Only the Indian Territory Farmers' Union, he argued, possessed a lawful charter.[27] Murray then applied to the National Farmers' Union for official recognition, receiving a charter on 9 March 1906. Armed with this endorsement, he again contacted Indiahoma Union secretaries in southeastern Oklahoma, advising them to renounce their original charters in favor of that of the new Indian Territory Farmers' Union.[28]

Indiahoma officials realized that most of the farmers in the Indian Territory were loyal to their organization, and they urged local secretaries to ignore Murray's arguments. Daws reminded members in the Indian Territory that they had overwhelmingly rejected the formation of a separate organization in a referendum and again at South McAlester. "All secretaries are required to obey the majority ruling," he maintained, "until the next convention."[29] He then called for a special convention to be held in Shawnee on 17 April 1906 to give locals in the Indian Territory a chance to respond officially to the formation of the Indian Territory Farmers' Union.[30]

The approximately one hundred delegates who attended the Shawnee convention that spring worked hard to sort out the dispute.[31] Shortly after the meeting began, news of Murray's latest theatrics transformed the debate over the merits of dividing the Indiahoma Union. Murray had taken his crusade for a separate organization to the courts, seeking an injunction preventing local secretaries in the Indian Territory from sending dues money to Indiahoma Farmers' Union headquarters in Shawnee. To the delegates gathered in Shawnee, Murray's action was deplorable, and it was made unforgivable by the fact that he attempted to use the injunction—which workers and those sympathetic to their cause considered one of the most blatant examples of illegitimate power held by the business class. A journalist covering the convention recorded the effect of Murray's action on the delegates: "Like a bolt this information electrified the members and whatever kind feeling they had for the Indian Territory state organization up to that time, withered like the leaf that curls before the heat of the sun." The vote against the formation of a separate Union was unanimous.[32]

Despite this consensus, however, Murray's injunction kept the issue of separate Farmers' Union organizations before the membership. Notwithstanding the clear mandate to remain in the Indiahoma Farmers' Union, some local secretaries in the Indian Territory wondered whether they were prevented by law from sending dues money to Shawnee. The *Signal*, speaking for Indiahoma Union officials, assured members that the court had not yet considered the injunction. The paper informed readers that copies of the injunction circulated by Murray and other Indian Territory Farmers' Union officials amounted to nothing more than a "cheap looking dodger."[33] In June of 1906, the court ruled in favor of the Indiahoma Union by refusing to issue the injunction, a development to which the Indian Territory Farmers' Union responded by reinstituting legal action to prevent the Indiahoma organization from operating in southeastern Oklahoma.[34]

Murray's complex legal maneuvering began to erode the prestige of the Indiahoma Farmers' Union. Notwithstanding the huge majority enjoyed by the Indiahoma organization, farmers like W. H. Ward, the secretary of a local affiliated with the Indiahoma Farmers' Union, could not help but be confused. "My Local, Fairview, No. 638 has ordered me to send for some buttons and a receipt book," Ward reported, "and they have had such a time in Shawnee I don't know who to send it to."[35]

III

This complicating interlude in the experience of the Indiahoma Farmers' Union soon gave way to a more serious development—the co-opting of the organization by those sympathetic to the interests of the large landowners. The confusion and ill will engendered by Murray's short-lived Indian Territory Farmers' Union persisted through 1907.[36] During that time, a number of other developments further disrupted the movement's equilibrium. The debate over tactics, the debacle at Tishomingo, "Farmer's Independence Day" and the creation of Farmers' Union Clearing Houses, the mines' refusal to sell coal to the organization, and the denial of the *Signal*'s second-class mailing privileges all occurred simultaneously with the debate over the creation of the Indian Territory Farmers' Union. These multiple dynamics had brought the Union to a crisis.

As the events of 1906 took their toll on the Farmers' Union, the consensus that the movement was best served through a united Indiahoma organization began to break down. In June of 1906 the *Durant Independent Farmer*, which previously had been a strong opponent of Murray and the separate Union, expressed its growing distrust of the Indiahoma organization's ability to represent the interests of the farmers in the Indian Territory: "The Indian Territory enjoys (?) about the same relations to the Indiahoma Union that a step child does to a big old spoony fool couple who have ushered into the world a second set of bawling brats. . . . In the Indiahoma

Union it seems that everybody has a graft but the Indian Territory. Thank the Lord, we still get the password."[37] This sentiment reflected the growing disenchantment of many tenants and smallholders in the Indian Territory with the leadership of the Indiahoma organization. At the root of their disillusionment was yet another development, the gradual rise of the large landowners to a position of dominance in the Indiahoma Union.

The transfer of organizational power to those sympathetic with the agenda of the large landowners was not achieved easily and did not reflect a significant demographic shift in the material conditions of most Union members. Rather, this transformation represented a virtual coup, carefully orchestrated by a minority faction within the Indiahoma Farmers' Union. The process began with the discrediting of Daws, the Union's president and the chief spokesman of the working farmer. Conservatives in the Union first attempted to remove Daws from his post as editor of the *Indiahoma Union Signal*, the movement's most widely read paper. They were able to do so by virtue of a rather complicated turn of events that dated to 1905.

In that year, Daws had found that his considerable duties as president of the Indiahoma Farmers' Union made him ineffective as editor of the *Indiahoma Union Signal*, and he hired Thomas B. Tobin, a veteran newspaper editor from Colorado, to oversee the publication of the *Signal* as its managing editor. Having entrusted the daily operation of the paper to Tobin, Daws turned his full attention to the rapidly growing Farmers' Union.[38] By the spring of 1906, however, Daws began to suspect that the *Signal* was being improperly managed. In June of that year, Daws initiated a lawsuit accusing Tobin of using over eleven thousand dollars of *Signal* funds for his own benefit and of being responsible, through his inept leadership, for the loss of second-class mailing privileges.[39] The controversy raged throughout the summer and was thoroughly aired in the Farmers' Union press.[40] After a season of bitter debate, both Daws and Tobin agreed to submit the matter to arbitration within the Farmers' Union.

As the formal arrangements for the arbitration were worked out, Daws realized he had made a serious tactical mistake, for representatives of the large landowners controlled the process. The three-member arbitration committee created by the executive committee to hear the debate was baldly partisan, its composition deliberately predetermined to ensure a ruling against Daws. The chairman of the committee was J. B. Connors, whose sympathies with the Democratic Party were openly touted in newspapers like the *Daily Oklahoman*.[41] The two remaining members were Russell, whose performance at the Tishomingo convention left little doubt as to his loyalties, and J. W. L. Corley, whose candidacy for the Farmers' Union Executive Committee in 1906 was opposed by the rank and file.[42]

It came as no surprise, then, when the arbitration committee dismissed the charges against Tobin and awarded him control of the *Signal*.[43] The settlement required Daws to formally apologize to Tobin in a statement published in both the *Indiahoma Union Signal* and the *Durant Independent Farmer*.[44] When Union members protested that this decision was obviously based on ideological differences rather than on any actual evidence of wrongdoing on Daws's part, the arbitration committee evasively referred to the existence of secret, damaging evidence against the Union's president. During the course of the hearings, committee members asserted, they had documented some one hundred pages of evidence of malfeasance on Daws's part. Since public disclosure of the evidence would do the Farmers' Union "much harm," the committee refused to give any specifics about the charges against Daws. Committee members assured farmers, however, that the matter would be fully aired at the upcoming annual convention of the Indiahoma Farmers' Union.[45]

This turn of events injected an added sense of drama to the 1906 annual convention, which was consumed with the Daws-Tobin controversy. If the large landowners held any hope that the actions of the arbitration committee had eroded the farmers' loyalty to Daws, convention delegates quickly and unceremoniously dispelled this notion. Their dealings with Tobin can be described only as openly hostile, and he was jeered loudly whenever he appeared publicly at convention proceedings. Even the arbitration committee's "secret" evidence against Daws failed to sway the delegates, who responded with an important vote of confidence for their president. Since Daws was not eligible for reelection to the office of president, having already served two terms, he was selected to serve as the Union's new state organizer and lecturer.[46]

Even so, it was undeniable that the Indiahoma Farmers' Union had been transformed by the experience. The *Indiahoma Union Signal*, the movement's principal organ, was now in the hands of those who represented the large landowners. The executive committee, also dominated by large landowners, proposed that the organization's constitution be amended to abolish the office of state organizer. Since this was the office to which Daws had just been elected, the proposal obviously represented yet another attempt to remove Daws from a position of leadership in the Union.

There was more to this action than a personal attack on Daws, however. Indeed, the abolition of the office of state organizer was quite in keeping with the agenda of the large landowners. Prior to this change, the Farmers' Union relied on individual organizers to carry the gospel of cooperation to farmers who had not yet joined the cause. The principal responsibility of the state organizer was to recruit and oversee the cadre of lecturers who performed this function. For a variety of reasons, conservatives within the Union found this system of recruiting to be unacceptable. For one thing, as long as the individual organizers operated under the direction of one state officer rather than the executive committee, they were potentially free of the influence of large landowners. In addition, organizers tended to be veteran activists with direct ties to the Farmers Alliance. As such, they were well-versed in the workings of the commercial agricultural system and were convinced that the working farmer's only hope lay in cooperative action. In short, these organizers—like Daws himself—stood in direct opposition to the new vision for the Farmers' Union advanced by large landowners. The distinction became clearer when the conservatives introduced their own preferred method of recruitment. "Good literature," they maintained, was a more appropriate way of presenting the Farmers' Union to nonmembers.⁴⁷

Abolishing the office of state organizer required approval of the membership via referendum vote, and the process of gaining that approval was in itself instructive. The constitution required that copies of proposed amendments be sent to all locals no more than thirty days following the annual convention, and locals were given an additional thirty days to vote on the changes and report the results to their county secretary-treasurer.⁴⁸ In this case, events moved more slowly. It was not until October that locals received ballots, and in early December state leaders expressed dismay that only three thousand members had thus far participated in the vote.⁴⁹

Ultimately, the executive committee achieved its goal of abolishing the office of state organizer, but this victory occurred amidst the demographic collapse of the Indiahoma Farmers' Union. The month before the change was ratified by referendum vote, only slightly more than twelve hundred members of the Union had paid their dues and were in good standing.⁵⁰ It seems safe to conclude that a disproportionate number of those leaving the Union were small farmers loyal to Daws.

The large landowners completed their victory with the resignation of J. W. Houchin, the sole representative of the working farmer on the executive committee. Houchin's resignation followed pressure applied in the pages of the *Signal*, now firmly under the control of the conservatives.⁵¹ With this action, the Indiahoma Farmers' Union had become a different organization, serving a different constituency and committed to a fundamentally different set of goals.

At this point, the question of politics, always a thorny issue in the agrarian movement, made its way to the top of the Farmers' Union's agenda. Union leaders like Russell and Murray, who represented the vanguard of the large landowners now in control of the organization, were also leaders in the Democratic Party, and they naturally sought closer and more formal ties between the two groups.

Some Union members, especially those with greater experience in the agrarian movement, were suspicious of the developing Farmers'

Union–Democratic Party alliance. After all, the decision to align with the Democrats in 1896 had virtually wrecked the Farmers Alliance. The bitter legacy of that election, in fact, was so compelling that Union organizers had added language to their constitution explicitly designed to prevent its recurrence.[52] The Indiahoma Farmers' Union constitution pledged that the organization would conduct its affairs "without in any sense permitting the discussion of partisan politics or partyism."[53] Now Union leaders were breaking that proscription.

On a deeper level, the Union's burgeoning alliance with the Democrats was especially troubling to those who tended to coalesce around Daws and the working farmer faction. The Democratic Party, after all, was dominated by large landowners, merchants, and small businessmen, hardly the kind of men small farmers could turn to for assistance in times of crisis. Indeed, in the Union's bitter internal struggle it was Democratic Party leaders who led the charge against working farmers, providing many in the rank and file with all the evidence they needed of the imprudence of the new alliance. The Farmers' Union of Russell and Murray was not a place where Daws and those he represented felt welcome.

Sure enough, the actions of the new leaders at the Indiahoma Farmers' Union annual convention of 1907 proved that a political alliance with the Democratic Party was a portent of profound change in the organization. Working farmers, who had so enthusiastically supported crop withholding and the clearing house system in 1905 and 1906, were scolded by their new leaders for believing the "silly twaddle going the rounds of the press about 'this age of commercialism' and this being a day of greed for dollars."[54] Then convention organizers directed the discussion to what they considered to be the most pressing issue facing the Farmers' Union—whether the organization should support Lee Cruce or Charles Haskell in the upcoming Democratic gubernatorial primary.[55]

Although the distinctions between the two leading Democratic candidates for governor might have been uppermost in the minds of large landowners, the majority of Oklahoma farmers were unenthusiastic about the new agenda. Yet with organizational authority firmly in the hands of conservatives, the prospect of turning the discussion to issues of more direct consequence for working farmers was dim. As a result, thousands of farmers, already stung by their brush with the coercive power of the institutions of commercial agriculture, responded by severing their ties with the Indiahoma Farmers' Union. The demographic effect of this development was staggering; the organization began 1906 with at least seventy-four thousand members but ended the year with only three thousand.[56]

IV

The decline from some seventy thousand to three thousand members in little more than one year was disastrous by any standard. One need not search far for an explanation for this development; the combined effects of coercion and co-optation had induced thousands of Farmers' Union members to abandon their organization in 1906 and 1907. Such a dramatic change had implications that went well beyond the Union, affecting the political development of the new state of Oklahoma. Where were these thousands of working farmers to go, now that the Indiahoma Farmers' Union no longer served their interests? As these alienated citizens explored their options after statehood, they infused the political arena with a volatility uncharacteristic of the American electoral system. Ultimately, this large group of voters—disaffected, yet sophisticated in their understanding of the workings of power—would bring their weight to another political organization, the Socialist Party of Oklahoma.[57]

CHAPTER 4

The Remaking of the Socialist Party of Oklahoma

1907–1912

The demise of the Indiahoma Farmers' Union was only one of the factors that made the 1907 and 1908 political seasons especially turbulent in the Sooner State. The Democratic Party's progressive alliance with the Farmers' Union and organized labor lasted scarcely a year, causing Democratic leaders to feel especially uneasy about their chances for success in 1908.[1] The results of that year's elections confirmed their fears. Democratic presidential candidate William Jennings Bryan carried Oklahoma in 1908, but he did so with only 48 percent of the popular vote. Of even greater concern, three of the state's five congressional seats went to Republicans that year.[2] Perhaps most disturbing of all to Democrats, the Socialist Party appeared to be an important beneficiary of this political realignment. As table 3 demonstrates, more than fifteen thousand fewer Oklahomans voted Democratic in 1908 than in 1907, whereas votes for socialist candidates jumped by more than eleven thousand over the same period.

Such developments called for unusual measures, and Democratic Party luminaries put together a secret strategy in the fall of 1908 to ensure success on election day. The plan specifically targeted the thousands of working farmers alienated by the demise of the Indiahoma Farmers' Union, voters who hovered uneasily between the party of Jefferson and the party of Marx and who Democratic

TABLE 3. *Oklahoma Election Returns, 1907 and 1908*

		No. of Votes	
	Dem.	GOP	Soc.
Gubernatorial Contest, 1907	137,663	110,296	9,836
Presidential Contest, 1908	122,362	110,473	21,425
Difference, 1908 over 1907 (%)	−15,301 (−11)	+177 (0)	+11,589 (+118)

leaders wanted desperately to attract into the fold. Party strategists realized, however, that the traditional practice of sending openly partisan Democrats to appeal to these potential voters would be ineffective. Democratic planners planned a bold new tactic; they would finance speakers to deliver nonpolitical addresses, speeches that mentioned no specific political party but praised the newly ratified state constitution and the laws passed in the recent session of the state legislature.[3] Traditional party candidates would follow these speakers, pointing out that since the Democratic Party dominated both the constitutional convention and the legislature, the electorate should continue to vote Democratic in order to ensure future advances.

To institute their strategy, Democratic leaders solicited Daws's help. They had reason to believe he would cooperate, for the Democratic governor had recently appointed him to the post of Oklahoma state librarian.[4] Indeed, Daws was the perfect choice. His past in the Farmers' Union provided credibility among the farmers who were the object of the strategy, and his present position as a political appointee guaranteed his loyalty to the Democratic Party.

Democratic strategists' confidence in Daws was not misplaced. Daws campaigned hard in 1908, but he did so in a way shrewdly designed to advance the Democrats' secret strategy. Although his speeches and writings during the campaign season included blistering attacks on the difficulties faced by farmers and workers, his condemnation of the responsible parties remained strangely circumspect. In a dramatic retreat from the presidential address he had delivered to the Union membership only two years earlier, when he had alluded to deep and systemic shortcomings within the capitalist system, Daws now limited his attack to those politicians who favored "conservatism, fewer laws and better laws." It was a thinly veiled reference to the ideological differences between Democrats and Republicans, completely in keeping with the secret agreement between Daws and Democratic Party leaders.[5]

I

Daws's anomalous behavior in 1908 provides a fascinating window into the complexities of political assertion in modern American life. While his service on behalf of the Democratic Party seems completely out of character, his actions during the remainder of his life refute the notion that he sold out his commitment to working farmers in return for an easier life within the patronage system controlled by the Democratic Party. Although he remained state librarian until January of 1915, Daws never lost his commitment to the worker. He continued as an active lecturer and writer in the Farmers' Union, writing militant pamphlets under the pen name "Swadso."[6] His stature within the labor movement remained high, and delegates to the annual convention of the Oklahoma State Federation of Labor eulogized him in 1916 as "a consistent union man and a strong and vigorous worker in behalf of the toilers to the day of his death."[7]

Whatever Daws's personal motivation, his surprising behavior from 1908 until his death eight years later points to truths of profound significance for agrarian insurgency in the Sooner State. Daws was, after all, the most visible spokesperson for working farmers in the movement, and his decision to support Democrats instead of socialists after 1908 is testament to the agony of American democratic politics. Like Daws, thousands of alienated tenants and indebted smallholders felt politically isolated by 1908. Neither the Democratic nor the Republican Party could claim to represent them, and the capture of the Indiahoma Farmers' Union by forces sympathetic to large landowners rendered that organization ineffectual as well.

The Socialist Party appeared more promising, and many former Union members ultimately transferred their allegiance there. As Daws's case makes clear, however, the transition from the Indiahoma Farmers' Union to the Socialist Party of Oklahoma was neither smooth nor immediate. It was not until after 1912 that the Oklahoma socialist movement began to enjoy the widespread support of the working farmers who had constituted the core of the Farmers' Union. Like Daws, many former Union members found it difficult to transfer their allegiance from the Farmers' Union to the Socialist Party. While thousands ultimately made this political sojourn, many—like Daws—were unable to make the shift.

The explanation for their reluctance lies in an important tendency within the Socialist Party itself. During the Party's early years, its ideological and strategic positions on the critical question of land ownership were singularly inhospitable to the interests and aspirations of Oklahoma's yeoman farmers. This dynamic produced a series of events that has long puzzled students of the movement. On the one hand, the practical radicalism of former Union members ultimately energized the Socialist Party in Oklahoma and made it one of the premier state organizations in America. On the other hand, this breakthrough was achieved over the objections of Party members who had long been committed to the cause of socialism. Indeed, the wisdom on agrarian issues that was brought to the Party by those who had been active in the Farmers' Union was at first dismissed by socialist leaders as being inconsistent with socialist ideology.

In addition, agrarian radicals came to the Socialist Party with democratic ideas of decentralized power firmly in place, ideas that were immediately at odds with the way Party leaders routinely exercised their authority. The existing leadership structures in the Socialist Party were, as events would reveal, inherently authoritarian.⁸ The subsequent democratization demanded by former Union members was essential to the flowering of socialism in Oklahoma.

As a result of these complicated dynamics, the Socialist Party was immersed in debate during its formative years, as its members struggled to reach consensus on important questions. Prior to 1912, this debate centered on two critical issues: (1) whether or not it was appropriate for the Party to promote (or even tolerate) the private ownership of farm land, an issue known to all as "the land question"; and (2) the debate over how power would be distributed within the organization. Reaching consensus on these crucial issues involved nothing less than remaking the Socialist Party of Oklahoma into a form consistent with the needs of its intended constituency. As this process unfolded, the Party was shaped in fundamental ways by the memory of the Farmers' Union.

II

Of course, the discussion of the relationship between the Socialist Party and the Farmer's Union presupposes that a socialist presence existed during the territorial period, when the Union was the more significant manifestation of agrarian activism. During the years preceding statehood, the territories hosted a loosely organized group of socialist locals and clubs, for the most part clustered near the Kansas border. The first such local, organized in 1895 in Medford, Grant County, was formally affiliated with Daniel DeLeon's Socialist Labor Party.⁹ There was also socialist activity in the town of Newkirk in Kay County on the Kansas border. There, the editor of the *Kay County Populist* converted to socialism around the turn of the century, renaming his paper the *Oklahoma Socialist* to reflect his new political philosophy. Early in 1900 thirty-two representatives of socialist locals in ten counties formed a permanent territorial organization, and by 1902 the socialist presence in the territories had grown to twenty-three locals. Such organizing bore fruit on election day, and socialist candidates received some nineteen hundred votes in 1902.¹⁰ Significantly, these locals were concentrated in the northern and western regions of what became the state of Oklahoma. Virtually no socialist locals existed in the Indian Territory, the southeastern cotton-growing region where the Farmers' Union was most active. In an attempt to redress this weakness, socialist leaders organized a series of lecture tours in the Indian Territory beginning in 1903.¹¹ In that year twelve locals were organized, and by December of 1904 there was sufficient activity in the cotton region to warrant uniting socialist locals from the two territories into one organization.¹²

At this point, the burgeoning Socialist Party in Oklahoma and the Indiahoma Farmers' Union were essentially parallel developments. Socialist organizers helped create a structure that by 1908 would host the fastest growing socialist organization in the nation. Undoubtedly, many recruited into the Party between 1900 and 1908 already belonged to the Farmers' Union. Since the Union was strictly nonpolitical, it coexisted peacefully with the Socialist Party in the lives of farmers who had an activist bent.¹³

The Marxist language often used by Union members and organizers facilitated this easy coexistence. For example, writing in the *Durant Independent Farmer* in 1906, Union member W. M. Stingley borrowed freely from Marxist theoretical concepts in making sense of Oklahoma society. "The capitalist masters own, not only the natural and mechanical machinery of production," Stingley proclaimed, "but they own the full machinery of our government from justice of the peace up." He concluded that all workers (farmers included) must unite in opposition to the "capitalist class."¹⁴ Others used language taken from the best-known Marxist document of all, *The Communist Manifesto*. In 1905 Union leader Wood Hubbard wrote in the closing sentence of one of his articles, "Let us be of good spirit for we have nothing to lose but our chains, but we have a world to gain."¹⁵

Some farmers in southeastern Oklahoma spoke openly of this coexistence. One who belonged to both the Indiahoma Farmers' Union and the Socialist Party wrote to the *Appeal to Reason* about his prosocialist Union local in the town of Trail. "We have organized a Farmers' Union at our school house," he reported, "and they are getting educated rapidly. As soon as [the farmer] gets his eyes open he becomes a socialist. Have a number who will take the *Appeal* as soon as I can get to them."[16] Indeed, one former Union member who had made the transition to the Socialist Party remembered that the two organizations had shared more than rhetoric. "It is a fact," he wrote in a socialist publication in 1913, "that the strongest agitators for the Farmers' Union were avowed Socialists."[17]

When the Union veered right in 1907, however, its relationship with the Socialist Party was forever altered. Those farmers who sympathized with the ideological precepts of socialism were no longer welcome in the Union, and they found it increasingly difficult to hold membership cards in both the Indiahoma Farmers' Union and the Socialist Party. In essence, they were forced to make a choice: they could remain active in the Farmers' Union, in practice renouncing their ties to socialism by becoming inextricably bound with the Democratic Party; or they could remain in the Socialist Party of Oklahoma and jettison their ties to the Union.

The dynamics of such a choice were troubling to all involved. The final resolution of this crucial dilemma in the lives of thousands of Oklahoma voters would influence the trajectory of Oklahoma's political future. As both the political evidence and the personal experiences of Oklahomans like Daws indicates, there was no single obvious solution. Over time, however, it became clear that thousands of farmers eased their political isolation by moving into the Socialist Party. Doing so, they participated in the remaking of the Socialist Party of Oklahoma, directly challenging its positions on issues central to farming life.

III

Union members making the transition into the Socialist Party had only to glance at the socialist press to see that the Party's responses to the agricultural crisis did not address the needs of working farmers. Given the level of debate that had existed in the Union over the relative merits of collective marketing, cooperative stores, and the clearing house system, former Union members must have been stunned to read in the pages of an Oklahoma socialist publication: "No person may own real estate. Every acre of land in the country is owned by the whole people through the national government—taxes are simply rent."[18] Gradually, the scope of the problem facing agrarian activists in the Oklahoma Socialist Party became clear. Inherent in the Marxist ideology that undergirded socialist rhetoric was a thinly veiled disdain for farmers so profound that it held sway even in rural states like Oklahoma. Until Oklahoma socialists could break free of this crippling precept, they could not expect serious agricultural reformers, men like Daws, to support their movement.

The problem was endemic to the American Socialist Party, where discussion of agrarian questions was limited to the issue of whether farmers could own land and still be legitimate members of the working class. Thus, socialist leader Job Harriman declared on the floor of the Social Democratic National Convention in 1900 that "the farmers do not belong to the working class, because the farmers own the farms."[19] Harriman's comment came just one year after members of the Social Democratic Party eliminated, by referendum vote, the demands of farmers from the party's platform.[20] In 1908 the Socialist Party of America institutionalized this concept with a resolution calling for government ownership of all land and labeling dissenting positions as "unsocialistic."[21] Such a conclusion was consistent with the Party's position, codified in its platform that year, that farmers did not belong in the working class.[22]

Some in the national movement were uncomfortable with the finality of this conclusion, suggesting that the Socialist Party of America would be well advised to explore more fully the place of farmers in the organization. Algie Martin Simons, the most prominent of the dissenters, took issue with the orthodox position that saw all farmers as members of the bourgeoisie. In *The American Farmer*, published in 1902, Simons argued forcefully that under capitalism small farmers were just as exploited as their urban counterparts; they were, he maintained, "no more capitalistic than the miners who owned their own picks." He assured farmers that the Socialist Party would welcome them and had no interest in expropriating their land.[23]

Yet Simons's position, while enlightened by contrast with prevailing opinion within the Socialist Party of America, seemed rather primitive to Oklahoma socialists with experience in the Farmers' Union. As the agricultural crisis deepened, even Simons concluded that the prospects of success for yeoman farmers had become so minuscule that only one viable option remained: Farmers must voluntarily consolidate into large-scale cooperative farms in order to compete with large capitalist landowners.[24]

This national debate over the place of farmers within the socialist movement highlighted the distance between working farmers and national socialist theorists. Even the most sympathetic of the national socialist leaders failed to understand the depth of farmers' ties to the land. In this sense, the editor of the *New Century*, an Oklahoma socialist paper, stated the case for working farmers much more effectively and with a greater degree of precision than did Simons or any other national Party leader: "Without land, man cannot exist. It is the first necessity of being. It is the exclusion of wage workers from the soil that places them at the mercy of their employers and binds the chains of slavery upon them. There can be no solution of the economic question that does not restore the land to the people."[25]

Borrowing equally from the ideological and rhetorical traditions of the American Revolution and Marxism, this remarkable passage exemplified Oklahoma socialists' marriage of Jefferson and Marx. It is significant that this editor almost effortlessly combined a Marxist understanding of the agricultural crisis—the loss of land places "wage workers . . . at the mercy of their employers"—with Jefferson's tenet that only through freehold tenure could a measure of equality be attained in American society—"Without land, man cannot exist. It is the first necessity of being."[26]

Here, in terms that could not be mistaken, was the fault line on the land question. Those who spoke of land collectivization simply did not understand the American agricultural system. After all, the most disturbing manifestation of the agricultural crisis was the demise of the yeoman farmer, resulting in the concentration of land into the hands of large landowners and merchants. The socialist strategy of land collectivization seemed to many to be only slightly less objectionable. Agrarian activists understood that the opposite tactic was called for; only by returning the land to those who worked it could the agricultural crisis be solved. The resolution of this crucial inconsistency—the Marxist demand for land collectivization versus the Jeffersonian ideal of autonomous yeomen farmers—was absolutely necessary if the Socialist Party was to survive in the Sooner State.

Judging by the Oklahoma Party's platform prior to 1910, such a resolution had yet to be accomplished. Borrowing heavily from other state platforms, the Oklahoma document barely acknowledged the existence of farmers in its intended constituency. Completely ignoring the vast majority of Oklahomans, it defined the working class as "the class that works in the industries, and who secure their income through the sale of their labor power to the class that owns the means of production (the mines, factories, shops, railroads, warehouses, etc.)." Far from pointing out that the current agricultural crisis forced farmers into exploitive relationships that resulted in the loss of land, the platform hinted that in a socialist state, parcels of land should be kept out of the hands of individual farmers. "School lands and other public lands," which politicians often saw as property that could be distributed to individual farmers, would "remain the property of the state" under the socialist system.[27]

Only in 1909 did the Oklahoma Socialist Party acknowledge the dominance of agrarians in its constituency by including a "Farmers Programme" in its platform.[28] But even this document represented only a partial recognition of a rural proletariat. Carefully written to avoid alienating hard-line Marxists, the Farmers Programme stopped short of openly promoting full land ownership for tenant farmers. Instead, the program proposed to provide farmers with the benefits of ownership by calling for state lands to be rented to landless farmers "at the prevailing rate of share rent or its equivalent." Once the amount of rent paid equaled the value of the land, the tenant and his children were given permanent right of occupancy, thereby enabling "every farmer to have the use and occupancy of the land sufficient for a home and the support of his family."[29]

As socialist organizer Oscar Ameringer explained, Party leaders looked to the Homestead Act for inspiration in drafting this part of the Farmers Programme: "The outstanding feature of the Homestead Act was that until the settler proved his use and occupancy, his presence constituted his only claim to the land. . . . Thus, only farmers who farmed the land could possess the gift of Uncle Sam. Under this form of land tenure, which, so far as I know, was a purely American invention, absentee ownership was excluded."[30] This compromise was acceptable to most within the organization; it deferred to the orthodox Marxists in the national Party by not officially endorsing the expansion of private property, and it also addressed the reality of the poverty faced by Oklahoma's landless farmers. Yet it was still a compromise, making it clear that Oklahoma socialist leaders were not yet ready to confront this serious inconsistency in their ideological heritage.

It was not until 1912 that the Socialist Party of Oklahoma began openly supporting the distribution of land to tenant farmers. This time, the Party platform endorsed a far different definition of the proletariat, stating succinctly that "[t]he working class of Oklahoma is largely made up of agricultural workers." In addition, the plan for allowing farmers to rent land from the state was expanded to include provisions for the "constant enlargement of the public domain." The most significant change in the platform was contained in its "Renters and Farmers Program." In a clear rejection of the position of the orthodox Marxists, the platform proclaimed openly that the Socialist Party's central mission was "to facilitate the passing of the land from the possession of the landlords into the hands of the actual tillers of the soil."[31]

By staking out this ideological and strategic position, the Oklahoma comrades changed the trajectory of the American socialist movement. In important ways, Party members in the Sooner State won the debate over farmers and their place in the movement. Although the national Party did not come close to speaking on this issue as clearly and forcefully as the Oklahoma organization, in 1912 the Socialist Party of America's platform did include farmers in the working class for the first time. The Party now urged working farmers to join wage earners in the socialist cause, explicitly pledging "to support the toilers of the fields as well as those in the shops, factories and mines of the nation in their struggles for economic justice."[32]

Those socialists who had been active in the Farmers' Union must have observed with a sense of irony the arduous process by which the Party included and refined the farmers' demands in its platform. In a very real sense, in 1912 the Oklahoma Socialist Party arrived at what had been the starting point for the Farmers' Union program a decade earlier. Having overcome the Marxist prohibition of land ownership, however, socialists were presented with another, more formidable offshoot of their ideological roots. The socialist reluctance to engage in capitalist enterprises and the fear of "reformist" solutions prevented the Party from pursuing the collective marketing and cooperative buying strategies employed by the Farmers' Union. At the Socialist Party state convention in 1916, delegates rejected "industrial and commercial cooperation," a prohibition that made irrelevant the considerable experience and expertise of much of the Party's constituency.[33]

It was in the context of this dilemma that a group of agrarian socialists formed the Renters' Union in 1909. As an organization intended to supplement the political activism of the Socialist Party by organizing on the social and economic front on behalf of tenants and yeoman farmers, it represented the attempt by agrarian activists to pursue the tactics they had learned in the Farmers' Union while remaining active members of the Socialist Party. As one proponent of the organization put it, the Renters' Union would work "on the industrial field and the Socialist party on the political field."[34]

In establishing the new organization, the founders of the Renters' Union borrowed freely from the experience and lessons of the Farmers' Union. Remembering the destructive role played by large landowners in the old Union, the new organization explicitly limited its membership to tenants, farm workers, and those landowners who worked the land.[35] The Renters' Union also employed tactics inspired by the Farmers' Union, including crop withholding efforts, working to reduce rents by setting a maximum to be paid by Union members, and circulating the names of dishonest or particularly exploitive landlords.[36] True to its intended purpose of serving as the economic arm of the socialist movement, the Renters' Union cultivated its ties with the Socialist Party.[37] Renters' Union business was often transacted at the Oklahoma Party's annual conventions, and the principal work of organizing for the Union was performed by avid socialists, including J. T. Cumbie, Leonard Johnson, Sam and Luke Spencer, and H. Grady Milner.[38]

Drawing upon the wisdom gained by those socialists who had been active in the Farmers' Union, the Socialist Party of Oklahoma refined its stand on issues related to the land and thus became the only true protector of the interests of tenants and smallholders on the state's political landscape. Even if the Party never achieved the sophistication of the Indiahoma Farmers' Union in addressing the problems of the agricultural system, its stand after 1912 on the land question represented a significant achievement. By staking out an ideological position that made room for both Marx and Jefferson, the Socialist Party offered working farmers an alternative far superior to those advanced in either the Democratic or Republican platform.

IV

But the remaking of the Party was not yet complete. Socialists with experience in the Union recognized that too much organizational authority was centralized at the state level. Even as the Party worked to correct this imbalance, it was embroiled in a debate over how power should be distributed. Like the discourse over the land question, this discussion was central to the remaking of the Socialist Party. The terms of the debate were shaped by both the memory of the Farmers' Union and the inherited traditions of American socialism.

As members of the Socialist Party of Oklahoma discussed this complicated question, they confronted a crucial dynamic. During the first decade of the twentieth century, internal leadership positions in the Party were dominated, not by Oklahomans, but by representatives of the Socialist Party of America sent to the state by national leaders to oversee the development of the movement. These leaders had their own plans for the Oklahoma Socialist Party, plans that were not always acceptable to the rank and file.

In conceptualizing the development of the Oklahoma organization, Party leaders turned to the one example of a working socialist administration then in existence in America, Victor Berger's Milwaukee socialist movement. Convinced that Berger's Milwaukee formula could be applied to Oklahoma with similar success, Party leaders outlined the lessons of that experience that seemed relevant to the Sooner State in what they called the "Milwaukee Plan." As they described it, the Plan was actually quite simple. The movement must maintain a newspaper "owned and controlled" by the Party; it must nurture and develop a strong organization at all levels, from the state to the precinct; and it must present a united front to the rest of society. This final requirement could be achieved by the Socialist Party taking a "definite stand" on "every question that concerns the worker," thereby speaking with authority as the voice of the working class.[39]

Although these recommendations seemed eminently reasonable to state socialist leaders, the reactions of many Party members ranged from suspicion to outright hostility. At the heart of the negative response on the part of the rank and file was the realization that implementing the Milwaukee Plan would require a greater concentration of authority in the hands of state Party leaders. Prior experience in the Farmers' Union had left many socialists with certain expectations about the democratic boundaries within which their leaders should operate. The proposals advanced in the Milwaukee Plan exceeded those boundaries, setting up an inevitable conflict between rank-and-file members and their state leaders. As a consequence, until 1912 the Socialist Party of Oklahoma was consumed by controversy on a baffling array of seemingly minor issues related to this central dynamic. Only in retrospect does it become clear that the disturbances were remarkably consistent. Without exception, all of the seemingly minor issues over which the members clashed were related in some way to the implementation of the Milwaukee Plan.

The most immediate conflict centered on the first recommendation, the call for the establishment of a Party-owned press. When in late December of 1909 a group of socialists formed a weekly paper pledged to "conform to the principles advocated by the Socialist party of Oklahoma," it briefly appeared that this goal would be met with a minimum of disturbance.[40] Although the incorporators of the newspaper were not members of the state executive committee (SEC), the principal governing body of the state socialist party, the publishers' initial conduct could hardly have been more agreeable to state leaders. The new paper, the *Industrial Democrat*, would be edited by Oscar Ameringer, an organizer with deep roots in the national socialist organization, the American labor movement, and—most importantly—Berger's Milwaukee socialist organization.[41]

But the amity between state leaders and the *Industrial Democrat* proved to be short-lived. It broke down, in fact, during the paper's first official assignment, the reporting of the events of the annual state Party convention held in Oklahoma City in December 1909. The fracture between the publishers of the *Democrat* and the SEC centered on the stand taken by convention delegates on an issue unrelated to the Party itself—a proposed amendment to Article 9 of the Oklahoma Constitution. Article 9 granted the state government considerable regulatory power over the corporations operating within its borders, and the proposed amendment sought to limit this authority, most importantly by allowing railroads with headquarters outside of the Sooner State to operate within its borders. Formal enactment of this "railroad amendment" required the endorsement of the state's voters, and a special election was scheduled for June of 1910 for this purpose. In preparation for the election, delegates to the Party convention debated at length the proper socialist stand on the amendment. Following an address critical of the measure by the Secretary of the Oklahoma Federation of Labor, the delegates decided that the Socialist Party of Oklahoma would take an official stand against the amendment, and Party members were advised to cast their votes in the negative at the upcoming special election.[42]

Not all Party members approved of the decision to oppose the railroad amendment, and a vocal minority of dissenters made it clear that they would vote according to their consciences on election day. The debate over the railroad amendment became entwined with the issue of a Party-owned press by virtue of the fact that C. H. Armstrong, the principal founder of the *Industrial Democrat*, led the charge against the convention decision. When Ameringer publicly sided with the majority on the convention floor in opposing the railroad amendment, Armstrong removed Ameringer from his position as editor of the paper.[43] With a new editor in place, the *Industrial Democrat* went on record as supporting the railroad amendment, criticizing the SEC for its role in the affair. With this, the *Democrat*'s status as the official organ of the Oklahoma Socialist Party ended, and state leaders began searching for another publication more suited to that distinction. In response, a group of socialists who considered themselves more receptive to the official interests of the Party formed the *Oklahoma Pioneer* to fill this void.[44]

In the months that followed the convention, a bitter and destructive feud between the supporters of these two publications over the railroad amendment dominated the Socialist Party's affairs. At the heart of the matter was the conflict between the view of state leaders, whose experience was rooted in urban-based socialist activism and a deep commitment to the labor movement, and the view of Oklahoma farmers schooled in the activist tradition of the Alliance and the Farmers' Union. Speaking for the SEC, the publishers of the *Oklahoma Pioneer* argued that the stand against the railroad amendment was the only reasonable alternative. Not only was it proper that the Oklahoma Socialist Party endorse the position taken by the State Federation of Labor, it seemed clear that the proposed amendment was actually little more than a transparent attempt by railroad companies to circumvent the relatively strong regulatory power vested in state government by the Oklahoma constitution. This position seemed so obvious to the editors of the *Oklahoma Pioneer* that they could scarcely imagine how true socialists could legitimately disagree. There remained only one explanation for the conduct of Party members who supported the railroad amendment, an explanation succinctly laid out in the pages of the *Pioneer*: "We are convinced that the *Industrial Democrat* was financed by the railroad interests of the state and as such it was absolutely necessary that they be exposed and the party saved from the domination or influence of the party press by the capitalistic interests of the state."[45]

To the supporters of the *Industrial Democrat*, however, favoring the amendment was fully justified—a conclusion that reflected the difference in perspective between supporters of the two publications. While the *Pioneer* spoke for the Milwaukee-style Party leaders, who automatically aligned socialist political activism with organized labor, supporters of the *Industrial Democrat* saw the world from the perspective of farmers. To them, it seemed obvious that admitting more railroad lines into the state would benefit farmers by making it easier for them to sell their crops free of the domination of local merchants. Thinking it strange that the four largest railroads already operating in the state took the same position as the American Federation of Labor on the measure, they saw resistance to the railroad amendment as an attempt by these companies to preserve their monopoly in the state. "If we are forced to take a stand," the editor of the paper proclaimed, "we prefer to stand by the little roads, the cripples and the bankrupts, as against the four big thieves which have already raped and ravaged this state to a queen's taste."[46]

Based on these differences, both sides in the debate developed arguments to prove that their opponents were acting improperly in the matter. For the publishers of the *Oklahoma Pioneer* the issue was simple; the actions taken by the supporters of the *Democrat* represented a blatant breach of Party discipline. By taking a stand on the railroad amendment that opposed the official Party position as decided at the state convention, the *Industrial Democrat* was pursuing a course of action that undermined the legitimacy of the socialist movement. To supporters of the *Democrat*, on the other hand, the railroad amendment was not itself the central issue. Rather, the central issue was whether or not Party leaders had the right to determine the opinions of individual socialists. Arguing that the proposed amendment was "simply a controversy between two factions of the capitalist class," they expressed their position with great indignation: "As if the Socialist convention presumed to debate how the membership should vote on non-Socialist and non-political questions."[47]

The bitterness of the debate gave Oklahoma socialists pause as they observed the invective flying in both directions. The *Pioneer*, for example, charged at different times that support for the *Industrial Democrat* came from the Santa Fe Railroad and from "every incompetent, discredited or crooked worker in the state."[48] The *Industrial Democrat*, for its part, published the equally unsubstantiated charge that State Secretary Otto Branstetter illicitly used Party funds to support the publication of the *Pioneer*.[49] If all of this was disturbing to Party members, its seriousness paled by comparison to the final developments in the dispute. The month before the special election on the railroad amendment, C. H. Armstrong, Marvin Brown, and G. W. (Pap) Davis, the publishers of the *Democrat*, were expelled from the Socialist Party by the Oklahoma City local to which they belonged.[50]

Given the seriousness of this conflict, it is evident that there were more fundamental issues than the railroad amendment at stake. Indeed, well before the Oklahoma electorate settled this question by rejecting the proposed amendment, the focus of the debate between the two publications had already shifted to the recent decision of the SEC to own and publish the *Pioneer* as its official organ.[51] The Committee declined to include the officers or subscribers of the *Industrial Democrat* in this arrangement because of their past history of "direct opposition to the expressed will of the party."[52]

At this point, Oklahoma socialists began conceptualizing the debate in terms of the legitimacy of the concept of the Party-owned press as articulated in the Milwaukee Plan and implemented in the recent decisions of the SEC. While virtually all Oklahoma socialists agreed that the movement's newspapers must be owned and operated by Party members, there was considerable opposition to the current arrangement with the *Pioneer* on the grounds that it gave too much power to state leaders.

With the *Pioneer*'s contributions to the railroad controversy fresh in their minds, many Party members argued that it would be more appropriate for this function to become the province of Party officers at the county, rather than the state, level. Indeed, in supporting this view they could point to the existence of the numerous county socialist papers published in Oklahoma, all of which provided space to Party leaders for news and comments from the perspective of state headquarters. In addition, they pointed out, the *Appeal to Reason* published a special Oklahoma Edition, which also made space available to the SEC. All of this adequately filled the movement's communications needs, they argued, making it unnecessary for the Party to support and finance an additional newspaper devoted solely to propagating the views of state leaders.

Despite these objections, the SEC began taking steps early in 1911 to further solidify the ties between the Socialist Party and the *Oklahoma Pioneer*. Arguing that the publication was experiencing financial difficulties, the Committee proposed that all socialist locals be required to purchase annual subscriptions to the *Pioneer* for each member. In this way, Party leaders reasoned, the paper would be granted both a reasonable amount of financial security and the assurance of circulation among all socialists. However, despite warnings from the editor of the *Pioneer* that this step would be crucial for the survival of the paper, the proposal was soundly rejected by the Party membership in a referendum vote.[53]

Even though Party members eventually recanted, allowing the SEC to allocate part of the revenue generated through dues payments to the *Oklahoma Pioneer*, the paper continued to operate at a deficit and on at least one occasion was unable to make publication.[54] To cut expenses, the *Pioneer* gradually reduced the frequency of publication, changing to a monthly format in October of 1912.[55] Those opposed to the operation of the newspaper were triumphant, and by the end of 1912 the *Oklahoma Pioneer* ceased publication.

It is impossible to understand the nature and tenor of this conflict apart from the experience of the Farmers' Union. Those socialists who had been Union members must have seen disturbing parallels between the demise of that organization and the current struggles in the Socialist Party. The Farmers' Union had been destroyed by the co-optive influence of conservative large landowners who succeeded in gaining control of the organization. Building upon their base of support within the executive committee, these members won control of *Indiahoma Union Signal* and used this advantage to mold the Union into their image. Of course, the attempt by the Socialist Party's SEC to establish the *Pioneer* as the organization's official newspaper and the leadership's attempt to dictate the "proper" stand on the railroad amendment immediately raised the suspicions of former Union members within the Socialist Party of Oklahoma.

Thus, the historical links between the Indiahoma Farmers' Union and the Socialist Party help to explain the negative reactions of many Oklahoma socialists to the official Party stand on the railroad amendment and to the establishment of the *Oklahoma Pioneer*, reactions that are not as completely out of proportion to the potential impact of these issues on the Party as they might otherwise seem. The same dynamic was at work in the response to Party leaders' most direct attempt to institute the tenets of the Milwaukee Plan, which was made at the state socialist convention in December of 1910. There members of the SEC mounted an ambitious campaign to convince the membership of the propriety of their position, inviting Victor Berger himself to deliver the keynote address at the convention. Berger informed the delegates that "the Milwaukee success was due in large measure to the fact that it was a splendid machine in which the membership conferred upon the party officials the power to go ahead and do things."[56]

Inspired by Berger's rhetoric, convention delegates adopted measures that strengthened the SEC. Among the most prominent was the restructuring of the dues system to provide more funds for the maintenance of the state office. Prior to the convention, Party members had paid dues of five cents per month, all of which was forwarded to national socialist headquarters in Chicago.[57] With no regular flow of money to the state office, the Oklahoma Party was constantly forced to solicit donations to support its headquarters in Oklahoma City, a system that had only limited success. To correct this imbalance, convention delegates agreed to dramatically increase Party dues in order to place the state office on a firm financial footing. Besides the amount sent to national headquarters, each Party member would pay an additional ten cents per month to support the state office. Furthermore, delegates imposed on each member an additional assessment of five cents per month, which would go to state headquarters to pay for literature.[58]

With the state office more financially secure, Party leaders took further steps to strengthen their authority. Through the passage of a measure called the Lecture Bureau Resolution, the SEC worked to bring all socialist lecturers and organizers active in the state under its direct control. Under the terms of the resolution, all socialist speakers had to be certified by the SEC in order to work in the state. In addition, all future lecture tours were to be arranged and scheduled through state headquarters.[59]

The new regulations represented a direct challenge to the existing practice of allowing socialist speakers to work in Oklahoma under the auspices of socialist publications such as the *Appeal to Reason* and the *Rip Saw*, peddling subscriptions to these publications while spreading the gospel of socialism. Prior to 1911, this system worked well enough to be supported by state leaders, since the speakers in question inevitably strengthened socialist locals in the process of boosting the circulations of various socialist newspapers. After Oklahoma leaders decided to follow the example of the Milwaukee movement, however, the practice quickly became unacceptable. For one thing, with the establishment of the *Oklahoma Pioneer* as the official Party paper, the SEC was unenthusiastic about the promotion of other publications. In addition, the presence of speakers over whom Party leaders had no control was inconsistent with the SEC's new policy of centralizing authority.

Party members who objected to these developments were subjected to bitter attack by state leaders and their sympathizers. For instance, George E. Owen, the editor of the *Oklahoma Pioneer* and a strong supporter of the SEC, dismissed those who disagreed with the actions of state leaders as "individualists" whose loyalty to the socialist cause was clearly in doubt.[60] An article by Patrick Nagle published in the *Pioneer* employed similar tactics, identifying six individuals for special consideration as leaders of a "ring" responsible for obstructing the efforts of the SEC. In each case, Nagle attempted to prove that the individual in question was acting only in his self-interest. According to Nagle, H. H. Stallard, a former vice president of the Farmers' Union and past editor of the *Farmers' Union Advocate*, opposed state leaders' plans to establish a Party-owned press because of his wish to edit a privately owned paper that would "boost him for Congress." Nagle also contended that J. T. Cumbie, who by virtue of his recent nomination as the socialist candidate for governor was the most prominent of the decentralizers, took his stand only because of his considerable ego. Besides running for office, Cumbie penned numerous socialist verses; his opposition to the SEC, Nagle charged, came "because his impossible 'poems' and 'songs' were not lauded to the skies" in the *Oklahoma Pioneer*. Yet another of the decentralizers, Stanley Clark, opposed state leaders because they possessed the authority to prevent him from "'working' the party and the individual comrades for the 'coin.'"[61] The SEC attacked Clark in a particularly vengeful manner, suspending him from the organization for allegedly stealing money from the Party.[62] When Local Sulphur, Clark's local, refused to expel him, its charter was revoked by the state leaders.[63]

Opponents of the Milwaukee Plan responded quickly and decisively to these developments, thus beginning the final battle over the distribution of authority within the Socialist Party. The editor of the *Beckham County Advocate* condemned the tactics employed by the SEC with rhetoric reminiscent of earlier struggles within the Farmers' Union. The "rank-and-file of the party," he warned, must never become subservient to "a few kid-glove dudes and parlor socialists who happen to occupy official positions in the party." The editor concluded with a few words of wisdom regarding the proper amount of deference to be paid to Party leaders: "Obedience to authority is dangerous—just as much so in the socialist as in any other party."[64]

Other Party members responded with specific proposals intended to undermine the strategy of the Milwaukee Plan by redistributing authority among county and local organizations. A county socialist officer named H. M. Sinclair (see photo 1) offered the most ambitious of these, proposing that the five-cent assessment currently used to subsidize the *Oklahoma Pioneer* and to purchase socialist literature be removed, thereby reducing dues by 25 percent. In addition, he proposed that the portion of monthly dues used to finance the state office be reduced from ten cents to three cents per Party member, with the remaining seven cents returned to county and district organizations. In this way, county and local organizations would not be forced to finance county activities by imposing assessments above the twenty cents per month already paid in dues, a system which Sinclair argued penalized socialists in areas where the Party was most active. Sinclair also proposed that in the future more organizational work, such as planning encampments and routing speakers, should be done by county officers rather than the SEC. Finally, the state headquarters for the Socialist Party should be moved from Oklahoma City to Shawnee.[65] All of these proposals had the clear purpose of weak-

Photo 1. H. M. Sinclair. One of the original "decentralizers" responsible for returning organizational autonomy to socialist organizations at the county level, Sinclair was the secretary of Pittsburg County's socialist organization. He later served as the state chairman of the Oklahoma Socialist Party. Courtesy Western History Collections, University of Oklahoma Libraries.

ening the state office and vesting additional responsibilities in the hands of county and local officials.

When these proposed changes were submitted to the Party membership for approval, it became clear that while the majority of Oklahoma socialists favored decentralization in theory, most were not prepared to support all of Sinclair's recommendations. The proposal to reallocate a portion of the dues to county organizations was approved, although by the narrow margin of 893 to 776. The amendment to abolish the dues of five cents per month in support of the *Oklahoma Pioneer*, however, was soundly defeated, and, by a margin of almost three to one, socialists declined to move Party headquarters to Shawnee.[66]

At the Party convention in 1911, state leaders encountered further opposition, this time in the form of a series of amendments to the Party constitution that reduced the authority of the SEC. Among the changes adopted at the convention, the power to expel members was removed from the hands of the SEC, greater authority in obtaining and routing speakers was granted to county organizations, and the

Party administrative structure was changed so that the state secretary was no longer under the supervision of the executive committee.[67] The editor of the *New Century* reported these developments enthusiastically: "The New Constitution wipes out ring rule, obliterates bossism, establishes County Autonomy and puts the power of the Socialist movement into the hands of the rank and file, and brings to that organization a pure form of democracy."[68]

The final victory for socialists opposed to the actions of the SEC came at the Party convention the following year. Keeping the issue before the membership with the help of a socialist weekly called the *New Century*, the decentralizers planned their strategy carefully. As the date of the convention approached in 1912, they introduced the "Texas Plan," an aptly named alternative to the Milwaukee strategy. As explained in a lengthy article in the *New Century* by "Red Tom" Hickey, the fiery Texas socialist, this new strategy was necessary to rescue the Party from those wishing to misuse their organizational authority. Hickey called for a direct assault on the agenda of the existing state leaders. All state committees with the "power to take a hand in party affairs" should be abolished. Regarding the *Pioneer*, Hickey was even more direct: "Shun a party owned press as you would the plague. It depends upon the party treasury and not upon merit for support, it always sides with the powers that be, and it never fails to cause trouble." Finally, Party members must establish "absolute county and local home rule" in order to prevent the Oklahoma City "machine" from controlling the "internal affairs of a local or a county."[69]

At the state convention, the preparation of the decentralizers bore fruit. Delegates refused to issue credentials to State Secretary Otto Branstetter because he was not an Oklahoma citizen, and the SEC was formally repudiated for its action in the Clark case.[70] In Branstetter's place, delegates chose Sinclair, an Oklahoman who had served as a local secretary and as chairman of his county organization and the author of the earlier decentralization plan. Finally, Party members decided to rescind the action taken by the SEC against Clark and Local Sulphur and to abolish the editorship of the *Pioneer* as a Party office.[71] In a final action taken by the membership in June of 1913, the victory achieved at the previous two conventions was further solidified. A clear majority of Oklahoma socialists voted by referendum to recall Ameringer, one of the last of the national organizers still remaining in Oklahoma, as the state's national committeeman and to reinstate Armstrong, Davis, and Brown, the original publishers of the *Industrial Democrat*, to full Party membership.[72] An internal organizational structure more accountable to the rank and file was finally in place.[73]

V

By 1913 Oklahoma socialists had completed the tumultuous process of remaking their party. In the process, Party members resolved troublesome inconsistencies on issues of fundamental importance, inconsistencies that had seriously inhibited the movement's success. On the most important of these—disputes over the ownership of land and over procedures for the internal distribution of power—Oklahoma Party members faced inherited forms of socialist practice that were at odds with the needs of the agrarian constituency of the Sooner State. Yet Oklahoma socialists overcame these obstacles, embracing an ideology that unambiguously supported the return of the land to the working farmer and putting into place a more democratic and less centralized internal leadership structure. It was a remarkable achievement, accomplished by members who had learned important lessons in movement building through their experience in the Farmers' Union.

Even so, Party members recognized that their task was not yet complete. The Socialist Party still did not articulate the message of socialism in a manner wholly compatible with the cultural folkways of Oklahoma farmers. As they began working to make their party more responsive to their own experience, Oklahoma socialists recognized that evangelical Christianity, the dominant religious folkway of the Oklahoma countryside, provided the perfect link between the Socialist Party and the culture. Indeed, for all who had eyes to see, the teachings of Jesus Christ were every bit as explosive as those of Karl Marx.

CHAPTER 5

"The Real Gospel of Christ"

The Religion of Socialism in Oklahoma

Those who had joined the Indiahoma Farmers' Union in the territorial years must have experienced a numbing variety of emotions as they participated in the rise and fall of their organization. From the euphoric early success of crop withholding and the clearing house system to the destructive coup engineered by the large landowners, these experiences became part of a valuable collective wisdom carried into the Socialist Party of Oklahoma by its members. Of course, Party members put this wisdom to use, and their skills as social activists profoundly influenced the Socialist Party.

Oklahoma socialists were not simply lumps of clay to be molded by Party leaders into "good socialists." Their past caused them to respond to the stimulus of Party developments in infinitely complicated ways. Nor were they cultural exiles who had somehow escaped the dominant folkways of early twentieth-century American life; they brought with them into the Party most of the same ideas, preconceptions, and values held by other southwestern farmers. While some of these cultural forms—for example, the racism and sectionalism internalized and exploited in the political rhetoric of the Democratic and Republican Parties—clearly worked at cross purposes with socialist ideology, others coexisted easily with the precepts of Marxist socialism. Among the most powerful of the latter were some of the traditions of evangelical Christianity.[1]

Embedded in these traditions are ideas that carry potentially rich, if seemingly ambiguous, political implications. In its very sweep, the tenets of the Christian faith necessarily embrace ideas that are infinitely powerful, but which seem to have directly contradictory implications. Thus, while the principles of Christianity lead some believers to renounce all wars, many other Christians regularly call upon their religious beliefs to justify engaging in warfare. Of no less importance for political activists, the Biblical tradition speaks with a certain authority to the poor and otherwise disfranchised of the world; in this garment, Christianity offers power, dignity, a sense of purpose, and a feeling of self-worth to those whose position in society provides no such comforts. At the same time, in another garment the Christian tradition can be used to legitimize existing hierarchical forms, thereby instilling in the dispossessed an added sense of inferiority in contrast to their social "betters."

It is a tribute to the sophistication of Oklahoma socialists that they recognized both garments in their inherited religious beliefs, embracing the former as a useful tool in nurturing social activism, while rejecting the latter out of hand as lending support to the status quo. By incorporating so enthusiastically their Christian faith into the political message of the Socialist Party, the Oklahoma comrades instilled into Sooner socialism a profoundly religious flavor. Indeed, a unique synergy resulted from the mixing of these seemingly disparate forces, a synergy that worked to the great advantage of the Socialist Party. Just as the teachings of Jesus of Nazareth took on a whole new meaning when filtered through the lens of Marxism, the Socialist Party of Oklahoma seemed all the more valid to its agrarian constituency because of the religious tenor of its message and the moral implications of the socialist gospel.[2]

In light of this, it is important to begin thinking about the interaction of religion and radicalism in more sophisticated ways.[3] The religious flavor of Oklahoma socialism must be treated as more than a historical curiosity.[4] Party members in the Sooner State did not just happen to be religious; the profoundly religious nature of the Oklahoma movement was pivotal to its success. Socialist activists in the

Sooner State recognized that, for a variety of reasons, evangelical, fundamentalist Christianity was a perfect vehicle for spreading their political message. Carrying within it powerful communitarian ideals, Christianity could be interpreted by political activists in a way that called into question the reigning presumptions of agrarian capitalism. In addition, because of its widespread acceptance in the Oklahoma countryside, evangelical Protestantism provided a cultural language that was readily accessible and universally understood by prospective socialists. For these reasons, the teachings of Jesus Christ were not only as radical as those of Karl Marx, they were more persuasive to Oklahoma farmers.

I

Consider the announcement by Christians in the town of Roll in July of 1917 that a visiting preacher, Reverend O. E. Enfield, would preach at the local schoolhouse the following Sunday. Those who read the announcement in the local paper did not have to be told that Roll was the site of one of Oklahoma's most active socialist locals, and they already knew that Reverend Enfield, a popular socialist organizer, was sometimes referred to as Comrade Enfield. According to the correspondent who attended the meeting, the most notable aspect of Enfield's sermon was his explanation of "why we should oppose war."[5]

This incident is striking in its clarity, but it was by no means an isolated case. A similar meeting took place later in the same county, also involving church services with preaching and "dinner on the ground." The speaker was John A. Currie, another minister and socialist leader. This meeting, the paper promised, would be "a rare treat both materially and spiritually."[6] The same phenomenon occurred at the other end of the state in Bryan County, where among the speakers at a socialist picnic held in Durant were a Methodist minister from Texas, a Baptist minister and Oklahoma socialist leader, and a Holiness preacher.[7] The Texan, Reverend M. A. Smith, specialized in what he called "socialism as taught in the Bible."⁸ When the revered American socialist leader Eugene Debs came to Durant in southeastern Oklahoma in 1906, he spoke in that city's Holiness Tabernacle.⁹ Another comrade writing to a socialist newspaper reported that his local met every week "at a hall that's used for a church, and it was the pastor of the church who invited us in."¹⁰

In these ways, Oklahoma socialists routinely incorporated the cultural form of Protestant Christianity into their political discourse, an association almost instinctive to Party members who were believers. To a socialist named J. S. Evans, for example, it seemed perfectly natural to close a letter to a local socialist newspaper by extolling "the benefits and pleasures to be derived from the harmonious laws and teachings of Christ and Socialism."¹¹ For those who linked socialism to Christianity in this way, the indiscriminate mixing of the language and metaphors of the two seemed perfectly natural. Thus, the masthead of the *Sword of Truth*, a socialist weekly published in Washita County, proclaimed that its prose was as "Refreshing as 'The Shadow of a Great Rock in a Weary Land.'"¹² Most of the paper's subscribers recognized the phrase as an excerpt from the nineteenth-century hymn, "Beneath the Cross of Jesus" and as a verse from the Old Testament book of Isaiah. The editor soon added two additional Bible verses to the masthead.¹³

Another socialist used the language of evangelicalism to articulate the Marxist concept of class struggle: "The Social Souls of the earth are about to roll away the stone that has hid the Christ of Humanity from the working class of the world."¹⁴ A Party member from Tulsa, writing to the *Appeal to Reason* in 1903, described socialism in openly religious terms: "Socialism is the only 'ism' to turn the wicked from the error of their ways. The bible is full of socialism, but the churches have departed from the faith, and we, the Socialists, must educate them with the true light Christ brought into this world."¹⁵ Another comrade contributed a prayer to the *Sword of Truth*, combining religious morality with the Marxist concept of an impending social revolution. The prayer implored: "Permeate our souls with divine discontent and righteous rebellion.

Strengthen within us the spirit of revolt; and may we continue to favor that which is fair and to rise in anger against the wrong, until the Great Revolution shall come to free men and women from their fetters and enable them to be good and kind and noble and human! O Lord, hasten the day!"[16]

Thus, the Christian reverence for Jesus Christ became part of Oklahoma socialists' political faith, and Jesus was celebrated as a great socialist hero. The *New Century*, a socialist weekly published in the town of Sulphur in southeastern Oklahoma, described Jesus as "the best man the world ever knew."[17] In a poem called "The Toilers," Jesus was described as the leader of "the legions of democracy." The final lines of the poem answered the rhetorical question of who would lead the people to democracy:

> I think he is a fellow working man-
> A carpenter they say, from Galilee[18]

Another socialist made the point even more explicitly, arguing that Jesus' life could best be interpreted in terms of the struggle against the usurers in the temple. Writing in the *Boswell Submarine*, he informed readers that "Christ mingled with the poor; the reason he was spiked to the cross was because he lashed the bankers and the money changers."[19] Some wrote about the martyred Christ with even more emotion: "When Pilate handed down the decision the master class demanded, they led the Man of the People away to the Hill of Golgotha, and there suspended betwixt heaven and earth, one of the first great labor leaders of the world gave up his life for his class."[20]

Oklahoma socialists consistently emphasized Jesus' roots in the working class, often referring to him as "the lowly Nazarene" or the "proletarian Jesus."[21] The fact that Christ was a fellow worker gave socialists in Oklahoma a sense of dignity. As the *Beckham County Advocate* reminded its socialist constituency, Jesus taught that "whosoever is greatest among you, let him be servant."[22]

Thinking of Jesus as a socialist provided Party members like J. T. Ketchum with a legitimacy generally denied to members of radical political organizations. "We are Socialist," Ketchum proclaimed in the *New Century,* "because Jesus Christ, our elder brother, was the first one to preach the Socialist doctrine, Peace on Earth and Good Will toward man."[23] Another Party member noted that Christ's disciples practiced a form of socialism characterized by the communal ownership of all possessions. Significantly, this writer stressed, among the disciples there were "none that lacked anything."[24] A similar sentiment was expressed by N. S. Mounts in his regular column, "Musings of the Old Kuss," which appeared in several Oklahoma socialist newspapers: "I note that some journals hint that the source of socialism is of questionable character. I have not traced the theory to its source but I have read the history of an individual who lived and practiced it some two thousand years ago and he was undoubtedly of lowly birth. In early life he worked at the carpenter trade. Later he became a teacher and selected twelve companions of equally low estate as himself. These thirteen practiced socialism in its extreme form."[25]

This is not to say that Oklahoma socialists abandoned the more traditional heroes of the left in their haste to classify Jesus as a socialist; Karl Marx often took his place beside the Galilean as an important hero. One article described socialism as "a far reaching principle that embraces every phase of life, that makes Christ and His teachings more comprehensible, that clusters Darwin, Engels, Drummond, Huxley and Marx in a group of thinkers that can be understood, that applies the Golden Rule and answers the prayer of Gethsemane."[26] In an article entitled, "Some Biblical and Historical Points Leading Up to This Time," socialist Coleman White quoted in its entirety Isaiah 2:20–21, a familiar prophetic passage that predicted the coming of the Messiah: "In that day a man shall cast his idols of silver, and his idols of gold which they made each one for himself to worship, to the moles and bats. To go into the clefts of the rocks, and into the top of the ragged rocks, for fear of the Lord, and for the glory of his majesty, when He ariseth to shake terribly the earth." White had his own idea, however, as to who the Messiah was. In response to the question, "Who was this man?" he wrote,

"His name was Karl Marx, born of Jewish parents at Treve, in the province of the Rhine, May 5, 1818."[27]

Oklahoma socialists knew intuitively that their use of religious imagery made the socialist message instantly recognizable to a constituency seeped in the traditions of fundamentalist Christianity. Yet religion did not merely serve to make socialism palatable to a rural constituency. Its contributions to Sooner socialism were often more direct, affecting the movement in organizational as well as ideological ways.[28] Party functions in the state often involved praying and the singing of hymns. Socialist encampments, important events in the structure of the Oklahoma movement, featured special music and nationally known speakers in a juxtaposition closely resembling its religious counterpart, the tent revival. The similarities between these two events become clear in one socialist's description of an encampment held in 1914: "In short, [I] will say the encampment was one of the best in the state. They opened with prayer. We had the finest singing you ever heard. I saw old men and women weep like children. They shouted for joy for the coming victories through cooperation. About 1500 were in attendance.[29]

The point was made even more explicitly by "Comrade Davis," who wrote to the *Appeal to Reason* about a socialist encampment held in the territories in 1903: "It makes one think of an old-fashioned Methodist camp meeting. Singing and speeches, interest and excitement ran so high that the event lasted until about one o'clock in the night."[30] The religious presence was also felt in a dinner and program held in Roll in 1918 to commemorate the fourteenth anniversary of the founding of that local. The program included the song, "Who is a Christian," to be sung by one of the local's most devout socialists.[31]

II

It is clear that Oklahoma socialists borrowed heavily from the language, values, and practices of Protestant evangelical Christianity, presenting the gospel of socialism in terms that were familiar to farmers and workers. Not all Party members, however, approved of this practice. Socialist leader Stanley Clark, in fact, unleashed a particularly vehement attack on Christianity as a twentieth-century vestige of the superstition of the Dark Ages. Claiming that the "truths" of the Christian religion were simply legends based only loosely on fact, Clark called for "the story of the cross" to "take its place beside that of William Tell." Socialism, on the other hand, was rooted firmly in a foundation of "science and rationalism," he maintained, making it the inherently superior alternative in the minds of the enlightened. Indeed, Clark found little justification for the argument that Christianity could coexist with socialism, calling instead for the active opposition to religion by Party members in Oklahoma. He voiced this sentiment in no uncertain terms, proclaiming that "Christianity must be destroyed, this can never be accomplished by stabbing it in the back. To attack from behind is the act of a coward. Some political party should make it clear that civilization and Christianity cannot dwell in the same world together. If socialism has become so prostituted that it has lost its spirit of revolt against Christianity, a start to the cemetery is in order, and socialism should lead the procession."

Clark went even further in his denunciation of religion by openly questioning the wisdom of allowing professed Christians to be Party members. "A Christian in the Socialist Party," he argued, "is a driftwood on the bosom of an intellectual stream, he muddies the waters and builds a dam across the current that obstructs passage to the further shore."[32] Another socialist, who preferred to think of himself as a "Rationalist," expressed the same sentiment in a less visceral manner. To this critic, the very foundation of the Christian religion seemed in serious doubt:

> To be orthodox it means you must accept the Bible as the word of God, does it not? The Bible, a book that not only sanctions wars of conquest . . . but gives its endorsements to the institutions of chattel slavery and polygamy. How any American can intelligently believe

such institutions now, or ever did have the sanction of a wise and just God is far beyond our comprehension. . . .

Do you believe Jonah was swallowed by a whale? Do you, in the face of modern scientific discovery, assert the story of creation as told in Genesis is true? Do you believe the atrocities of the Jews, related in Genesis chapter 31, were commanded by a just God?

I hope you are not orthodox.[33]

Most Oklahoma socialists, however, made it clear that they did not support such stark secularism. For one thing, pronouncements like these violated the ground rules on religion established by the national Socialist Party in 1908 when it asserted that since socialism and religion were wholly separate forces, the Party neither supported nor rejected any religion.[34] Furthermore, the majority of Oklahoma Party members were quite comfortable with the peaceful coexistence of religion and socialism. To them, the official position adopted in 1908 served, not to protect the Socialist Party from excessive religious influence, but to prevent overtly antireligious sentiment—such as the views expressed by Clark—from being sanctioned by the Party.

These distinctions became clear in a series of official actions on the proper place for religion in the Oklahoma socialist movement. In 1911, for example, the Party's Muskogee local passed a resolution protesting the lack of enthusiasm toward religion displayed by the state leadership. While socialism "has nothing to do with anything spiritual or with a hereafter," the resolution concluded, it was, after all, "in entire harmony with that part of the Bible that teaches of man's rights and duties to his fellow man."[35] At the Oklahoma Socialist Party's state convention held in 1913, delegates adopted a resolution that made this the Party's official position on religion:

> We do not think it good tactics to drag religious questions into our political movement. We, therefore, disapprove the method of some who indiscriminately denounce the church, the Bible and the Christian

religion; but instead, we recommend that every individual be left to exercise his own religious views, regardless of creed or order.

But that each and every speaker have the unanimous consent of the party to take the hide off of every capitalist-minded preacher or politician who misrepresents the socialist party.[36]

A resolution adopted by delegates to the 1916 state convention went even further. This time, they recommended that "Socialist locals, agitators or party members in their capacity as Socialists should refrain from attacking on the platform or through the press the various established institutions of religion."[37]

III

Clearly, Oklahoma socialists were conscious that Christianity was an integral part of their movement. Their frequent use of the language, symbolism, and forms of Christianity was entirely consistent with the fact that a large number of ministers in Oklahoma were active in radical politics. One Party member, in fact, estimated in 1912 that a majority of the ministers in his county supported the socialist movement.[38] The same commentator remarked that the Party was gaining "more recruits from the ranks of the ministry than from any other profession."[39] These socialist ministers, whether or not they represented a significant portion of their profession, made important contributions to the success of the movement in Oklahoma. Under the direction of ministers like Thomas W. Woodrow, the Christian Socialist Fellowship actively sought to "proclaim socialism to churches and other religious organizations" in the state.[40] The effort seemed to be working. Woodrow described in the *Industrial Democrat* his experience preaching in a Baptist church where "most of the Baptists [were] Socialists."[41] The Oklahoma Conference of the Pentecostal-Holiness Church was also affected by the spread of radical doctrines. At its annual convention in 1911, denominational leaders grappled with the proliferation of socialist pastors, a development they found troubling. They admonished the offending preachers to "entirely abandon their doctrine of Socialism, as our doctrines are Christ and Him only."[42]

These ministers were invaluable to the Party, serving as leaders, candidates, speakers, and organizers. J. T. Cumbie, one of the movement's foremost leaders, was a Baptist minister. Cumbie was the socialist candidate for U.S. Representative in 1907, 1912, and 1914, he was the candidate for governor in 1910, served as the county organizer in Bryan County, and was elected to represent Oklahoma as a member of the national committee. Cumbie's status as a minister was well-known; he was sometimes referred to by his comrades as "John the Baptist."[43]

Reverend Enfield, the minister who addressed the Party faithful in Roll in 1917, was also a socialist candidate for Congress and governor. A vehement opponent of U.S. involvement in World War I, he was arrested in 1918 and charged with promoting armed resistance to the United States government.[44] Thomas H. McLemore of Beckham County, who was elected as a socialist to the Oklahoma House of Representatives in 1914, was a Church of Christ preacher. McLemore also served as secretary of his Party local and of the Beckham County socialist organization.[45] Reverend Leonard Johnson was a veteran organizer who worked actively for the Farmers' Union, the Renters' Union, and the Socialist Party. Preaching became one of his essential recruiting tools. Johnson traveled the state organizing locals, stopping on Sundays to preach in local churches.[46] George W. Hutton, the editor of an important socialist weekly in Roger Mills County, authored a regular column containing religious news and arguments entitled "Sunday Morning Thoughts."[47] Another minister, Reverend George G. Hamilton, the associate editor of a widely read weekly called the *Social Democrat*, served as a Party lecturer in 1912 and 1913 and was the socialist candidate for lieutenant governor in 1914.[48]

The dozens of ministers occupying prominent positions in the Socialist Party was merely another indication of how intimately the organization shared the religious values of the Oklahoma countryside.

This quality made it difficult for the enemies of the Party to successfully portray socialists as immoral and antireligious, the standard antisocialist weapon then in vogue in the United States. Even so, spokesmen for the Democratic and Republican Parties in the state gamely repeated charges that socialists wryly referred to as the "free love and atheism bugaboo."[49] The editor of the *Roger Mills Sentinel*, a partisan Democrat, demonstrated his mastery of the technique in an editorial charging that "Socialism was founded by infidels, and has been conducted by infidels, and today it is led by a bunch of infidels." Karl Marx, the editor continued, was "an infidel Jew," and Morris Hillquit—a prominent socialist from New York— was an agnostic. The editorial also pointed out that the Socialist Party regularly held meetings on Sunday, thereby "desecrat[ing] the Sabbath." Finally, socialism was evil because it denied the divinity of Christ.[50] The editor repeated the attack in a later edition, charging that the avowed objective of socialism was to "reck [sic] this free government bequeathed us by our forefathers, to crush and to turn back the hands on the dial of time when the Socialists had full sway in France." As was often the case with antisocialist attacks based on the accusation of atheism, ministers were enjoined to lead the charge against socialism.[51]

In light of the large numbers of ministers in the movement and given socialists' persistent references to the Bible in their rhetoric, the charge was patently absurd. It was thus with some exasperation that one socialist weekly asserted that socialism was in actuality "the great *bulwark* of society, Christianity and the home." Only under a socialist system, the paper maintained, would it be "possible for a man to do unto others as he would have them do unto him, as taught by the Carpenter."[52] There was a certain irony in this exchange, since the paper defending itself against the charge of atheism was called the *Sword of Truth*.

Other socialists responded more aggressively to these attacks by turning the charges against their accusers. The *New Century*, for example, charged that the Democratic Party was "the party of slavery, the party of polygamy, the party of booze and boodle, and yet they say you Socialists would 'break up the church.'"[53] H. Grady Milner, the paper's associate editor, developed an elaborate argument based on "Jefferson's Bible" to prove that this founder and hero of the Democratic Party did not believe in the deity of Christ and spurned Christian morals.[54] N. S. Mounts, the writer of a column appearing in several socialist newspapers in Oklahoma, lambasted Billy Sunday for the hypocrisy of his antisocialist position: "The language attributed to Sunday is blasphemous, a libel upon Him who footprinted the sands of Galilee in the long ago. And, the ho-bo, blaspheming, ecclesiastic clown insists that socialism is the avowed enemy of Christianity and would destroy the home."[55] As this bitter attack on Billy Sunday illustrates, the exchanges over the inherent morality of socialism were not conducted solely by journalists and politicians.

IV

It would be a mistake, however, to assume that Oklahoma Party leaders seized upon the language and forms of Christianity solely in a Machiavellian attempt to attract religious farmers into the Socialist Party or to condemn its enemies. Such an interpretation presupposes that Christian arguments lacked the substance of Marxist ideology and played only a supporting role in the Oklahoma socialist movement. In fact, Marxism and Christianity achieved a synergy in the Party, combining in a unique way to strengthen the movement. Thus, while the Marxist ideas that socialists brought to Christianity energized the democratic, communitarian strains in evangelical Protestantism, religion simultaneously deepened and made relevant the Marxist ideological core of the Socialist Party. The resulting message became all the more powerful.

The Oklahoma Party's stand on the agricultural crisis that crippled southern states for decades following the Civil War provides the most revealing example of how the joining of Christianity and Marxism strengthened both traditions. Building on the Marxist notion of class conflict, socialist leaders in the Sooner State argued persuasively that the inequities of the existing system resulted from shortcomings systemic to capitalism. Such an analysis helped draw farmers into the Party by explaining the poverty endemic in the Oklahoma countryside in terms that emphasized the shortcomings of the system rather than the shortcomings of its victims.

Interestingly, fundamentalism—the particular form of evangelical Protestantism practiced by most Christian socialists in the state— also attracted those bruised by the inequities of the existing system. For this reason, the worship patterns of Oklahomans were deeply divided along class lines. Those most likely to vote socialist could generally be found on Sundays in Primitive Baptist, Pentecostal, and Holiness churches, groups characterized by H. Richard Niebuhr in his study of denominationalism as "churches of the disinherited." On the other hand, the business and political leaders who actively opposed socialism were more likely to be members of the established, mainline Presbyterian, Baptist, and Methodist denominations.[56]

Oklahoma Party members understood this dynamic and incorporated the class-based component of denominationalism into their message. They considered it only natural for ministers associated with the mainline denominations like the Methodist, Presbyterian, and Baptist churches to oppose socialism, since they belonged "body and soul to the capitalists" and their attacks on the Socialist Party "may be regarded as merely an effort to earn their daily bread."[57] Such sentiment had long been part of the socialists' arsenal; as early as 1895, the *Appeal to Reason* argued that "modern Christianity is little better than a fraud and a humbug and used by the preachers on orders of the wealthy class, to force the common herd to bear with patience the daily outrages placed upon them, so as to better prepare the toilers of the nation to accept that serfdom into which they are rapidly drifting."[58] A socialist named Vance Cook denounced mainline religion as the "church of greed" that worshiped the "god of gold." Cook was at pains to make himself clear: "I here and now declare war on them both—war to the death—and this church and this God we will destroy with the help of Almighty Jehovah."[59]

As biting as this political analysis of denominationalism was, its theological premise provided an additional edge. Theologically, the major difference between the "churches of the disinherited" and mainline evangelical, Protestant denominations centered on a phenomenon known as the *baptism of the Spirit*. While all evangelical Protestants accepted the notion that all who had been born again were saved and would go to heaven, some fundamentalists believed that only a few, select Christians displayed evidence of having reached a higher plane of Christianity by receiving the baptism of the Spirit.[60]

The pragmatic implications of this theological distinction became clear on Sunday mornings. The values associated with the higher place of spiritualism accompanying baptism of the Spirit translated into such worship practices as faith healing, speaking in tongues, and increased emotionalism. Significantly, these were practices that mainline denominations seldom engaged in. For some Christians associated with fundamentalist churches, this distinction provided insight into a mystery that was both religious and political in nature: How could local furnishing merchants, bankers, and politicians—those most directly responsible for the impoverishment of the working farmer—gain such widespread acceptance in the mainline denominations, even serving as the very pillars of their respective congregations?

The answer was clear to those in the churches of the disinherited: Such Christians might think themselves pious, but the fact that they refrained from healing and tongues could only mean that the Holy Spirit was withholding his gifts. Thus, God himself understood what the rest of society seemed to have missed; in God's eyes, the impoverished farmers who worshipped in fundamentalist churches were superior to their political and economic enemies. Here, the theology of fundamentalism meshed seamlessly with the politics of Marxism. In their own way, each helped the dispossessed make sense of the world's imperfections.[61]

The resulting link between fundamentalist Christianity and Marxist socialism made the Oklahoma Socialist Party extraordinarily powerful. Socialism made sense to thousands of Oklahoma farmers because it was the only political option consistent with the values of Christianity. As "the most moral organization in the world," the Socialist Party, alone among the three major political parties in Oklahoma, remained true to the teachings of Christ.[62] Oklahomans must accept the doctrines of the Socialist Party, one comrade argued, because "God is the author and founder of the economic social cooperative commonwealth of the nation."[63] So fundamental was this connection between morality and socialism that the lines between them began to blur in the minds of some socialists.

As the editor of the *New Century* admitted, "To us socialism is both a science and a religion. It is a religion because it teaches the fulfillment of the natural laws and prepares a man so that he can truthfully pray, 'Thy Kingdom come. Thy will be done, in earth as it is in heaven.' It teaches the brotherhood of man. . . . It is a science of government that must prevail that the whole human family may have access to the means of life."[64] When asked to share his reasons for becoming a Party member, the same editor replied that he had joined "because the ethics of Socialism and the ethics of Christianity are identical."[65]

For those who equated socialism with morality, it followed that rejecting socialism was as great a sin as renouncing Christ. One socialist editor was explicit about the connection between moral and political apostasy, condemning those who dismissed socialism without investigating its merits as being "in the same category with those who crucified Christ."[66] Another socialist argument, this time directed at Oklahoma's ministers, couched the dilemma over whether to support or oppose socialism in similar terms: "The day is at hand, Mr. Preacher, when you must line up, must show your colors. If you are with the crowd that Jesus drove from the temple, you will have to show it, and if you want to come out from among the thieves and money changers and join the battle for humanity its [sic] time to show your hands. The fight is on and you are either with the masses or with the classes. Where do you stand?"[67]

George Fowler, a socialist from Harrah in Lincoln County, also pointed to these biblical enemies in his critique of twentieth-century

America: "'Awake thou that sleepeth, for thine enemy is upon thee.' The very 'wickedness in high places' that Christ fought, bled and died for is flourishing in all of its vile effects among you today. We have the competitive, money changing, private ownership system that Moses, the prophets, Christ, and the apostles died fighting against."[68] In similar fashion, a socialist named J. H. Hawkins developed an argument based on the Bible to prove that "the two thieves crucified with Christ represented the Democratic and Republican parties."[69] An article in the *Beckham County Advocate* provided perhaps the most direct articulation of the notion that, since socialism was equated with morality, those opposed to it represented the forces of evil. The Socialist Party, the paper asserted, was "fighting the powers of hell."[70]

For Oklahoma farmers, the "powers of hell" were all too present in the world around them. Through Marxist class analysis, made even more powerful by the moral authority of Christianity, Oklahoma socialists denounced tenancy, the crop lien, and rural poverty. Their attack on usury—the cornerstone of the exploitive relationship that trapped Oklahoma farmers in a cycle of tenancy and indebtedness— shows with exceptional clarity just how powerful this mix could be.[71]

Oklahoma socialists began by confirming that usury was condemned in the Bible. The *Appeal to Reason* quoted verses from Deuteronomy and Leviticus denouncing usury, and Oklahoma socialist minister Currie outlined a carefully conceived argument proving that Jesus opposed the charging of usurious interest.[72] A socialist writing to the *Beckham County Advocate* describing two recent sermons preached by socialist ministers also began with a biblically based condemnation of usury. In this case, however, the condemnation was merely the foundation of an argument denouncing bankers and merchants as robbers: "Both of these preachers told what the bible says about the man who is extortionate in dealing with his brother in distress. . . . When we see a man or a church professing the name of Christ and at the same time doing things the bible explicitly forbids, we know they are hellish frauds seeking to hide behind Jesus to carry on their robbery."[73]

The *Boswell Submarine* continued this line of reasoning, arguing that "In the sight of God theft is theft whether legalized or otherwise. The most abominable deception practiced," said the paper, "is upheld by the church when it harbors the usury monger who steals from your babies (through interest) that which justly belongs to them."[74] When another socialist weekly issued a challenge to non-socialist preachers for a debate on the question of whether "a church can uphold rents, interest, and profits and still be a scriptural church," the argument had come full circle.[75] The moral standards of Christianity were now invoked to denounce, not just the charging of excessive interest, but the right to charge any interest at all. In doing so, socialists used the Bible to condemn the principles central to the capitalist system.

This line of reasoning led to a powerful political conclusion: Capitalism was an inherently unchristian system. For J. H. Vandiver, the central flaw in the system was its dependence upon competition rather than cooperation: "To be a true follower of Christ one must be in favor of brotherly cooperation and against competition, for competition puts every man against his brother, competition makes every man to be his brother's killer."[76] Socialist columnist George Fowler reached the same conclusion: "'Love thy neighbor as thyself.' Rejoice in his prosperity the same as thy own. How can this be under competition which means strife? 'Look not everyone on his own things, but also upon the things of another.' Such is possible only under co-operation."[77]

The *Sayre Social Democrat* expressed a similar sentiment, characterizing capitalism as a "ghastly fraud" and a "horrid mockery." "The present system is not Christianity," the paper concluded, "it is cannibalism."[78] It seemed ironic to a writer for Beckham County's socialist newspaper that America considered itself to be a Christian nation when "all business is based on the very opposite to what was taught by the lowly Nazarene."[79] The twenty-third Psalm was used by a socialist minister as the inspiration for a bitter parody highlighting the exploitive nature of the existing agricultural system:

The (land) Lord is my shepherd;
I shall not want (for shearing).
He maketh me to lie down in (his) green pastures;
He leadeth me (by the nose) beside the still waters (of his political mud-puddle)
He exploiteth my soul; he leadeth me in the paths of capitalism for his game sake.
Yea, though I walk through the valley of starvation and death,
I will fear no less evil; for thou art with me (to skin me); thy rod and thy party lash they come fast upon me.
Thou preparest a table before me and bank-queteth me in the presence of mine enemies; thou annointeth my head with toil; my cup of sorrow runneth over.
Surely curses and poverty shall follow me all the days of my life;
And I will dwell in the (rented) house of the (land) Lord forever.[80]

An even more direct attack appeared in the *New Century* in 1913: "Since the Good Book says: 'The land is mine; it shall not be sold forever,' it is quite clear that capitalism has had a head-on collision with Holy Writ, and that a bunch of fellows are in possession of stolen property."[81]

One socialist newspaper editor summed up the explosive power of fundamentalist Christianity when mixed with the message of socialism. "There is enough dynamic force in the New Testament, if preached," he proclaimed, "to blow every existing social institution to atoms."[82]

V

This fascinating juxtaposition of Christianity and Marxist socialism was a unique part of the Oklahoma movement. In the Sooner State, we are treated to the spectacle of Eugene Debs addressing his constituency from the pulpits of Pentecostal churches, the picture of O. E. Enfield delivering stirring antiwar messages at church picnics, and the vision of thousands of comrades gathered for socialist encampments with their heads bowed in prayer.

This rich tapestry of evidence makes it clear that religion was centrally important to the Oklahoma socialist movement. For many socialists, in fact, the connection was so intimate that socialism simply became equated with Christianity. Thus, when the editor of the *New Century* called for ministers to preach socialism, he did so with the admonition, "The *New Century* would like to see the ministers preach the real Gospel of Christ."[83]

By freely borrowing from Christianity, Party members in Oklahoma produced a movement that remained overtly socialist while giving expression to deep-seated cultural and religious values. Not only did the Party's statement on land ownership unabashedly proclaim a message that was true to the experiences of working farmers, it now spoke in a cultural form that was instantly recognizable and that carried the moral authority of the Gospel itself. As a result, by 1912, the Socialist Party of Oklahoma was in a unique position in the history of American politics; it could no longer be dismissed as a "third party" with only a remote chance of political success.

CHAPTER 6

Power and Insurgency

Democrats and the Socialist Movement, 1910–1916

All of the pieces were now in place, and Socialist Party leaders in Oklahoma looked expectantly to the future. By 1912 they had built an organizational structure that shared power with members at the local and county levels. They were sophisticated enough as activists to present their message in the widely recognized cultural form of evangelical, fundamentalist Protestantism, creating a synergetic relationship with the inherited, Marxist-based message of socialism. And perhaps most importantly, the Socialist Party did not equivocate in the Sooner State on the crucial question of land ownership; it embraced the Jeffersonian ideal of a democracy rooted in a strong yeoman class. All of this made the Socialist Party of Oklahoma uniquely qualified to serve as the political voice of working farmers, the clear demographic majority in the state.[1]

I

At the center of the political drama in the Sooner State were the specters of tenancy and indebtedness, which haunted the lives of most farmers.[2] In this context, the Socialist Party's stand on the land question was inherently superior to that of its principal opponent, the Democratic Party. Most Democratic officials were members of the agricultural and business elite, making that party's position in agricultural society at best an ambiguous one. The case of Robert L. Williams, a veteran Democratic Party activist who was elected governor in 1914, illustrates perfectly this ambiguity. Hardly "a man of the people," Williams owned three thousand acres of farmland in Bryan County, land that was worked by numerous tenants. In addition, he held "substantial interests" in several banks and controlling interests in cottonseed oil and insurance companies.[3]

As long as the Democratic Party remained dominated by men like Williams, it faced serious challenges from the flourishing Socialist Party. After all, such men were profiting handsomely under the existing agricultural system and could hardly be expected to support reforms that would undermine the institutions of this system. At the same time, however, their continued political success was contingent upon the ongoing loyalty of tenants and smallholders, those who suffered most profoundly under the status quo. Given this ambivalence—relying on the support of tenants and smallholders for their political existence while at the same time defending a system that kept this group in peonage—Democratic officials found themselves in an interesting dilemma whenever the political debate turned to the crisis on the land. At these junctures they displayed a noticeable lack of urgency, relying on abstractions and platitudes in place of meaningful discussion. Disaffected farmers must work harder, they admonished their constituency, live more frugally, and—above all—participate in the electoral process by voting for Democratic candidates on election day.

The Socialist Party, on the other hand, unencumbered by this structural contradiction between the needs of its constituency and those of its leadership, spoke on agricultural issues with an authority unavailable to the Democrats. Socialist organizers ridiculed the platitudes repeated endlessly by Democratic and Republican leaders, pointing skillfully to their crippling inconsistencies. As one socialist caustically remarked, "The Democrat has nothing to offer the renter, save an admonition to 'love Joe Baily and hate the nigger,' funny stories and a five cent cigar."[4] Ameringer used humor to illustrate the absurdity of the Democratic and

Republican positions. "The trouble with you tenant farmers in the south," Ameringer wrote in a satirical account of a politician's speech to a group of tenant farmers, "is that you spend your money foolishly. Take your table, for instance. What's the use to squander good money on such luxuries as baking powder, biscuits, corn pones and salted swine's bosom. Or, what is still worse, black coffee with real sugar in it."[5]

For impoverished farmers, Ameringer's parody led to a liberating conclusion—their poverty resulted from the shortcomings of the system, not their own failings. Far from being "lazy" or "extravagant," one socialist editor asserted, farmers who happen to be poor were "hard-working, frugal, honest souls that have labored hard all these years, and are to-day without a legal right to stay upon the earth, simply because they have been robbed of the greater amount of the products of their labor."[6]

Not content to merely identify the inconsistencies in their opponents' stands, socialists articulated clearly why such inconsistencies occurred. The Democratic and Republican Parties' unsatisfying responses to the agricultural crisis, socialist organizers pointed out, were actually quite understandable, given the fact that both organizations were dominated by bankers and large landowners. On this point, the Socialist Party could speak without ambiguity. Unlike the other political parties in the state, one socialist editor pointed out, the Socialist Party "does not pretend to represent both the capitalist and the worker. It represents only the worker and says so plainly, and asks no capitalist to vote its ticket."[7]

During the heat of political campaigns, the Party relentlessly exploited this advantage. For example, the Socialist Party campaign book, distributed to thousands of voters during the election season in 1916, contained photographs of tenant shacks on the estates of prominent Democratic officials juxtaposed with renderings of the officials' residences (see photos 2–5). On one page was pictured the home of Jake Loveall, a tenant on the estate of Governor Williams. Along with the picture were the following questions:

How does the Democratic Home Ownership Law help this tenant? Is the interest of tenant Loveall and Landlord Williams identical? Do they belong to the same class?
Does the Democratic party legislate in favor of the Williams class or the Loveall class?[8]

Having reached this logical threshold, the Socialist Party of Oklahoma began staking out ideological territory uncharted by Democratic or Republican Party politicians. Socialists like Patrick Nagle (see photo 6), a lawyer and former Democrat who edited a socialist newspaper called the *Tenant Farmer*, spoke to Oklahoma's tenantry with a directness generally absent from American political discourse:

> Under the institution called "capitalism," which holds you in its grip, every two years out of three, is an absolute and complete failure so far as you are concerned. You labor three years on a rented farm—one year's labor goes to the landlord—one year's labor goes to the money loaner, the transportation, storage, implement companies and middle men, and one year's labor you retain for yourself and your family.
> The Socialist party stands unalterably for the tenant farmer and unalterably against the farmer who farms the farmer.[9]

Whereas Democrats and Republicans were forced to rely on abstraction, socialists described the reality of the agricultural crisis using imagery that heightened the immorality of the system. "The children of the tenant must pick cotton on cold November days until the blood drips from the ends of their fingers," one socialist publication asserted, "so that the banker, landlords and parasites of the electric towns may revel in luxury."[10] (See photo 5.)

Then came the ideological centerpiece of the socialist program. The agricultural crisis could be resolved, socialist organizers proclaimed, only by fundamentally restructuring the institutions of agrarian society. The Socialist Party platform was explicit on this point. A massive redistribution of land "from the possession of the landlords into the hands of the actual tillers of the soil" would be required to end agrarian poverty.[11]

The skill with which the Socialist Party made its case to Oklahoma farmers was not lost on Democratic officials, who often referred to socialist leaders with a grudging respect. The haunting simplicity of testaments like a letter addressed to the Democratic candidate for governor during his campaign in 1914 could not help but affect Democratic Party leaders. "Now Mr. Williams," the letter began, "if you want to know how the People is going to vote down here you go to the State head quarters of the Socialist Party an you will find that there Platform has got you skined a city Block an then some [*sic*]."[12] Much of the socialist literature, one Democrat reluctantly admitted, was "shrewd beyond comparison with any other political material that has ever appeared in the state."[13] When responding to questions about the "socialist threat," the leader of the progressive wing of the Democratic Party warned fellow Democrats not to engage in public debate with socialist candidates: "But the leaders of socialism, the men who direct the affairs of the party in this state and who represent it in the public forum, are in the great majority of instances highly informed and acute minds, shifty antagonists in debate, with whom it must be admitted there are few democratic speakers competent to cope."[14]

Despite the Democrats' inability to speak for small farmers, however, they were not about to allow the socialist message to go unchallenged. "It will take hard and persistent work," one Democratic official argued, "to counteract this enemy."[15] And local Democrats did work persistently, having long experimented with ways of diffusing the socialist menace. Officers in Coal County, for example, responded decisively when Stanley Clark brought the socialist message to the town of Coalgate in 1904, as did the town fathers in Shawnee five years later when confronted with socialist organizer Oscar Ameringer's rhetoric. In both cases, the offending parties were quickly arrested.[16] Local officials in Okmulgee displayed a particular penchant for creativity in the arrest of a socialist organizer named Jack Wood in 1906. Since Wood happened to be

2   OKLAHOMA RESIDENCE OF SENATOR ROBT. L. OWEN.

3   HOME OF TENANT J. BECK (5 in family).
    On Senator Owen's estate.

Illustrations from the Socialist Party of Oklahoma's Campaign Book, 1916. The party's Campaign Book for 1916 made skillful use of photographs to promote socialist solutions and discredit the Democratic Party. In these illustrations, the sprawling home of Democratic Senator Robert Owen (photo 2) is juxtaposed with the shack of a tenant family on Owen's estate (photo 3). The Lee Huckins' Hotel in Oklahoma City, where Governor Robert Williams often stayed (photo 4), contrasts dramatically with the home of one of Willimas's tenants (photo 5). Courtesy the Special Collections Library, Duke University, Durham, North Carolina.

LEE HUCKINS' HOTEL.
The Home of Bob Williams and the Democratic Machine.

HOME OF TENANT BENEFIELD (11 in family.)
On estate of Governor Williams

Photo 6. Patrick S. Nagle. Editor of the Tenant Farmer *and socialist candidate for governor and U.S. Senate, Nagle was an important Oklahoma socialist leader. This photograph is taken from the party's Campaign Book for 1916, when Nagle was a candidate for the criminal court of appeals. Courtesy the Special Collections Library, Duke University, North Carolina.*

addressing a crowd from a sidewalk located one block from the county courthouse, peace officers arrested him for "disturbing the United States court by loud talking."[17] As if to stress that these local actions were not enough, the Democratic press bureau in 1909 began to send an increasing quantity of overtly antisocialist material to partisan newspaper editors, urging local editors and officials to "cooperate in eliminating this danger which threatens the democratic party."[18]

These developments illustrate that local Democratic politicians were quite willing to use their control over governmental institutions to their own political advantage. Among the most prized advantages held by elected officials was their dominance over the electoral machinery in the state, and Democratic leaders proved themselves quite capable of misusing that dominance. As a result socialist candidates consistently found themselves the victims of electoral fraud. One allegation focused on the conduct of election officials in Custer County in 1906. According to a formal complaint filed by socialists in the case, local poll watchers blatantly disregarded state regulations, permitting the ballots to be tampered with by "some unauthorized person."[19] Not providing enough ballots to precincts that were known to be strongly socialist was another popular tactic employed by election officials. This was the case in seven precincts in Kingfisher County in the primary election of 1908; one precinct in Le Flore County received enough ballots for only one-third of its socialist voters.[20]

The situation was so bad in Murray County that socialist leaders were forced to provide Party members with exact instructions on how to prevent their votes from being disqualified. Comrades were warned to be especially alert to election officials who used a pencil to push ballots into the box. These officials were "well acquainted with the people of the precinct," socialist leaders pointed out, and could predict with reasonable certainty those who were voting for socialist candidates. Officials would use the lead end of the pencil to push these suspicious ballots into the box. After all of the votes had been cast, it was a simple matter for them to identify the ballots containing pencil markings and disqualify them as being mutilated.[21] Using such tactics, over two hundred socialist votes were disqualified in Blaine County in the election of 1912.[22] In the same election, the socialist candidate for township treasurer in Murray County defeated his Democratic opponent only to have the Board of Elections award the victory to the Democrat after the contest—even though the Democratic candidate had already conceded victory to his socialist opponent![23] Two years later, election officials refused to allow socialist poll watchers to observe the voting in the primaries, an action that Party officials complained was repeated in the general election.[24]

In these ways Democratic officials used their dominance over the State Board of Elections to deprive socialists of a portion of their vote. Thus, a letter from a local Democrat to the governor thanking him for state officials' help in defeating local socialists is unusual only in its candor. The socialist defeat in his area, he reported, was "due to the reorganization of the County Election Board, for which all good democrats here thank you."[25]

II

These attempts by Democrats to deal with the "socialist problem" notwithstanding, prior to 1912 Democratic leaders saw the Republicans, not the socialists, as their greatest threat. The election of 1908, in which Republicans were victorious in three of the state's five congressional districts, served to illustrate this in a most disturbing manner. Oklahoma Democrats followed a time-honored southern strategy for dealing with this kind of electoral scare; they attempted to weaken the GOP by disfranchising black voters.[26] Estimating that such a tactic would deprive the Republican Party of more than twenty-five thousand voters, Democratic strategists assured their constituency of the strategic merits of this course of action.[27]

In 1910 Democratic politicians drafted their own version of the literacy test and grandfather clause, legislation used elsewhere in the nation to disfranchise blacks, and offered it as an amendment to Oklahoma's constitution. The proposed amendment sought to disqualify black voters by making literacy a prerequisite for voting. In order to prevent this provision from having the unintended effect of disfranchising the large number of Democratic white voters who were also illiterate, the grandfather clause specified that descendants of those eligible to vote on 1 January 1866 were not subject to the literacy qualification.[28] To satisfy the state's constitutional requirement that prospective amendments be submitted to the populace for a referendum vote, party officials arranged for the measure to appear on ballots in the primary elections of 1910.[29]

Democratic officials made no attempt to hide the underlying purpose of the literacy test and grandfather clause, assuring white voters that they had nothing to fear from the measure. "Its sole effect," one partisan editor informed his readers, "is to properly limit the suffrage right of our Negroid voters."[30] The author of a broadside distributed to Democratic voters agreed, assuring whites that "the illiterate negro is the only person in any way affected by the amendment." Those who implied otherwise, this Democrat warned, were unscrupulous, designing politicians who were motivated by the desire to "retain the negro in politics for the purpose of using his vote for corrupt purposes."[31]

Although the literacy test and grandfather clause was intended to weaken the Republican Party, Oklahoma socialists made it clear that they, like the Republicans, opposed the proposed amendment. As the *Industrial Democrat* pointed out, "the measure was purely and simply the result of race hatred and race prejudice accounted for on the grounds that the negro simply cannot be induced to vote the Democratic ticket." The paper admonished its readers to vote against the provision on election day, "thereby vindicat[ing] the principle for which our revolutionary forefathers fought."[32] Other socialist arguments against the literacy test and grandfather clause were more firmly grounded in Marxist theoretical precepts. "The socialist as a matter of course," one editor argued, "views the proposition from the standpoint of the class struggle and will oppose it from that standpoint, realizing that the negro belongs to the working class."[33] The Oklahoma Socialist Party's official position on the measure was equally clear: "We are opposed to the disfranchisement of the negro, because the negro belongs to the working class. If we stand for the working class we must stand for the whole of the working class and not a part of it, and consequently we must stand for the negro. If he is disfranchised it weakens the voting strength of the working class."[34] The editor of the *Oklahoma Pioneer* used similar reasoning, warning that the provision represented "the thin edge of the wedge that eventually leads to the disfranchisement of the whole working class, irrespective of race, color or degree of knowledge."[35]

Democratic leaders had expected opposition from the Republican Party, but they were surprised by the severity of the socialist response.[36] Black voters, after all, traditionally supported Republican candidates, and very few blacks in Oklahoma had joined socialist locals. The fact that both socialists and Republicans were working against the literacy test and grandfather clause sparked Democratic leaders to go to extraordinary lengths to ensure its approval. On the ballots drawn up by the election board, the other measures to be considered in the primary elections in 1910 under the constitution's referendum provision were listed according to past procedure; the title and text of each measure were provided, along with separate boxes for the voter to register approval or disapproval. The literacy test and grandfather clause, however, appeared on the ballot in quite different form. In place of the text of the provision was only the phrase, "State Question 18." Instead of providing separate boxes for affirmative and negative votes, there were only the words, "FOR THE AMENDMENT."[37] On election day, a negative vote could be cast only by striking through this phrase.

Since the passage of referendum measures required a majority of the total votes cast, the unique treatment afforded the literacy test played an important role in the final outcome. In normal referendum contests, electors who voted for any of the candidates for office but failed to vote on a particular referendum were in effect voting against the measure by increasing the number of total votes cast without also increasing the affirmative votes for the referendum in question. Through their manipulation of the ballot, however, Democratic officials succeeded in circumventing this "silent vote," which had proved disastrous to previous referenda. The silent vote was recorded in favor of, rather than against, the referendum on the literacy test and grandfather clause.[38]

The Democratic strategy paid off on election day; the literacy test and grandfather clause passed by a vote of 135,000 to 106,000.[39] The Socialist Party responded by filing suit, charging that the peculiar way the measure was listed on the ballot represented an unconstitutional use of power on the part of state election officials. The state supreme court rejected the claim, blandly ruling that the ballot used in the election was "neither illegal or unusual."[40] The literacy test and grandfather clause remained in effect in the state until 1915, when the United States Supreme Court ruled it unconstitutional in the case of *Guinn and Beal v. U.S.*[41]

The reaction of the Socialist Party to this attempt to disfranchise blacks provides useful insight into the state of race relations within the Party. While its insistence that blacks should be treated as fellow members of the working class represented the Socialist Party's

Photo 7. H. H. Stallard. A member of the Farmers' Union who moved into the Socialist Party after Oklahoma achieved statehood, Stallard was a socialist candidate for U.S. Congress on four occastions. His views on race and war, however, made him one of Oklahoma Party's most controversial leaders. Courtesy the Special Collections Library, Duke University, Durham, North Carolina.

official position, this was not necessarily the opinion of all socialists. Some Party members expressed serious misgivings about any stand that appeared to espouse racial equality, sparking a messy and somewhat disturbing internal debate on the "race question."

One of the most prominent dissenters from the official Party position was H. H. Stallard (see photo 7), a former Farmers' Union official who became a frequent Socialist Party candidate and a member of the SEC. Stallard favored the segregation of blacks and whites within the Socialist Party, arguing that "if enlisting one negro or pushing him to the front will prevent ten white men from studying socialism we have done the negro as well as the whiteman an injury. Socialism is what we all want, then let us adopt a resolution declaring for segregation of the negro and let him work out his own destiny."[42]

Clearly, many Oklahoma socialists considered Stallard's remarks to be outside the mainstream of socialist ideology. The socialist local in Wilburton, for example, passed a resolution condemning Stallard and affirming the right of blacks to be Party members.[43] Other socialists articulated similar expressions of support for blacks. John M. Work condemned Jim Crow laws as "an absurdity and an insult to a race which deserves our sympathy and assistance instead of our malice and contempt," concluding that "prejudice can not find any lodgement in a broad mind."[44] H. Grady Milner condemned the absurdity of the Democratic Party's efforts to "submerge politically all the workers who by chance of birth happens [sic] to be black."[45]

This is not to say that the socialist debate on race was always conducted in such rational terms. On the contrary, examples of blatant racism on the part of socialists in Oklahoma abound. The editor of the *Otter Valley Socialist*, for example, criticized President Wilson in 1916 for removing the widow of a Confederate general from the office of postmistress in Georgia and replacing her with a "thick lipped Georgia coon."[46] The editor of the *Kiowa Breeze* offered his own, equally racist, insight into the debate: "When the South learns that a 'nigger' can't be controlled when he is full of cocaine or bad whiskey, without first injecting the contents of a shot gun into his black hide, the 'race question' will about be solved.[47]

Other socialists were inordinately quick to defend themselves against the charge that they favored racial equality, betraying their true feelings in the process. The editor of the *New Century*, for example, attempted to prove that the Democrats were also guilty of this charge. Interracial marriages, he pointed out, were presently occurring in states controlled, not by socialists, but by Democrats.[48] Another socialist offered a rhetorical question as a response to the Democratic Party's charge that socialists favored racial equality: "How about that nigger your national leader, Woodrow Wilson, appointed Registrar of the United States Treasury?"[49] The *Ellis County Socialist* was at pains to point out that it was a Democratic judge who performed the marriage ceremony joining the mayor of Chicago with a "coal black 'nigger gal.'"[50]

This conflicting evidence regarding the Socialist Party of Oklahoma and race defies easy generalization. Yet despite the ravings of Stallard and other racist socialists, the fact remains that the Party worked hard to defend the franchise for blacks at a time when it was politically dangerous to do so. Even given the openly racist sentiments of some socialists, the Socialist Party was the most hospitable political institution available for black Oklahomans in the early twentieth century. The Republican Party, the traditional home for black voters, disassociated itself in 1906 from this portion of its constituency through the efforts of a group called the "Lily White Republicans." Their success became evident at the state party convention in 1907; blacks who attended were denied admission to the central committee meeting, they were excluded from all appointed committees at the convention, and a separate headquarters was established for black Republicans.[51]

Faced with this kind of alienation from both the Democratic and Republican Parties, many blacks saw the Socialist Party's opposition to the literacy test and grandfather clause as all the evidence they needed of the socialists' commitment to racial fairness. As a result, a group of prominent black leaders met in convention following the election of 1910 to make a significant recommendation: "Therefore, Be It Resolved, That we hereby endorse the platforms put out by our Socialist brothers and recommend that all the colored people of Oklahoma vote the Socialist ticket and align themselves with our Socialistic brethren of Oklahoma."[52]

The Socialist Party platform adopted in 1912 vindicated the position taken by these black leaders, committing the Party to unambiguous support for a racially united working class. "The safety and advancement of the working class depends upon its solidarity and class consciousness," the platform proclaimed. "Those who would engender or foster race hatred or animosity between the white and black sections of the working class are the enemies of both; and we assure the black section of the working class that under the coming civilization which is Socialism, they will be accorded every political and economic right which we now demand and eventually shall secure for ourselves."[53]

It is this position, not the ravings of a few individual socialists who happened to be racists, for which the organization should be remembered. The Socialist Party of Oklahoma stood alone in the

Sooner State on this issue, and it took a highly visible place among its American comrades in promoting a Marxist vision of a unified working class that transcended ethnic and racial barriers.[54]

In retrospect, the Socialist Party's stand on the literacy test and grandfather clause and the resulting debate over black-white relations within the Party proved instructive to all concerned. Democrats, who seemed almost incredulous that the Socialist Party would take such a politically risky stand on this issue, began learning that their socialist opponents were not ordinary political enemies. Six years later, a leading Democratic strategist still struggled with this lesson: "Socialism is not merely a political doctrine; it is a broadly founded philosophy, a combination of highly theoretical considerations, metaphysical, psychological and biological, with emphasis on a number of maladjustments in modern society which the old political parties have heretofore ignored."[55]

Republicans, equally surprised by the Socialist Party's opposition to the literacy test and grandfather clause, realized that a mutually beneficial, if ideologically strained, coalition with the socialists might be possible. Indeed, the two parties did cooperate on occasion to counteract the Democrats. This, in turn, led periodically to the charge by the latter of socialist-Republican fusion.[56]

The response of black Oklahomans to this episode was necessarily complex. Those who met in 1910 to call for an alliance with the Socialist Party soon learned that not all African Americans supported their position. Shortly after this meeting, a counterresolution favorable to the Republican Party was drawn up and adopted by other black leaders in the state.[57] For all of the rhetoric suggesting an alliance between blacks and socialists, in fact, very little actual cooperation occurred. As one interpreter points out, most black Oklahomans continued to see the Republican Party as their best political option: "Oklahoma's Negroes, when they could vote, rejected class politics and consistently supported the GOP. The socialist press never once referred to the activities or existence of a Negro local, nor were any blacks ever elected to state or county executive committees. There were no socialist weeklies edited by or intended for

Negroes; the 'colored press' was dominated completely by the Republican oriented *Boley Progress, Black Dispatch,* and *Muskogee Cimeter.*"⁵⁸

This episode was most instructive for socialists. The Democratic Party's handling of the referendum on the literacy test and grandfather clause gave socialists their first real taste of the use of political and economic power to defeat insurgent movements. It was a lesson that some socialists remembered well from their days in the Farmers' Union and that all Party members would learn again in the coming years.

III

The socialist opposition to the literacy test and grandfather clause served notice to Democrats and Republicans that the Socialist Party had become a significant force in Oklahoma politics. The Party had an impressive organization in place, bolstered by dozens of local and state socialist newspapers. Indeed, by 1908 more copies of the national socialist weekly, *The Appeal to Reason,* were sold in Oklahoma than in any other state.⁵⁹ Party membership increased dramatically, from some ten thousand at statehood to more than twenty-four thousand in 1910.⁶⁰ The socialist faithful were revitalized each summer at socialist encampments. Generally held in August, when fieldwork on the cotton crop was completed, encampments gave Oklahoma farmers the opportunity to hear socialist speakers of national repute. Eugene Debs himself, the most beloved socialist of all, spoke at numerous Oklahoma encampments. More than two hundred such meetings were held in 1915 alone, several of which attracted ten thousand farmers each.⁶¹ An observer to an encampment held in Sulphur Springs in 1913 counted some seven hundred covered wagons, a spectacle this witness likened to "the gold rush days."⁶² Socialists who attended these encampments were treated to much more than socialist propaganda; an advertisement for an encampment held in Sayre in 1910 promised not only prominent socialist speakers, but music, "merry-go-round, shows, and all other forms of innocent amusement" as well.[63]

The extent of socialist organization in rural Oklahoma can be seen through the experiences of an agrarian organizer who traveled through the southeastern cotton-growing region of the state in the spring of 1912. The organizer described his arrival in the town of Shay in Marshall County, "a socialist hot bed" where virtually all municipal officials, including the postmaster and the members of the school board, were Party members. He found that Ravia, in nearby Johnston County, had "had several Socialist mayors and administrations." In Wapanucka, also in Johnston County, the town's largest mercantile establishment was run by an "active and loyal socialist."[64] The town of Mankomis was another pocket of socialist strength. There, town officials, the majority of whom were members of the Socialist Party, hung a huge crimson banner with the slogan, "Debs for President in 1912," from the top of the municipal water tower.[65]

Having reached this organizational plateau, the Socialist Party expected to achieve dramatic electoral success in the elections of 1912. In that year, Debs gathered more than forty-one thousand votes in the state, over 16 percent of the total votes cast. In the regions where socialism was strongest, the gains achieved since 1910 made it clear that the socialists, not the Republicans, were the major challengers for the position of power occupied by the Democratic Party. In both Marshall and Roger Mills Counties there were only two candidates, a Democrat and a socialist, for state representative. The socialist candidate for that office in Marshall County received 43 percent of the total vote, more than doubling his performance of two years earlier. The numbers were only slightly less dramatic in other counties, where increases over 1910 averaged more than 40 percent (see table 4). In addition, as table 5 demonstrates, the ongoing Socialist Party tradition of electing candidates to county and local offices was stronger than ever in 1912. (See map 2 for a sense of the geographical distribution of Socialist Party strength.)

Building on this strong performance, the Socialist Party immediately set its sights on the 1914 elections, fully expecting to capture

TABLE 4. *Election Returns in Selected Counties, 1910 and 1912*

County	Votes received by Socialist Candidate		% Change
	1910	1912	
Beckham	633	963	+ 52
Bryan	543	843	+ 55
Dewey	577	766	+ 33
Johnston	425	771	+ 81
Marshall	350	731	+109
Murray	532	599	+ 13
Roger Mills	415	590	+ 42
State Totals	24,655	41,424	+ 70

Source: Oklahoma State Archives, Oklahoma City, Oklahoma

Note: State totals for 1910 reflect votes received by the socialist candidate for governor; totals for 1912 are votes received by the socialist candidate for president. All county totals are votes received by socialist candidates for representative

important political offices at that time. Such was the optimism prevailing among socialists that one delegate brought to the state convention in 1913 a handmade oak chair that was "highly polished and decorated with horns." He had crafted the chair for use by the first socialist governor of the state, to be elected in 1914.[66]

To reach that goal, the Party mounted a massive organizing campaign, an effort that bore fruit by the beginning of election year. Over one hundred new locals were organized in the first five weeks of 1914.[67] In the first six months of 1914 alone, 834 new Socialist Party locals were organized.[68] These new locals were incorporated into a carefully conceived Party structure consisting of county organizations and, during the campaign season in statewide elections, campaign committees for each congressional district. In anticipation of the campaign, Oklahoma socialists raised money for a "Red Automobile," which would tour the state "filled with socialist speakers." In each county, the Party's official nominees for public office would join the Red Automobile for a tour of the area.[69]

TABLE 5. *Socialists Elected to County and Local Offices, 1904–1913*

YEAR	LOCATION	OFFICE
1904	Stillwater (Payne Co.)	Councilman
1904	Grove (Delaware Co.)	3 Councilmen
1906	Stillwater (Payne Co.)	Alderman
1909	Krebs (Pittsburg Co.)	Police Judge, Mayor
1910	Marshall County	Sheriff
1911	Coalgate (Coal Co.)	Assessor, 2 School Directors, 2 Aldermen
1911	Krebs (Pittsburg Co.)	3 Aldermen
1911	Harrah (Lincoln Co.)	Marshall, Police Judge
1911	McAlester (Pittsburg Co.)	2 Aldermen
1911	Wilburton (Latimer Co.)	Alderman
1912	Krebs (Pittsburg Co.)	2 Aldermen
1912	Dougherty (Murray Co.)	Sheriff
1912	Love County	Sheriff
1912	Blue (Bryan County)	Constable, Justice of the Peace
1912	Oologah (Rogers Co.)	Township Clerk
1912	Wilson (Pushmataha Co.)	2 Justices of the Peace
1912	Skiatook (Tulsa Co.)	Township Trustee
1912	Collinsville (Tulsa Co.)	Justice of the Peace
1912	Kiowa County	Co. Commissioner
1912	Savanna (Pittsburg Co.)	5 Township Offices
1912	Seiling (Dewey Co.)	Justice of the Peace, Township Clerk
1913	Yale (Payne Co.)	Trustee
1913	Saline (Delaware Co.)	School Director
1913	Collinsville (Rogers Co.)	City Clerk, City Attorney, 4 City Councilmen
1913	Chant (Haskell Co.)	Mayor, Treasurer, Clerk, Marshall, 5 City Councilmen
1913	Kiefer (Creek Co.)	Justice of Peace, Trustee

Source: Socialist Party Papers, Duke; *Appeal to Reason*, 7 May 1904, 21 April 1906, 8 May 1909, 15 May 1909, 24 September 1910, 15 April 1911, 20 May 1911, 23 November 1912, 7 December 1912, 12 April 1913, 21 June 1913; *New Century*, 5 April 1912, 8 November 1912, 28 February 1913, 11 April 1913.

Note: This list is compiled from information provided in socialist publications. It is not comprehensive.

Strong Socialist Counties, 1912 to 1914

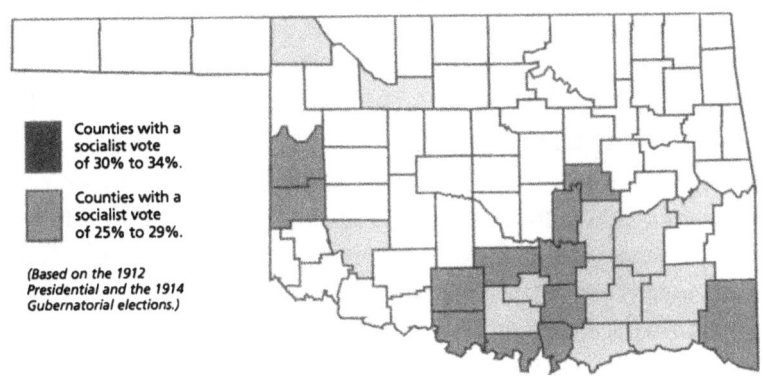

Map 2

Oklahomans who joined the Socialist Party pledged themselves to an organization that embraced Marxist ideology. Publicly affirming their support for "the principles of international Socialism," delegates to the state Socialist Party's annual convention in 1913 were unambiguous about their commitment to Marxism. "The Socialist party of Oklahoma declares its object to be the political organization of the working class of this state and those in sympathy with it," the delegates affirmed, "for the purpose of seizing the powers of government of the State of Oklahoma and using such powers for the immediate betterment of the condition of the workers and eventually bringing about a classless society."[70]

Democratic Party leaders witnessed socialist organizing with a growing sense of alarm. The editor of *Harlow's Weekly* noted with concern that in twenty counties socialist candidates had surpassed their Republican opponents in 1912, entitling them to the second position on the ballot in 1914.[71] As November approached, the outbreak of war in Europe made the Democrats even more uneasy. With the European cotton markets temporarily closed to American farmers due to the hostilities, cotton prices in Oklahoma plummeted to below five cents per pound.[72]

Although the Socialist Party failed to elect its candidate for governor in 1914, its performance in that year's election stunned major party observers. In a feat unmatched in any other state, Fred W. Holt, the socialist candidate in the gubernatorial contest, received over 20 percent of the votes cast.[73] In Marshall and Roger Mills Counties, Holt received 41 and 35 percent of the votes respectively. An examination of the socialist performance at the precinct level in these counties illustrates the depth of support for the Party in these areas. As seen in table 6, some precincts saw as many as 78 percent of the voters supporting socialist candidates. The Socialist Party candidate for representative in Roger Mills County was elected, and the state legislative candidate in Marshall County lost by only thirteen votes. All told, over 175 socialist candidates were elected to county and local offices in the state, including six to the Oklahoma legislature. Roger Mills County voters elected a socialist administration in 1914, with Party members assuming the offices of county judge, county treasurer, county weigher, county assessor, justice of the peace, and all three county commissioner seats.[74]

As the euphoria of the success of 1914 wore off, Oklahoma socialists saw no reason why the growth of their party should not continue. When 471 delegates gathered in Oklahoma City in late December of 1915 for their annual state convention, they came from every county in the state, representing a paid-up membership of more than 13,500.[75] Already the second largest state socialist party in the nation, State Secretary Sinclair predicted that by the following year the Oklahoma Party would "rank first all the way."[76] Leaving nothing to chance, Party leaders immediately began planning for the 1916 elections. By January of that year, the Party had in place a meticulously planned political organization, with socialist precinct chairmen assigned to virtually every voting precinct in the state. These precinct leaders were drawn from the more than eight hundred locals active in the Socialist Party of Oklahoma at that time.[77]

A series of misfortunes beset the Party in the early months of 1915, however, tempering the hardy optimism of the convention. Holt, who headed the Socialist Party ticket in 1914 as its guber-

TABLE 6. *Election Returns in Selected Strong Socialist Precincts, Contest for Representative, 1914*

PRECINCT	VOTES CAST			% RECEIVED
	DEM.	GOP	SOCIALIST	BY SOCIALIST
Marshall County				
Linn	11	10	48	70
Powell	13	26	56	59
Tyler	17	17	32	48
McMillan	13	12	49	66
Lark	16	8	73	75
Shay	15	8	45	66
Isom Springs	6	13	68	78
County Total	1020	316	1007	43
Roger Mills County				
Berlin #1	14	10	58	71
Kiowa #3	9	23	33	51
Dewey #1	30	27	34	37
Bowman #2	11	11	18	45
Meridian #2	22	22	37	46
Bar X	11	12	44	66
County Total	602	548	752	40

Source: Election Returns, Oklahoma State Archives, Oklahoma City, Oklahoma.

natorial candidate, received a six-month prison sentence in the spring of 1915 for giving arms to striking miners at McAlester.[78] Then Party leaders began to discover firsthand that political success could carry with it a high price. The six socialists who took their seats in the state legislature found themselves in a parliamentary situation that gave them little choice but to play broker politics with Democrats and Republicans. While socialist legislators worked hard to advance their party's political agenda, their efforts failed to move the Sooner State noticeably closer to the cooperative commonwealth. The sole socialist bill to become law was a measure limiting the hunting of deer, bear, and wild turkey in western Oklahoma. Even so, the socialist legislators were occasionally able to influence the outcome of parliamentary voting, and they consistently and

Photo 8. Oklahoma's First Socialist Legislative Group. In 1914 these six socialists were elected to the Oklahoma state legislature, one of the most impressive electoral achievements of any American state socialist organization. Courtesy the Special Collections Library, Duke University, Durham, North Carolina.

unambiguously represented the interests of tenants, smallholders, and workers.⁷⁹

In Roger Mills County, where a socialist administration was in place, success proved to be even more perilous. First, socialist F. M. Ogle, the county weigher, broke Party rules by appointing a Republican as deputy weigher. The Socialist Party constitution strictly forbade cooperation with capitalist organizations, and state Party officials promptly called for his resignation. Ogle flatly refused, announcing in the local press that he would not allow himself to become "a tool for the socialists."⁸⁰ Then, citizens of Roger Mills County began to rebel when socialist officials raised taxes in order to implement their program. In one town, county socialist officials were burned in effigy.⁸¹

These relatively minor setbacks provided little comfort to Democrats, who seemed at a loss in their efforts to stop the socialist advance. Amid the din of competing Democratic plans for meeting the socialist challenge, the voice of publisher Victor Harlow began to emerge as the most credible. The owner and publisher of *Harlow's Weekly*, he spoke for the progressive wing of the Democratic Party. Harlow's advice was simple and concise: "With the steadily increasing realization of the importance of Socialism in Oklahoma and its threat to the existing order," he declared, "should come a realization that the only successful method of meeting such radical tendencies is to modify the conditions which produce them. There must be a fundamental change in the methods of dealing with land ownership, land loans and tenancy in Oklahoma, if there is any real desire to stem the steadily rising tide of socialism."⁸²

One of the Democratic Party's most prominent office holders, United States Senator Robert Owen, apparently agreed with Harlow's assessment. The owner of a vast estate employing dozens of tenant farmers in private life, Senator Owen's position was particularly untenable given the socialists' proclivity for portraying the Democratic Party as the party of large landowners. In response, he announced in the pages of *Harlow's Weekly* late in 1916 that he would begin selling his estate in parcels to small farmers.⁸³

Whether or not progressives like Harlow and Owen were motivated completely by their concern for the plight of Oklahoma's small farmers, there is no denying the potential political advantages of their proposed course of action. Democrats, after all, had learned in 1896 and again in 1907 that co-optation was a particularly effective way of responding to challenges from the left. In this regard, the plans of the chairman of the Democratic Party in Payne County were unique only in their frankness: "I expect to call our County Central Committee to gether [sic] to plan for the approaching campaign and we expect to pass resolutions endorsing all we possibly can of the Socialists thunder but of course it will be labeled Democracy."[84]

But Democrats did not confine their responses to discussions of socialist ideology. To some Democratic leaders, the growing strength of the Socialist Party required a more forceful reaction. For example, one official in Bryan County, where the Socialist Party was especially strong, proposed that voting districts be changed so as to dilute socialist voting strength.[85] Other Democrats were equally direct, calling for the use of more extreme measures to prevent the "vice of socialism" from "overwhelming the state." "We have dallied with and pandered to it long enough," one functionary declared; it was now time to oppose the Socialist Party with deadly seriousness.[86]

Editors of Democratic newspapers in the state provided valuable service in this cause, mounting an unwavering series of attacks on the Socialist Party in their publications. Following the socialists' successes in Roger Mills County, for example, the Democratic editor of the *Sentinel*, the leading weekly in that county, instituted a policy of regularly running openly antisocialist articles on the paper's front page, a practice that continued for two years.[87] In Marshall County, the other great hotbed of socialist activity, the editor of the Democratic newspaper was equally aggressive. Among the stories published there were the following: "Socialism Means the Disintegration of Our Homes," "NY Aglow with Socialist Deviltry," "Socialists Officially Repudiate Religion in National Convention," "Socialism is Atheistic Philosophy," and "Officers Intercept the Course of Free Love."[88] Those editors who found such forms of responsible journalism too confining established papers that had as their sole purpose the destruction of the Socialist Party, and publications like the *Remonstrator,* the *Band Saw* (an obvious parody of the *Rip-Saw,* a socialist journal), the *Gnostic,* and the *Socialist Antidote* were born.[89]

IV

After 1912, as this ongoing struggle between Democrats and socialists raged, the Socialist Party quietly began working on a measure that would forever alter the relationship between them. Realizing that they could never triumph through the ballot as long as partisan Democrats controlled the election machinery in the state so directly, socialists drafted a "Fair Election Law" that proposed to dramatically change the state's political structure. This proposal, which the socialists hoped to enact through the initiative provision of the Oklahoma Constitution, would assure the Socialist Party of representation on election boards by specifying that each of the *three* parties, not two, receiving the highest number of votes in the most recent gubernatorial contest would be equally represented on state, county, and precinct election boards. In addition, the measure proposed to remove from the governor the power of appointment to these boards, shifting this responsibility to the state and county secretaries of each of the three parties.[90]

Work on the Fair Election Law began as early as 1913, but the Oklahoma Constitution's requirement of 50,000 signatures in order to gain a place on the ballot seemed daunting.[91] Using their superb organization, however, Oklahoma socialists surpassed this goal, collecting more than sixty-four thousand signatures by 1916.[92] Democrats, already stung by the recent decision of the United States Supreme Court to strike down the literacy test and grandfather clause, were stunned by the Socialist Party's achievement.

As Democrats searched for possible solutions to this crisis, the advice of Representative T. F. Hensley, published in the pages of

Harlow's Weekly, stood out. Hensley proposed that the governor convene a special session of the state legislature with a simple, dual agenda: first, to enact legislation to take the place of the literacy test and grandfather clause, thereby ending "the importation of ignorant negroes from the south into the state for election purposes"; and secondly, to "amend the elections laws, to the end that there may be no excuse left for socialistically inclined democrats to vote for that so-called 'Fair Election Bill' initiated by republicans and socialists."[93] Governor Williams obliged, calling state legislators together in February of 1916 to carry out Hensley's agenda. The timing of the session was hardly accidental; any changes enacted by the legislature would be safely in place in time for the upcoming elections, and those requiring approval by referendum could be considered at the August primary and still be in effect for the important general elections in November.

As legislators gathered in Oklahoma City for their special session, they first turned their attention to the void left by the demise of the literacy test and grandfather clause. Democratic lawmakers drafted a new registration bill that preserved the spirit of the old law by continuing to make literacy a prerequisite for voting. As for the provision protecting illiterate white Democrats from inadvertent disfranchisement, the new legislation was only slightly less transparent than the grandfather clause had been. This time, it was descendants of those who had served at any time in the military, whether in the armed services of the United States or of a foreign nation, who were declared exempt from the literacy provision. In an effort to prevent further interference by the courts, the lawmakers inserted a clause blandly stating that no portion of the law was intended to "conflict with the provisions of the Constitution of the United States."[94]

As with the literacy test and grandfather clause, the enactment of the new registration law was contingent upon the approval of the electorate. To ensure that it would be successful, Democratic leaders repeated the ploy that had worked so well in 1910 by substituting for the usual boxes on the ballot the phrase, "FOR THE

AMENDMENT," to mark affirmative or negative votes. The Socialist Party strongly opposed the new registration law, repeating the arguments made six years earlier and informing voters of the importance of striking through the phrase in order to vote against the measure.[95]

Having addressed the "negro problem," Democratic legislators then turned their attention to the "socialist problem." In an unprecedented move, they began drafting a "New Election Law" only after using their majority status to clear the legislative chamber of Republicans and socialists. The resulting legislation was so controversial and blatantly partisan that its reading to the readmitted Republicans and socialists sparked a melee in the legislative chamber, described vividly if in understated language by one reporter who witnessed the scene: "During the debate a near riot was precipitated as the result of a lively colloquy between Representatives Sams and Nesbitt. Serious trouble was barely averted after a few blows had failed to do damage and no less than three ink wells had missed their marks, to say nothing of those few who were deterred from drawing pistols. As a result of this bad temper a few minutes later State Republican Chairman Geissler was struck a blow which rendered him unconscious for a few minutes, by Representative Bryant of Osage."[96] Despite the severity of the socialist and Republican reaction, the Democratic majority in the legislature was sufficient to ensure its passage by a vote of sixty-nine to twenty.[97]

The central purpose of the newly enacted law could not be missed. It was explicitly designed to disfranchise those Oklahomans most likely to support socialist candidates, and it succeeded admirably in achieving that goal through a series of thinly veiled rules and procedures that greatly complicated the process of registering to vote. Instead of entrusting an existing municipal or county office with the responsibility of handling voter registration, the new law instructed the secretary of the state senate—who had always been a Democrat—to appoint a county registrar for each county. These officials, in turn, were given the power to appoint and remove the precinct registrars, the functionaries actually responsible for registering voters. Those wishing to register, therefore, were now forced to seek out the individual registrar in their precinct in order to gain the right to vote. Of no less importance, the county registrar was a political appointee loyal to the Democratic majority in the state legislature.

Even this failed to satisfy the authors of the new law, who further restricted the registration process by specifying that voter registration could occur only during a ten-day period before each election.[98] Clearly, this requirement struck directly at the Socialist Party's strategy of recruiting previously inactive voters. Its impact was magnified by Section 8 of the law, which specified that voters who had changed their residencies since the last election must cancel their existing registrations and register again in their new precincts. These individuals became, in effect, new voters, with their re-registration carried out according to the restrictive measures outlined in the new law.

Needless to say, none of these provisions was accidental. The Democratic election law was explicitly designed to make voting more difficult for tenant farmers, for whom mobility was a fact of life and who were joining the Socialist Party in droves. Their large-scale movement from farm to farm following the harvesting of the cotton was a regular event each year, a folkway that annually wrecked the subscription lists of the state's socialist newspapers. A study commissioned by the Oklahoma Agricultural and Mechanical College in 1929 adds a degree of precision to the somewhat impressionistic observations of socialist newspaper editors. In that year, according to the study, 49.8 percent of the state's white tenant farmers and 51 percent of the black tenants moved to new locations. In southeastern Oklahoma, the core of the socialist strength, the figures jumped to 58 and 62 percent respectively.[99] The new restrictions on voter registration, therefore, applied to a majority of the socialist constituency in the southeast in any given year. In fact, virtually all tenant farmers would have been affected by this provision at some time in their lives.

Apart from the mechanics of the voter registration process, yet another aspect of the new law served to weaken the electoral strength of the Socialist Party. Among the information that prospective voters had to supply on the new registration certificates were name, address, occupation, and party affiliation. Following the close of the registration period, election officials delivered duplicates of the completed certificates to the county clerk, where they became public record, making it possible for local merchants, landlords, and bankers to obtain lists of socialist voters. It was not difficult for tenant farmers, who often worked the land without the protection of a lease and who depended upon the local merchant for credit, to imagine the negative consequences of publicly disclosing their affiliation with the Socialist Party. While smallholders exercised slightly more autonomy over their fates, they too were dependent upon the banker and the merchant and could scarcely afford to register as socialists without considering the possible consequences of their actions.

The policy of depriving socialists of access to the land and to credit had been pursued by landlords, bankers, and merchants for a number of years. Reports of individuals refusing to deal with socialists were numerous, and there was evidence that a bank in Murray County had even discussed this strategy at a board meeting. The matter was dropped "for the sake of policy," but a "tacit agreement to this effect" remained.[100] Landowners had successfully used the same tactic in McIntosh County in 1914, where according to one newspaper the number of socialists declined noticeably.[101] Logistical complications, however, made this tactic difficult to implement, since it required a concerted effort on the part of a landlord or merchant to ascertain the political leanings of potential customers. Governor Williams, for example, found three letters of inquiry about a potential tenant necessary in order to discover that the farmer in question was indeed a socialist.[102]

The new law streamlined this process considerably. Civic leaders in Johnston County now had only to read the paper to discover which of their customers were socialists, since the *Johnston County Capital-Democrat* printed lists "of every varmint in the county" who registered as a member of the Socialist Party.[103] In nearby Marshall

County, the election law facilitated a boycott against socialists by "landlords, bankers and business institutions generally," which caused many Party members to leave the county.[104]

Voters sympathetic to the socialist cause could always avoid this dilemma by registering as Democrats and voting for the socialist candidates in the general election. Even this option, however, was not without its consequences, since Oklahoma election regulations specified that 27 percent of the votes received by each party's candidates must be cast in the subsequent primary in order for that party to remain on the ballot.[105]

Since the New Election Law took effect immediately, it not only reduced the support future socialist candidates could expect to receive on election day but it had immediate implications for the socialists' Fair Election Law as well. Obviously, the chances of success for this initiative were diminished considerably under the new rules for registering and voting. Even so, Democratic leaders left nothing to chance in their effort to defeat the socialist initiative. The Democratic-controlled legislature gave the governor the power to decide when initiative measures would be voted upon. Governor Williams promptly announced that the Fair Election Law would be considered in the November general election instead of in the primary, a decision that limited the socialists in two crucial ways. First, the Democrats' restrictive registration procedures would be in effect, thereby limiting the pool of registered socialist voters. In addition, even if the initiative were approved, it would not affect statewide elections until 1918.[106]

Outraged by this blatant manipulation of the electoral process, Socialist Party leaders responded in an ingenious way. Availing themselves yet again of the state constitution's initiative provision, socialists drafted a constitutional amendment that would, in effect, overturn the Democratic-sponsored New Election Law and they repeated the process of collecting enough signatures to gain a place on the ballot.[107] Mobilizing in a remarkably efficient and timely manner, state Party officials mailed blank petitions to local socialist leaders in early March. Completed petitions soon began pouring in to state Party headquarters at the rate of two thousand signatures a day. When socialist officials formally filed their petition on 5 May 1916, it had 81,613 signatures.[108] As a result, both socialist initiatives—the Fair Election Law and the constitutional amendment overturning the Democratic New Election Law—appeared on the ballot in the general elections held in November of 1916.

In the meantime, the summer primary elections gave socialists a chance to experience life under the new rules specified in the Democratic election law. In seven counties, the Socialist Party suffered a decline over the previous election in the primary, while eight counties experienced a gain of at least two hundred registered voters over 1914. It is striking that in every case, the losing counties had unusually high rates of tenancy, while tenancy rates tended to be lower in the counties that gained socialist votes; the average tenancy rate in the seven losing counties (76.2 percent) was a full 25 percent higher than in the counties that made significant gains (see table 7). Clearly, the Democratic election law proved to be very effective in disenfranchising tenant farmers, a critical part of the socialist electoral base. In areas where the core of socialist support came from this class, as in the southeastern cotton-growing region, the Party was significantly weakened.

Anecdotal evidence supplied by triumphant Democrats lends credence to this statistical portrait. Even in Washita County, where tenancy rates were considerably lower than in the southeast, a local Democratic official boasted of the new law's effectiveness: "The Registration Law has proven a great success in this county. There is a great fall-off in the socialist registration, and since its close I have not heard one who will confess that he is a socialist in public."[109] Another of the Democratic faithful was even more enthusiastic: "We wiped the socialists off the face of the earth in Kiowa County."[110]

Even so, the Socialist Party made careful preparations to carry its agenda in November. To guard against expected electoral fraud, the Party designated one member in each precinct in the state to serve as an unofficial election observer. Supplied with duplicates of the forms used by sanctioned election officials to report precinct returns,

TABLE 7. *Tenancy Rates and the Primary Election of 1916*

COUNTIES THAT LOST SOCIALIST VOTERS

COUNTY	TENANCY RATE
Bryan	78.1%
Haskell	81.4%
Love	82.3%
Le Flore	78.8%
Marshall	80.5%
McCurtain	68.4%
Ottawa	64.2%
Average	76.2%

COUNTIES THAT GAINED OVER 200 SOCIALIST VOTERS

COUNTY	TENANCY RATE
Beckham	35.2%
Caddo	53.5%
Lincoln	52.8%
Logan	44.6%
Oklahoma	49.5%
Payne	50.5%
Pottawatomie	52.5%
Rogers	58.1%
Average	50.0%

Source: Registration figures are from *Harlow's Weekly*, 20 May 1916; tenancy rates are listed in Bureau of the Census, *Thirteenth Census of the United States Taken in the Year 1910* (Washington, D.C.: Government Printing Office, 1912), 372–378.

they were instructed to observe the count, report the results on their forms, and submit them to state socialist headquarters. In this way, the Socialist Party could compile a semiofficial vote count as a check on state officials. The precinct observers also received a supply of ballots, printed at the expense of the Socialist Party, to be used in the event of a shortage of official ballots in their precinct.[111]

As Oklahoma voters went to the polls in November, it seemed that the socialist strategy was working. Despite instances of electoral fraud similar to that experienced by socialist voters in previous elections, the socialist initiatives received widespread support. The provision designed to overturn the New Election Law received 140,366 affirmative votes and 114,824 negative votes. The portion of the initiative containing the provisions of the Fair Election Law fared even better, winning by a margin of 147,067 to 119,602.

Like the literacy test and grandfather clause enacted six years earlier, both measures required a majority of the total votes cast in the election to succeed. To determine the total votes cast, officials in past elections had used the voter turnout in the campaign receiving the greatest number of votes. In 1916 this was the presidential contest. Under this criterion, the socialist initiatives needed to receive at least 146,214 affirmative votes to be enacted. While the attempt to negate the Democratic registration law failed to receive this number, the socialists' Fair Election Law exceeded the mark, winning narrowly by a margin of some 850 votes.[112]

Realizing that the enactment of the socialist election provision placed their control over the electoral process in jeopardy, Democratic officials resorted to extreme measures to reverse the socialist victory. In this case, the Democratic-controlled state election board issued a remarkable ruling that had just this effect. Breaking from past practice, the board ruled that in this case it would use the total number of ballots issued in determining the total votes cast. Since just over three hundred thousand ballots were printed and distributed to the precincts, the election board maintained that the socialist provisions needed 152,054 affirmative votes in order to be enacted. Of course, neither of the provisions received this number of votes, and the state election board declared them both defeated.[113] As socialists were quick to point out, the position taken by the election board was patently absurd. Since there was no way of knowing exactly how large the voter turnout would be in each precinct, election officials routinely provided a few spare ballots at each polling place. The ruling of the election board meant that the Socialist Party would be penalized for any unused ballots, as well as for any spoiled ballots. Indeed, this amounted to some 11,600 ballots, generating a significant silent vote against the measure, an obstacle that the socialists were unable to overcome.[114]

Even these measures did not enable the state election board to prevent Oklahoma voters from supporting the Socialist Party on election day. Socialist presidential candidate Allan Benson received almost forty-seven thousand votes in the state, a remarkable showing that represented an increase of 90 percent over Debs's total four years earlier.[115] Yet in aggregate terms, support for socialist candidates in 1916 dropped over 1914 levels, the first decrease in the history of the Oklahoma Party—clearly revealing the impact of the New Election Law. As table 8 illustrates, the Party's vote increased slightly in strongly socialist counties over 1912 levels in western Oklahoma, while in the southeast, socialist candidates suffered a decline.

The explanation for this difference in voting pattern lies in tenancy rates, which in turn connects the election results to the Democratic Party's new electoral procedures. In the three western counties where socialist voting increased, the tenancy rate averaged 27 percent. In the four southeastern counties, where the tenancy rate

TABLE 8. *Election Returns, Contest for President in Selected Counties, 1912 and 1916*

COUNTY	VOTES RECEIVED BY SOCIALIST CANDIDATE		% CHANGE
	1912	1916	
Western Counties			
Beckham	871	889	+ 2
Dewey	768	854	+11
Roger Mills	555	565	+ 2
Southeastern Counties			
Bryan	816	757	− 7
Johnston	741	670	−10
Marshall	700	618	−12
Murray	550	350	−36
State Totals	24,665	46,917	+90

Source: Election Returns, Oklahoma State Archives, Oklahoma City, Oklahoma.

hovered around 80 percent, votes cast for Socialist Party candidates decreased. The conclusion is obvious—by making it more difficult for tenant farmers to vote, the New Election Law had exactly the impact its designers intended, depriving the Socialist Party of Oklahoma of a crucial segment of its natural constituency.

V

The Socialist Party's effort to institute the Fair Election Law represented the pinnacle of its success in Oklahoma. With their remarkable organization and sophisticated skills as activists, socialists shook the confidence of Democratic leaders and moved closer to sharing political power in the Sooner State than anywhere else in America. On the eve of the Democratic state convention in 1916, Victor Harlow spoke for many in his party when he wrote that "The shadow of the socialists lay heavy over the gathering."[116]

That year, the Democratic Party demonstrated its willingness to use extralegal measures, if necessary, to prevent socialists from gaining political power in the state. Socialist leaders, indignantly expressing their outrage over these injustices, had no way of knowing that within a few short months, the United States would be involved as an active partner in the European war. Under the new rules of political engagement that accompanied the declaration of war, repressive measures loomed on the horizon that made the New Election Law seem mild by comparison. In this new environment, the Socialist Party of Oklahoma found itself virtually defenseless.

CHAPTER 7

The Politics of Crisis

The Destruction of the Socialist Party of Oklahoma, 1917–1920

In the early months of 1916, there occurred in the cotton region just west of the Arkansas border a series of events that foreshadowed the bitter developments of the war years. Sequoyah County in that region seemed to be on the verge of open class warfare. The merchants, bankers, and large landowners who comprised the county's economic and social elite found that the considerable tenant population in the region no longer displayed the deference that leaders had come to expect. At the root of the tenant farmers' newfound confidence was their involvement in a secret, direct-actionist group, the Working Class Union (WCU), which claimed as many as thirty-five thousand Oklahoma and Arkansas farmers among its membership in 1916.[1] The incident that had civic leaders most concerned involved the WCU and a former county judge named L. C. McNabb.[2] McNabb had been elected as a Democrat to that post in 1914, but soon displayed a lack of detachment in the performance of his duties that his fellow elected officials found to be unacceptable. The plight of smallholders and tenants in Sequoyah County so disturbed the judge, in fact, that within a year of his election he resigned his office and began offering his services to the WCU on behalf of these exploited farmers.

With McNabb's help, the WCU developed a simple, effective strategy that brought immediate results to farmers. In action coordinated by the WCU and made possible by McNabb's legal skills, farmers in the region began filing suit against bankers and landlords for violations of Oklahoma's anti-usury law. The law, tightened considerably at the special legislative session in February of 1916, set 6 percent as the maximum legal interest rate and provided that violators would repay double the amount of usurious interest they had charged.[3] By March of 1916, some sixty suits had been initiated, with nearly fifty resulting in verdicts favorable to the plaintiffs.

Of course, this strategy did not go unopposed; county leaders responded by instituting disbarment proceedings against McNabb. To prevent the WCU from interfering with the disbarment, the leaders arranged for the hearings to take place in the county seat of nearby Muskogee County. On the day of the hearings, however, some two thousand WCU members in Sequoyah County took to the streets of Sallisaw, the Sequoyah county seat, in a massive demonstration of support for McNabb. Some of these farmers even made their way to Muskogee on the day of the hearing, "wearing red shirts," a disturbed newspaper editor reported, "and depicting a bold desperation that is almost unbelievable in Oklahoma."[4] Anonymous notes were posted throughout the area warning that barns would be burned and banks dynamited if the disbarment proceeding continued. Local leaders, understanding the seriousness of these demonstrations, suspended the hearings.[5]

Additional evidence pointed to widespread unrest among working farmers in Sequoyah County. Organized groups of night riders regularly took direct action against those involved in foreclosures, a tactic that gave pause to banks and companies offering mortgage loans. A representative of one such company described in a letter to his superiors the gravity of the situation:

> I understand that in the event a loan company has to take over property under foreclosure these "night riders" prevent the company taking charge of the property either by threatening the one who is moving in, or if this is not effective, will then burn the buildings on the

land. It seems that one of the principal objects of this organization is to prevent any one taking charge of a property on which a mortgage has been foreclosed.

Considered from a loaning viewpoint, this condition places the moral hazards of Sequoyah County below the average and if you are to continue making loans there, I believe a thorough investigation as to the moral risk should be made in each and every case.[6]

For the president of the loan company in question, the "moral risks" were simply too great for his firm to continue conducting business in Sequoyah County.

To local leaders, the tacit acceptance of the night riders by much of the citizenry seemed almost as disturbing as the violence itself. The WCU enjoyed such widespread support in Sequoyah County that law enforcement officials found it difficult to seat juries willing to convict those accused of night riding.[7] Even the sheriff himself was reported to be a member of the WCU in that county.[8] Local farmers harbored such deep resentment against banks that they at times sheltered and protected bank robbers. Under such conditions, insurance companies found it necessary in 1916 to cancel all bank burglary policies in fifteen eastern counties.[9]

The actions of the WCU were not limited to Sequoyah County, nor were they directed only against banks and loan companies. T. G. McMahan, a state legislator from Le Flore County in the southeastern corner of Oklahoma, reported the destruction of his engine and grist mill by members of the WCU in 1916.[10] In southern Bryan County, notices that were signed "Night Riders" warned farmers not to sell their cotton for less than ten cents per pound, harkening back to the crop withholding efforts of the Farmers' Union. Those who ignored this minimum price, the notices threatened, would "suffer by fire."[11] The following year, owners of cotton gins reported a rash of fires of suspicious origin, with "as many as five gins in the same town catch[ing] fire in one day."[12] A similar warning appeared on the door of a church in Washita County:

Warning to Land Lord[:] any man that rents his land for more than one third and pay his part of thrashing grain where renter furnishes seed or rents for money will get his land seeded to Johnson grass and his houses and barns burned[.] or tries to dodge this by working big bodies himself and any renter agrees to give more will be looked after in a way that will not be pleasing to him[.] any gin or thrasher that gins or thrashes on land that fails to heed this warning will also be burned and if this notice is concealed from the public this church house will go up in flames[.] we mean business[.] from seven determined men that know how to keep a still mouth and carry out this warning to the letter.[13]

The WCU also opposed the state's newly initiated program of mandatory cattle dipping intended to prevent the spread of disease from Texas. The inevitable loss of some stock in the dipping process made the program unpopular with the renters and small farmers, who felt such losses more profoundly than did ranchers or large landowners. As a result, the vats used in the program were prime targets of the night riders, who in Adair County destroyed three dipping vats in one week early in 1916.[14]

For state political leaders, these incidents formed a disturbing pattern that pointed to the existence of a widespread social crisis in much of the cotton region of southeastern Oklahoma. At the heart of this crisis, of course, were the material hardships suffered by farmers under the system of commercial agriculture dominant throughout the American South. In 1914 the outbreak of war in Europe further destabilized this already explosive situation. When the combatants on both sides in the conflict sought to deprive the other of precious war materiel by blockading each other's ports, the European war began to directly affect the lives of Oklahoma farmers. Chief among the commodities cut off by the blockades was cotton, causing the world market to be flooded with the supplies that would ordinarily have been sold in Europe. As a result, Oklahoma farmers saw a precipitous drop in the prices they received for their crops. In the space of a year, cotton prices in Oklahoma dropped from thirteen cents per pound to seven cents, with the figure dipping as low as five cents in some regions.[15] For farmers barely surviving with thirteen-cent cotton, such a development resulted in hardships that caused many to turn to the WCU and the Socialist Party.

I

The fact that those near the bottom of the economic system in a location as far removed from the battlefields of Europe as rural Oklahoma would feel so directly the effects of the war was a sobering lesson in the workings of the capitalist system. The initial reaction of Americans was almost universal—the United States must not become involved in the European conflict. As the implications of neutrality became apparent, however, the nation's leaders began to reconsider their commitment to noninvolvement, thus beginning a national journey from neutrality to preparedness and war in the months following August 1914.

Those at the head of the procession, however, were not at all certain about the level of commitment they could reasonably expect on the part of the populace. President Wilson's reelection in 1916, after all, resulted in large part from his promise to keep the United States out of the European war. With this uncertainty deepened in Oklahoma by the crisis in the cotton region, a haunting question emerged. How would a citizenry already dangerously prone to anarchic acts of violence respond to the increased sacrifices demanded during wartime?

The reaction of American socialists to the onset of hostilities in Europe was hardly encouraging. The national socialist organization made its position clear almost immediately after the German invasion of Belgium, declaring that the European conflict resulted solely from "'imperialist' rivalry between the capitalist powers in Europe."[16] The implication was obvious; workers in the affected nations, as members of the same class, had no stake in the conflict and thus had no business killing each other over what amounted to a quarrel between competing members of the ruling class. As the United States drifted toward a declaration of war, however, this general statement of Marxist principles became inadequate, and socialists gathered in St. Louis in April of 1917 to draft a more concrete policy statement. This time, they specifically addressed the issue of how the American working class should respond to the declaration of war, concluding that

> the Socialist Party of the United States in the present grave crisis solemnly reaffirms its allegiance to the principle of internationalism and working-class solidarity the world over and proclaims its unalterable opposition to the war just declared by the Government of the United States.
>
> The Socialist Party of the United States is unalterably opposed to the system of exploitation and class rule which is upheld and strengthened by military power and sham national patriotism. We, therefore, call upon the workers of all countries to refuse to support their governments in their wars. The wars of contending national groups of capitalists are not the concern of the workers. The only struggle which would justify the workers in taking up arms is the great struggle of the working class of the world to free itself from economic exploitation and political oppression.[17]

Following the American declaration of war in April of 1917, Oklahoma socialists made their support for the St. Louis resolution explicit, pledging "continuous, active and public opposition to the war, through public demonstrations [and] mass meetings."[18] Oklahoma socialist columnist N. S. Mounts wholeheartedly agreed, couching his Marxist critique of the war in considerably more colorful language. To him, the war was being fought only to "vouchsafe the safe conduct of a few score money grabbers across the big pond." "The aristocracy has ever held," Mounts continued, "that it is the business of the masses to toil and die that rulers and nobles may live in idle luxury."[19] In another article, the columnist noted that those who were most vigorous in the "shouting and flag-waving" were "never the first in the trenches, where the dance of death is timed to the groans and shrieks of the mangled and dying."[20]

Party members in Oklahoma reserved their strongest rhetoric, however, for the attack on conscription. At the state Party convention held in December of 1914, they made their position brutally clear: "Resolved; that if war is declared, the Socialists of Oklahoma shall refuse to enlist; but if forced to enter the military service to murder fellow workers, we shall choose to die fighting the enemies of humanity within our own ranks rather than to perish fighting our fellow workers. We further pledge ourselves to use our influence to the end that all toilers shall refuse to work for the master class during such war."[21]

The intensity of this position went beyond a commitment to the Marxist principles of class and internationalism inherent in the ideology of the Socialist Party. At the heart of the resolution was the sense of desperation felt by many Oklahoma socialists over the potential effects of conscription on their lives. Oklahoma farmers knew full well that even the subsistence level of existence they currently endured was contingent upon long hours of work in the fields. They could only imagine the deprivations their families would suffer if compulsory military service prevented them from working their crops. A terse report in a socialist newspaper illustrated graphically the potential effects of this cruel dilemma: "Driven crazy over the draft questionnaire, Chas. E. Logan, a Muskogee county farmer, killed his wife and baby, committed suicide and burned his home."[22] Socialist leaders understood this dynamic, and after the declaration of war they began emphasizing the inordinate sacrifices that would be demanded of farmers during wartime. To one organizer, American involvement in the war gave the Socialist Party a tremendous advantage: "Now is the accepted time. That neighbor who a year ago was cursing you is now ready to listen to you. Carry to him the message. Hold picnics and encampments this season as you never did before. Order literature by the bundle and hand out. Put some in all wagons, buggies, auto's [sic]. Talk PEACE and you will have an audience."[23]

Such exchanges must have been on the minds of the state's political leaders as President Wilson announced his plan to raise the United States army to fighting strength through universal conscription. As Congress moved closer to the passage of a conscription act, the question of how Oklahomans would respond to the draft assumed paramount importance. Oklahoma socialists participated enthusiastically in their national party's effort to submit conscription to a national referendum, circulating petitions to that effect widely in the late spring of 1917.[24] Such activism became especially disconcerting when state officials realized that much of the antidraft sentiment came, not only from socialists and members of the WCU, but also from within the Democratic Party.[25] When the citizens of Beckham County, far from the tumultuous cotton region, held a mass meting in April of 1917 to discuss the matter, only three of the more than five hundred citizens present openly admitted to being in favor of conscription, and the anticonscription speakers, many of whom were Democrats, outnumbered those supporting it by a margin of seven to one.[26]

Following the passage of the Conscription Act by Congress, state leaders' considerable anxiety centered on 5 June 1917, the day all men of draft age across the nation were required by law to register for conscription in the county of their residence. A worried official in Dewey County was only one of the many who expressed concern about how the people in his district would respond. Socialists throughout his county, he informed the governor, were advising residents not to register on June 5.[27] The Socialist Party of Oklahoma assisted those who opposed the draft by establishing a legal bureau to help individuals, regardless of political affiliation, gain exemptions from conscription.[28]

To the great relief of state and local political leaders, however, things went relatively smoothly on registration day. While a few arrests were made in Oklahoma, no organized antidraft rallies occurred.[29] Even so, civic leaders could hardly characterize the day as a total success. Only slightly more than half of the 215,000 Oklahomans expected to register by federal officials actually did so, and 72 percent of the registrants attempted to escape military service by claiming exemption.[30] These figures left no room for doubt. The vast majority of Oklahomans were not willing to fight in the European war, leaving state officials troubled at the prospect of enforcing conscription on an unwilling populace.

In at least one county, the antiwar sentiment seemed to go deeper than the unenthusiastic response to conscription. In Seminole County in the heart of the cotton region, the situation had become so tense that a local citizen dispatched a frantic letter warning the governor of possible revolution: "There is an uprising here among our farmers, and I feel that you should know. . . . They say as soon as the Draft begins that they will start in Burning, Corn Cribs, houses, and have threatened to destroy the Town [of Seminole]. And that they will Die at home before they will be Drafted. We all know that they have been having secrete [sic] Meetings and that they have been buying all the Guns and Ammunition they could get. Parties tell me that they are Hundreds Strong, and will fight untill [sic] the end."[31] While there is no evidence that the governor heeded this warning, the letter proved to be prophetic. In the town of Dewar in nearby Okmulgee County, eleven members of the WCU were arrested for dynamiting the town's water works.[32] Then, seven members of another radical organization known as the Jones Family were arrested for attempting to obstruct the conscription law by inciting men of draft age to rebel.[33] These incidents pointed to much deeper resentment, and in August of 1917 farmers loyal to the WCU in Seminole and surrounding counties led an armed uprising against conscription that became known as the Green Corn Rebellion.

Figuring prominently in the Rebellion were H. H. Munson and Homer Spence, two veteran organizers who had been arrested on registration day for encouraging resistance to conscription. Released from jail on bond by early August, Munson and Spence immediately began organizing opposition to the war effort in the southeastern counties clustered near the Canadian River. It was in this region that the first incident of the Green Corn Rebellion occurred. On 2 August 1917 a group of black farmers loyal to the WCU engaged Seminole

County Sheriff Frank Grall and his deputy in a brief gun battle. The following morning, heavily armed WCU members gathered at several locations in the area, prepared to take whatever means necessary to prevent conscription.

Their plan was to cripple the ability of officials to enforce the draft by burning bridges, cutting telephone and telegraph wires, and destroying oil pipelines. Then they would begin a march to Washington, joining forces along the way with other workers and farmers sympathetic to their cause. By the time they reached the capital, they predicted, their numbers would be so great that President Wilson would be forced to abandon the war effort. On their march, the militants intended to survive by eating corn picked from the fields every evening, thus giving the rebellion its name.[34]

Local authorities reacted quickly and decisively to the Green Corn Rebellion, and the rebels' planned march to Washington never materialized. Hastily formed posses routed members of the WCU wherever they congregated, crushing the abortive rebellion within a week. Disturbed by what they perceived as evidence of a well-organized and dangerous threat, officials began making wholesale arrests in the wake of the uprising. In one location in Seminole County, investigators discovered a cache containing seventy-five sticks of dynamite, eight ounces of strychnine, and one Winchester rifle.[35] Officials issued blanket indictments against participants in the rebellion for draft resistance, and leaders were indicted under the more serious charge of "seditious conspiracy."[36] Even with the Oklahoma State Penitentiary crowded with 450 suspects arrested following the Green Corn Rebellion, *Harlow's Weekly* warned that the incarcerated probably represented "only a modicum of those involved in the seditious plans."[37]

In the days following the Rebellion, state and local officials cast a wide net; all known radicals in the region, irrespective of the extent of their participation in the uprising, were considered to be suspects by local authorities and were subject to arrest. H. M. Sinclair, the state secretary of the Socialist Party of Oklahoma, realized that Party members in the affected region would be among the most immediate suspects, and he quickly took steps to distance the organization from the Rebellion. In a formal statement on the insurrection and the arrests that followed, Sinclair pointed out that while socialists were sympathetic with the farmers who participated in the insurrection, the Socialist Party believed in political action as a more effective way of promoting the interests of the working class. Lest there be any misunderstanding, Sinclair plainly asserted that the "Socialist party organization [had] nothing whatever to do" with the Green Corn Rebellion. "We will continue the fight for working class emancipation along political lines," the statement concluded, "and invite all who are in sympathy with our platform to join with us and by *intelligent* action pave the way for a better day."[38]

This lesson in the intricacies of left-wing politics was completely lost on officials responding to the insurrection. Governor Williams could see no distinction between the Socialist Party and the WCU, claiming in a letter to federal authorities that the Green Corn Rebellion was caused "by the I.W.W., the Working Class Union, the socialists and anarchists."[39] Although Democratic Party leader Victor Harlow concluded that the Socialist Party had not been directly involved in the rebellion, he too was unwilling to accept Sinclair's disclaimer. "It is interesting to note," Harlow pointed out, "that in the counties nearly free from socialist influences there is an absence of Working Class Union disturbances, and that the disturbances are limited to communities in which there is a large socialistic influence."[40]

As a result of sentiments like these, known socialists in the Canadian River Valley were included in the post-rebellion roundup even though they had not been involved in the insurrection. Hardest hit was the socialist organization in Hughes County, where two of the three highest officials in the Party—O. A. Fisk, the county secretary, and State Committeeman J. C. Edge—were among those arrested. In addition, the secretaries of eight of the twenty-four active locals in Hughes County were incarcerated. Six local secretaries in Seminole County were arrested, as were a socialist justice of the peace and a county commissioner. These arrests were not confined to the areas where the Green Corn Rebellion occurred. Others incarcerated included J. D. Allen of Marshall County; Ed Blaylock, a former socialist candidate for treasurer in Carter County; George Owen, formerly the editor of the *Oklahoma Pioneer*; and recent gubernatorial candidate J. T. Cumbie. All told, over forty socialists were arrested in the days following the rebellion.[41]

II

For those opposed to the Socialist Party, the Green Corn Rebellion was a seminal event. The growth of the Party had reached alarming proportions in recent years, and although in 1916 Democratic officials finally succeeded in reversing the trend of steadily improving performance by socialist candidates on election day, the Socialist Party's near-successful attempt to implement the Fair Election Law had represented a challenge of a different kind. The socialists' impressive effort to use the electoral system to their advantage forced Democratic leaders to turn to uncomfortably extralegal methods. As they pondered this situation, the conscription crisis and the Green Corn Rebellion provided even more pressing cause for concern. Indeed, it suddenly seemed to many Democratic leaders that the very existence of the state's social, political, and economic system was at stake. The wholesale arrest of known activists in the days following the Rebellion can be seen as the response of state and local leaders to what they perceived to be a grave crisis.

As the hysteria died down, however, Democratic leaders realized that in the excitement of the Rebellion they had overestimated the strength of the insurgents. They also noted with interest that the arrests of law-abiding socialists following the Rebellion had failed to generate any significant protest over the denial of the socialists' constitutional rights. In this way, Oklahoma Democratic leaders learned the primary lesson of the politics of crisis: Under crisis conditions—when there is a perceived, imminent threat to the maintenance of the existing order—suppression, even outright illegal repression, can be employed with relative impunity in the effort to protect the status quo.

There was, of course, great uncertainty about key elements of this formula. What were the limits of the action that the Democrats, as defenders of the existing system, could take against the perpetrators of the threat? How much latitude would authority figures be granted in identifying the group or groups that personified this threat? At what point would general agreement as to the existence of a crisis situation end? If Democratic leaders in Oklahoma could not answer these questions with authority in the fall of 1917, they could point with confidence to two assurances. First, the weapon of repression could be employed against the perceived enemy with little fear of political or legal reprisal. In addition, Democratic authorities felt confident that the Socialist Party could be safely identified as a public enemy.

Here, then, was the long-awaited answer to the question of how to prevent the Socialist Party from reaching its goal of effecting fundamental change in the economic and political system in Oklahoma. During the months following the Green Corn Rebellion, Democratic officials experimented freely with this new weapon, testing its limits and invoking a variety of repressive tactics. In the end, they employed the politics of crisis with brutal effectiveness against the Socialist Party of Oklahoma.[42]

The editors of Oklahoma's capitalist newspapers played a vital role in this process by informing the citizenry that, during these special times, the rights it normally enjoyed, especially the right of free speech, were no longer in effect. These lessons were carefully laid out in an editorial published in Beckham County two months after the declaration of war:

> In time of peace and plenty no one cared enough about [the Socialist Party's] railings to realize just how contemptible and dangerous it really was. Under the present conditions, when our Nation is overcast with the clouds of war, when the very life of the Nation is threatened, when

every one will sooner or later feel the pinch of want and grief for loved ones lost, when every man that's half a man should and will do all within their power to do our bit, we are in a bad temper to listen to this much mouthed "free speech" and there is going to be much less of it or we are fooled in the signs of the times.[43]

As another editor warned, open criticism of the government was "getting tiresome with the better citizenship."[44]

Now the papers began alluding directly to the Socialist Party's open opposition to the war. Shortly after the Green Corn Rebellion, for example, the *Beckham County Democrat* declared that those who opposed conscription were traitors, warning ominously that "IN TIMES OF WAR, TREASON IS PUNISHABLE BY DEATH."[45] In November of 1917, the paper openly called for mob action against those opposed to the war, asserting that "[i]t's tar feathers and the whip now, it will be the end of a rope if it does not stop."[46] An editorial published in April of 1918 used the imagery of the noose even more graphically: "For, mark our words, the time is right here where you are going to be a man, an American citizen and a loyal patriotic citizen or you are going to be in a Government internment camp or decorating the end of a tightly drawn rope."[47]

This kind of rhetoric permeated the state's editorial pages, illustrating the overpowering mood of suspicion and hostility that infected American society during the war years. Under such conditions, anyone who publicly disagreed with the nation's war policy bore the brunt of this hostility. For example, J. C. Thurmond, a veteran member of the Oklahoma legislature, was arrested because he remarked in a speech that he had "not heard of any young man in this community enlisting" and that he hoped widespread enlistments would not occur. Following his arrest, Governor Williams informed Thurmond that his only defense would be "to prove that he had not uttered the unpatriotic language attributed to him."[48] Carl Albert, an Oklahoman well known for his long service in the U.S. House of Representatives, recalls in his autobiography how his grandfather, Robert Carleton Scott, had felt the burden of intolerance.

When Scott's fundamentalist religion prevented him from taking a loyalty oath or signing a loyalty pledge (because "in his view, swearing violated the Commandments, and that [loyalty] card was the mark of the beast, Revelation's symbol of fealty to the Antichrist"), he was thrown in jail, seized by a mob, and given two hundred lashes. Albert's conclusion regarding this incident must accurately reflect the experiences of untold numbers of Oklahomans during the war years: "Grandpa Scott asked the Lord to forgive him and signed the card. He did it with his soul's reservation that he would recant if the Lord asked it of him. The Lord must have understood."[49]

It was in this context that socialist commentator N. S. Mounts offered a sarcastic evaluation of the state of public discourse in Oklahoma: "In these days of strained nerve tension, two Dutchmen seen in close conversation over a stein of beer will throw the population of a great city into a state of feverish excitement, send the entire police force scurrying hither and thither in search of culprits, and fill the first page of every jingo [newspaper] of another German plot uncovered."[50] At times, suspicions exploded into mob action taken against socialists or other known radicals. A farmer named O. E. Westbrook was whipped, tarred, and feathered for his antiwar opinions by an armed mob near Altus, and similar incidents occurred near Muskogee, Elk City, and Henryetta.[51] One Henry Rheimer was "hanged by [a] mob till almost dead" in the town of Collinsville, and in Wynnewood, a dissenter was tarred and feathered and a "Negro was hired to lash his back."[52] In Tulsa, an enraged citizen shot and killed a waiter named Joe String for "uttering the hope that all the American soldiers would go to France and would be killed."[53]

In the same city, some eleven IWW (Industrial Workers of the World) members who had been arrested for vagrancy were forcibly taken from police officials by members of a patriotic group known as the Knights of Liberty. The Wobblies were taken out of town and whipped, tarred, and feathered.[54] Tensions in Tulsa were at a boiling point at the time of this incident because of the bombing of the home of wealthy oil man J. Edgar Pew. The local press blamed the IWW for the bombing, calling on the citizenry to take direct action against the organization rather than wasting money on "trials and continuances and things like that."[55] Newspapers like the *Madill Record* applauded the action taken by the Knights of Liberty and suggested that "more such organizations would not be one bit harmful to the cause of liberty."[56]

Although wonderfully efficient, mob violence had its limitations as a means of suppressing dissent, and political leaders across the nation searched for a way of harnessing the energy of public hysteria into a more manageable form. With the help of the federal government, civic leaders arrived at the perfect solution—a network of semi-official agencies called *councils of defense* created especially to promote the war effort.[57] The organization of this huge network of state and local entities, which by the war's end encompassed nearly one million citizens, began at a conference in Washington in May of 1917 that was directed by the Council of National Defense and attended by representatives from all of the states.[58]

Oklahoma's representative was J. M. Aydelotte of Oklahoma City, a banker and manufacturer who, upon his return, helped organize the Oklahoma State Council of Defense. Headed by Aydelotte and consisting of some of the state's most respected citizens, the Oklahoma Council was given the task of supervising the war effort in the state by aiding the National Council "in any possible way."[59] This body quickly set about its most important task, the creation of the network of county boards that would supervise war work on the local level. These county councils, directed by the leading banker, editor, and attorney in each region, then organized numerous community councils of defense to promote the war effort in their respective locations.[60]

The Oklahoma State Council of Defense and its subordinate agencies were charged with the following specific responsibilities: promoting the sale of Liberty Bonds, supporting the work of the Red Cross, aiding in the conservation of food, assisting in recruitment for the armed forces, and disseminating government propaganda.[61]

All of these functions, of course, assumed that unanimous support for the war effort would be required of the citizenry, and dealing with the thorny problem of how to handle "disloyalty" was considered to be well within the province of the councils of defense. Indeed, the suppression of dissent came to be the councils' principal contribution to the war effort, an activity made necessary, according to newspapers like the *Daily Oklahoman*, by the presence of large numbers of citizens who "the law cannot touch, but [who] nevertheless need touching for loyalty's sake."[62] In the words of one of the organization's official publications, it was imperative that the Council "decide upon a plan of taking care of those who are pro-German in their sympathies, but do not go far enough to be handled by the federal authorities."[63] The key problem, said one county official, was the need to develop ways of dealing with "the different phases of the disloyalty we have in our country."[64]

Thus, the community and county councils of defense were instructed to be vigilant in detecting and reporting disloyalty wherever it appeared. In this effort, however, there was never any official clarification of what action made an individual disloyal, and local patriots exercised a great amount of discretion in reporting the unfaithful to their superiors. One county leader expressed this lack of precision, describing his task as pursuing any action necessary to "take care of the slacker, the slicker and the dissenter."[65] Among those included on the rolls of the disloyal were a man who made an "unpatriotic talk" in the fall of 1917, three persons who "made talks injurious to the cause," and anyone who "said and did things that were calculated" to turn people against the war effort.[66]

The Oklahoma State Council of Defense made an attempt to codify patriotism by printing and distributing loyalty pledge cards, and county and community council leaders were charged with the responsibility of making sure that cards were signed by all citizens in their districts.[67] Obviously, refusal to sign meant immediate categorization as disloyal, as in the case of one J. W. Merrell, who refused for religious reasons. His refusal to sign was quickly reported by the community official to his immediate superior, the chairman of the county council.[68] Such reports were made easier by the supply of "slacker cards" distributed by the State Council of Defense. Local patriots had only to supply information about people who refused to sign loyalty pledges and forward the cards to state officials.[69]

Another criterion used by council members in evaluating the patriotism of the members of their communities was the active support of the sale of government bonds. The sale of Liberty Bonds and War Savings Stamps was an important source of financing for the war effort, and government officials responsible for this aspect of the cause eagerly recruited the help of the councils of defense.[70] Thus, the connection between loyalty and the purchase of government bonds became explicit for the chairman of the Oklahoma State Council of Defense in the fall of 1917:

> You will find that the purchase of United States securities is the ·strongest possible antidote for the poison of sedition which German propaganda is constantly attempting to spread.
> You will also find that the people of that county which takes the strongest share of Liberty Bonds stand highest in citizenship.[71]

Government officials did not stop there in the promotion of the sale of bonds, resorting to less subtle tactics as the government's fiscal needs became more profound. State War Savings Committee Director George W. Barnes, for example, sent a letter to all county directors reminding them of their obligation in an upcoming sale of bonds. Maintaining that he would hold them personally responsible for their county's performance, he warned that he would "not accept any excuses for any county not doing its part."[72] Responding to this pressure, the director of Beckham County's committee corresponded with representatives of a district that failed to meet its quota. "You cannot afford," the letter informed them, "nor will your district be permitted to fail your Government in this perilous hour." All of the citizens of the district were ordered to attend a meeting that would not end until the proper amount of Liberty Bonds had been sold.[73] In the face of such pressure, excesses were bound to occur. One small farmer complained of the extreme measures resorted to in his town: "The poor people that did not own any property at all and did not have a Doller to there name," he wrote, "was Bull Dozed and made to pay as much as men that was worth 10 to 15 teen thousan Dollars [*sic*]."[74] In Muskogee, one man was tarred and feathered twice within three months for refusing to buy war bonds.[75]

The State Council of Defense, therefore, arrived at a working definition of disloyalty in its effort to promote universal patriotism. Among the key elements in this formula were making public statements that questioned government policy with respect to the war, refusing to sign loyalty oaths, and the less-than-enthusiastic support of government bond sales. Once disloyal citizens had been identified and reported by county and community councils, state leaders then had to decide what further action to take. In most cases, the initial step taken by the State Council of Defense was to warn disloyal individuals of the possible consequences of their actions. Often, members of the State Council sent letters filled with such warnings to citizens accused of disloyalty:

> It has been reported to the Oklahoma State Council of Defense that you have not been entirely loyal to the United States during the past few months. It is reported to us that you have made statements that loyal Americans should not make and that you have hindered rather than helped your country in time of war.
>
> Although these reports have been made to us from authentic sources, we trust that they are not correct. It may be that you have made statements which you did not mean, or it may be that you did not realize the seriousness of making statements of this kind.
>
> This is merely a friendly letter to you, and a warning that you are being watched. In case no statements of an undesirable nature are made in the future the matter will probably be dropped. If conditions warrant it, of course, the Department of Justice now has machinery to care for the situation.

We trust you can report to us by return mail that the reports we have received are not true. We shall expect a report from you within three days.[76]

Similar warnings were sent by the director of the State War Savings Committee to citizens identified by local authorities as being unenthusiastic in the sale of Liberty Bonds. James E. Graves of Texola, for example, received a letter informing him that his purchase of $650 worth of Liberty Bonds was not enough. In the next bond drive, the letter continued, he would "be expected" to purchase $1,000 worth of bonds and to donate to the Red Cross as well.[77]

To demonstrate that these were not idle threats, officials pointed to specific government action that could be taken against the disloyal. When the chairman of the Beckham County Council of Defense complained that he had no authority to send slackers to jail, a state official hastily replied that he would send a "government man" to assist in the county by beginning a "government investigation" against those identified as being disloyal.[78] In July of 1917 a federal agent was dispatched to the town of Woodrow to investigate a socialist named I. C. Hicks. Hicks was considered to be disloyal by virtue of a letter he had written to President Wilson urging peace.[79] Sam Williams, the chairman of Beckham County's War Savings Stamp Committee, received numerous requests for government action against "disloyal" citizens. "If a Government inspector would visit Beckham County and spend a week here investigating these things and have two or three of the ring leaders taken away for awhile," he wrote to a state official, "it would work a wholesome relief."[80]

The U.S. Congress assisted mightily in the effort through the passage of the Espionage and Sedition Acts in 1917 and 1918. The Espionage Act, which became law in May of 1917, made it a crime to "cause or attempt to cause insubordination, disloyalty, mutiny, or refusal of duty" in the armed forces and was used to prosecute those who spoke out in opposition to the country's involvement in the war. With punishment for violation of the law ranging to twenty years in prison and a fine of up to $10,000, it was indeed an effective weapon against dissent. Many officials, however, did not feel that the Espionage Act went far enough; the need to prove that the disloyal were attempting to cause insubordination, they felt, was too great a constraint. As a result of this concern, Congress amended the act the following year to give the government even greater power. The resulting amendment, known as the Sedition Act, added the following actions to the list of illegal activities included in the initial legislation: the use of "disloyal, profane, or abusive language" in reference to the form of government, the Constitution, the military forces, or the flag of the United States; the use of language (spoken or written) to "urge, incite, or advocate" the curtailment of the production of goods necessary for the war effort; and the support, "by word or act," of the cause of any nation at war with the United States.[81] Oklahoma officials quickly took advantage of these powers, reminding county chairmen that the Espionage and Sedition Acts could be used against those obstructing the sale of U.S. bonds or securities.[82]

In cases where even this degree of official power was not enough, the councils of defense willingly took extralegal action against those opposed to the war. As members of the State Council of Defense advised their subordinates, "We are convinced . . . and we have so instructed those who inquire for information that when a man, especially a stranger, is suspected of disloyalty the thing to do is to get him behind the bars, then find out what to do about it." The council in Washita County decided that the students, faculty, and board of regents of Cordell Christian College were disloyal, and closed the institution. In Texas County, representatives of the county and local committees visited in the home of a preacher who was opposed to the war. They were accompanied on their visit by the sheriff and the county attorney, and persuaded the preacher to leave the area. The members of a community council in Comanche County were equally persuasive in the case of a man who refused to sign a loyalty pledge. The man was taken by force to a meeting where he "was placed on an organ stool in the middle of the rostrum and asked to explain to his neighbors why he refused to sign the pledge card. He attempted explanations but failed; finally he wanted to sign the pledge card. They made him kiss the flag and take an oath of allegiance and made him a member of the school district council."[83] In Roger Mills County, a man who declined to purchase the prescribed amount of War Savings Stamps was forced by his banker to withdraw his funds. After "other firms with whom he had dealings expressed their displeasure," the man agreed to purchase $1,000 worth of War Savings Stamps and an undisclosed amount of Liberty Bonds, as well as to contribute "liberally" to the Red Cross."[84]

III

After the war ended, the Oklahoma State Council of Defense was given one final task, to compile and publish an account of the work it had done in the previous two years. The resulting volume, *Sooners in the War*, celebrated the contribution the Council made to the war effort: "With unfaltering directness it struck at the very roots of disloyalty and apathy, alert at the slightest sign or inclination on the part of individuals or communities to evade such sacrifices or to shirk such responsibilities as are laid on men in times of great national stress."[85]

Oklahoma socialists, of course, saw things differently. In their view, the actions of the superpatriots were anything but noble. "Mob violence has been done with no present redress for the victim" one socialist editor protested. "Yellow striped and black hearted cowards, loudly boasting patriotism, have insulted the manhood of America till it may be more tolerable for Sodom and Gomorrah in the day of judgement than for those who have violated, not merely the law, but common decency as well."[86] As opponents of the war, socialists were automatically singled out by councils of defense at all levels searching for the disloyal. Indeed, local patriots identifying disloyal individuals often felt that little incriminating evidence was necessary beyond the fact that the individuals in question were "radical socialists."[87] Oklahoma socialists observed the resulting instances of mob violence and repression directed at their comrades and wondered if they were willing to pay the price of continued activism. The case of one prominent socialist, William Madison Hicks, was particularly disturbing.

Hicks, a frequent speaker at socialist encampments, had been a member of the important committee on resolutions at the socialist state convention in 1916.[88] He was one of the many socialists arrested by authorities in the wave of repression immediately following the Green Corn Rebellion, standing trial in Ellis County for encouraging young men to resist conscription by "picturing to them the horrors of war."[89] To save himself from incarceration, Hicks publicly rescinded his antiwar position in the months following his trial; by December of 1917, he was reportedly making speeches defending President Wilson and eliciting support for war bonds and the Red Cross.[90] Hicks's conversion was short-lived, however, and by early 1918 he was again preaching active resistance to the war, leading to a second arrest for encouraging resistance to conscription.[91]

While in custody on this charge, Hicks was seized by a mob of some one hundred men, most of whom were known to be members of the local council of defense, and taken into the country, where he was tarred and feathered.[92] The mob released Hicks after inflicting its punishment, but, fearing for his life, he immediately surrendered to law enforcement authorities. This time, Hicks was convicted of violation of the Espionage Act and sentenced to a twenty-year term in the federal penitentiary in Leavenworth.[93] Also given a twenty-year prison term was O. E. Enfield, another prominent socialist organizer; Enfield's offense was "attempting to organize a revolt in Ellis County" and obstructing the operation of the Selective Service Act.[94]

The fate suffered by Hicks and Enfield may be the most dramatic evidence of the danger associated with active involvement in the

Socialist Party during the war years, but the forty socialists rounded up following the Green Corn Rebellion learned that one did not have to engage in active antiwar protest to court arrest. As one socialist wryly observed, "Language is a dangerous gift; a man can say enough in five minutes to keep him in stripes the rest of his life."[95]

Even those socialists who managed to avoid incarceration and mob violence were subjected to other punishments, ranging from the loss of credit in local stores to public humiliation, meted out by a hysterical citizenry. Under these conditions, most comrades found it wise to avoid public actions that called attention to their political affiliation, and, as the Oklahoma State Council of Defense triumphantly reported in 1918, socialists became "quiet though largely through fear."[96] As a result, the Socialist Party began a precipitous decline following the declaration of war in April of 1917. By January of 1918 the number of active socialist locals in the state had been cut in half, a reality confirmed by State Secretary Sinclair when he admitted that during the war years "a greater part of the locals" in the state ceased to exist.[97]

These reductions translated into lost votes on election day. In the election of 1918, in fact, the staggering impact of wartime hysteria on the Socialist Party of Oklahoma became clear. Where almost forty-seven thousand Oklahomans voted socialist in 1916, only seven thousand did so two years later (see table 9). No mere statistical anomaly, this 84 percent reduction in the socialist vote had just one cause; the atmosphere of hostility toward any dissent created by the politics of crisis made it exceedingly difficult for the vast majority of socialists to support their party in the election.

As Party leaders discovered in 1916, this decline was more pronounced in the southeastern counties, where as tenant farmers, socialist voters were most vulnerable to the burden of repression. In 1918 in Marshall County, for example, socialists did not even field a candidate for the important office of representative, a contest in which the socialist nominee just four years earlier had received 43 percent of the vote. In Murray County, the Party was virtually wiped out; only twenty voters there could be persuaded to vote socialist in 1918.

TABLE 9. Election Returns in Selected Counties, 1916 and 1918

COUNTY	VOTES RECEIVED BY SOCIALIST CANDIDATE		% CHANGE
	1916	1918	
Eastern Counties			
Bryan	915 (R)	109 (G)	–88
Johnston	778 (R)	66 (G)	–92
Marshall	698 (R)	90 (G)	–87
Murray	377 (R)	20 (G)	–95
Western Counties			
Beckham	986 (R)	150	–85
Dewey	890 (R)	304 (G)	–66
Roger Mills	627 (R)	207 (R)	–67
State Totals	46,979 (P)	7,433 (G)	–84

Source: Election Returns, Oklahoma State Archives, Oklahoma City, Oklahoma

Notes: Votes received by socialist candidates for governor or president are listed for state totals and for counties in which the Socialist Party did not field a candidate for representative.

R = representative
G = governor
P = president

In effect, the Democratic Party's efforts at franchise restriction, tested earlier through the Democratic election law, reached their apex in the wartime repression of the socialists. The ultimate restriction was to put a movement spokesman in jail, thereby discrediting the entire socialist constituency and the ideals they had come to treasure. This dynamic becomes even clearer when voter turnout is added to the equation (see table 10). Fully one-third of those who had voted in 1916 chose not to participate in the 1918 elections. The politics of crisis, it seems, was brutally effective at keeping certain voters away from the polls. Indeed, as one political activist noted, despite the fact than at least one hundred thousand males of voting age had come to Oklahoma since statehood, fewer males voted in 1920 than in 1907.[98] Since every county that had enjoyed strong socialist support in 1914 saw a more precipitous decline in voter turnout than the state average, it is reasonable to conclude that socialists bore a disproportionate share of the burden of the hysteria. The process of disfranchising potential socialist voters, especially those who were tenant farmers—hardly a new phenomenon, since it began in 1916 with the passage of the Democratic New Election Law—was aided enormously by the politics of crisis. The same individuals who were most vulnerable to the threat of boycott in 1916 by virtue of their lack of economic independence were also most subject to the repressive measures of the hysteria of 1917–1920.

Of course, the Socialist Party of Oklahoma had lost forever its position as a legitimate contender for political power in the Sooner State. The Republican Party, which had been supportive of the socialists' Fair Election Law, quickly made it clear that it would never again cooperate with the Socialist Party. Although at one time the Party had "numbered many sincere persons," a state GOP leader contended,

> today, socialism stands throughout the world as opposed to any stable government: opposed to personal freedom and even to the defense to the last of the liberties we have so unthoughtedly [sic]

TABLE 10. *Voter Turnout in Selected Counties, 1916 and 1918*

County	1916 Pres. Contest	1918 Gov. Contest	% Change
Beckham	3,261	1,991	–39
Bryan	5,007	2,961	–41
Dewey	2,692	1,741	–35
Johnston	3,152	1,737	–45
Marshall	2,425	1,300	–46
Murray	2,117	1,259	–41
Roger Mills	2,260	1,390	–38
State Totals	292,335	194,562	–33

Source: Election Returns, Oklahoma State Archives, Oklahoma City, Oklahoma

enjoyed, and which we are so dearly at this time defending: opposed even to the security for which we organize government.

As a theory, or a party, it is a headless, heedless, unorganized mass, no longer to be countenanced or endured.[99]

Even Harlow, the progressive Democrat who had previously counseled moderation in dealing with the socialist threat, now rejected socialism as a legitimate political alternative. Any man who continued to remain a socialist, he maintained in 1918, was "not in sympathy with his country."[100]

It was transparently obvious that the Socialist Party's antiwar stand was at the root of the repression suffered by Party members. As long as the Party remained staunchly opposed to American involvement in the World War, those who belonged to the organization risked, in the words of one socialist leader, "invit[ing] themselves into the penitentiary."[101] Under such conditions, it was inevitable that some Oklahoma comrades would question the wisdom of their party's antiwar stand. The most visible Oklahoma socialist to do so was H. H. Stallard. "In our excitement of the early period of the war," Stallard asserted, "we made a mistake and it is injuring our organization at a time when we have the best opportunity we have ever had to get our political and economic ideas before the people.... I find socialists every where working for the Red Cross and buying liberty bonds. Then why not reverse our position on the war? I believe that ninety-nine percent of the socialists would vote to repeal the war program."[102]

Stallard's position rang true to the experiences of many Oklahoma socialists, who found the repression of local patriots too great a burden. Under such pressure, for example, the socialist candidate for state Senate in the 27th District in 1918 decided to remove himself from the socialist ballot because of his inability to accept the Party's antiwar stand.[103] The editor of the *Ellis County Advocate*, a socialist publication, openly disputed the Socialist Party's official position on the war: "We stand for the successful prosecution of the war, we stand for the Red Cross, for the Y.M.C.A., for the food administration, Liberty Bond issues, War Savings Stamps and all that is necessary for the prosecution of the war for Democracy, to secure peace upon the terms enunciated by Pres. Wilson."[104]

Despite the fervor of statements like these, and irrespective of Stallard's estimate that 99 percent of Oklahoma socialist were prowar, some Party members continued to support their organization's antiwar stand. One socialist, for example, expressed what he considered to be his party's superior logic on the war:

> All the twaddle about this being the end of wars is but the silly prating of soulless politicians or misguided zealots of a dying regime. The idea that Capitalism can end war is about as preposterous as that Satan will usher in the millennium.
> The essence of war is inherent in the Capitalist system.
> So put it down under your hat socialists are going to put an end to war by abolishing the profit system.[105]

Another declared that all of the repression and hysteria in the world could not make him change his opinion: "You may cuss us, discuss us, recuss us and cross cuss us but our hands are free from the blood of all men and that's more than you can say who voted for him who kept us out of war."[106]

Although the Socialist Party of Oklahoma never officially rescinded its antiwar stand, Party leaders concluded that the organization's interests were best served by as little public discussion as possible regarding the conflict. In order to prevent themselves from "unconsciously violat[ing] the espionage or other laws of the United States or this state," the SEC counseled, "it is the reasoned judgment of this committee that the membership should not at this time allow themselves to be drawn into a discussion of the war."[107]

The SEC had not exaggerated. Throughout the state, the survival of the Socialist Party during the war hinged upon its resolution of this thorny issue. In the southeastern counties, the Party chose not to rescind its commitment to the St. Louis resolution. As a result, socialists there bore the full burden of hysteria and repression after

1917. Under this pressure, the once flourishing socialist organization in the cotton region dwindled to virtual nonexistence in 1918.

In the midst of the wartime repression, there was even talk of disbanding the Socialist Party of Oklahoma. Oscar Ameringer reports in his autobiography that Pat Nagle, the socialist leader and attorney for many of the Green Corn rebels, suggested the idea of dissolving the Party in 1918 to protect socialists from possible conspiracy convictions. At the time the idea was introduced, Ameringer explains, Victor Berger and the national executive committee of the Socialist Party of America were on trial for conspiracy, which prosecutors defined liberally as "the collusive action of persons toward definite purpose, even though said persons had never actually met." Since prosecutors in Chicago, where the Berger trial was held, would likely be able to prove that some of the Green Corn rebels had read the Milwaukee *Leader*, socialist leaders undoubtedly feared that Berger would somehow be connected to events in Oklahoma.[108] There is no evidence, however, that socialists in the Sooner State were willing to commit organizational suicide in order to protect their comrades in other states. The SEC continued to meet in 1918, and no indication of the disbanding of the Party appeared in its published minutes.[109]

The situation was different in the western part of the state, however, where most socialists were smallholders who held more social and economic options than did their comrades in the east. With a greater chance of surviving the trauma of the war years, local socialist organizations in western counties made their peace with American involvement in the European war. As early as the spring of 1917, the *Strong City Herald*, Roger Mills County's socialist newspaper, stopped running the vehemently antiwar column, "Musings of the Old Kuss," and shortly afterward announced that it would begin printing Edward W. Pickard's pro-Entente articles on the war.[110] In December, the paper urged its readers to give War Savings Stamps as Christmas gifts and early in 1918 printed an article praising the councils of defense, complete with the slogan, "Let us make the world safe for democracy and let us begin at home."[111] When Stallard traveled throughout western Oklahoma on a lecture tour in March of 1918, his message was far removed from the sentiments contained in the St. Louis resolution. In a speech entitled, "Can We Beat the Kaiser," Stallard argued that only through the socialization of America's industries could the United States emerge victorious in its struggle with Germany.[112] Socialists in Roger Mills County took the final step toward complete renunciation of the Socialist Party's antiwar position at their county convention in 1918. In a resolution adopted at the meeting, these socialists pledged their "undivided support" for the U.S. government in its "effort to bring about a lasting peace." The pledge was prefaced with a condemnation of the "autocracy and junkerism of Germany" as the "worst enemies of liberty and democracy."[113]

Having arrived at this position, socialists in western counties began to grasp the magnitude of their reversal on the war. In September of 1918, for example, the socialists of Roll held a basket dinner that illustrated starkly the implications of this change. Unlike earlier dinners held by the local, at which O. E. Enfield had delivered stirring antiwar messages, this one was given in honor of those from the community who were entering the armed forces. One of the speakers was J. W. Goin, the chairman of the county socialist organization and the Party nominee for representative in the upcoming election. Goin was among those entering the military.[114] The supreme irony, however, involved the local council of defense in Roger Mills County. This organization, which was responsible for much of the hysteria directed against socialists during the war years, was directed in Strong City by Floyd Wheeler, a local socialist leader and the editor of the county's socialist newspaper.[115]

Such a dramatic transformation obviously made socialists in Roger Mills County less vulnerable to wartime hysteria. The Party in that county even had cause to be optimistic in 1917, holding county conventions in March and May to begin the process of fielding candidates for the 1918 elections and scheduling a series of six socialist picnics to take place in the summer.[116] The county socialist convention held in April of 1918 was said to be the "largest and most enthusiastic convention held in this country for many a day."[117] Local Roll, Roger Mills County's strongest local, even seemed to thrive during the war years. The local reported at its meeting of 3 February 1918 that it had thirty-eight members in good standing, a number that increased to over fifty by May 19.[118] In the 1918 elections, some two hundred voters supported the socialist candidate for representative in Roger Mills County, a total that represented 16 percent of the vote county-wide and as much as 28 percent in some precincts. While this performance was a marked decline from 1916, when almost one-third of the votes in Roger Mills County were cast for socialist candidates, it was considerably stronger than the miserable performance of socialist candidates in the cotton counties.

IV

However, even the complete reversal of their position on the war had only a temporary effect on western socialists. Ultimately, socialists in both the cotton counties and the western region were equally vulnerable to the superpatriotism of the war years. Even though the Socialist Party experienced a resurgence in 1920 relative to its dismal performance two years earlier, the increased socialist vote was largely a show of support for Eugene Debs, who ran for president that year from his prison cell in Atlanta.[119] As table 11 demonstrates, although the socialist vote more than trebled in 1920 over 1918, Debs's total nevertheless represented a reduction of 45 percent over the socialist performance in 1916. Indeed, it must be noted that the 1920 totals were partially a reflection of the effects of the Nineteenth Amendment, which in effect doubled the electorate by giving women the right to vote. Taken as a percentage of the total votes cast, the socialist performance in 1920, when socialist candidates received just over 5 percent of the vote, represented a mere fraction of the portion of the electorate claimed by the Socialist Party between 1912 and 1916.

Table 11. Election Returns in Selected Counties, 1916–1920

COUNTY	VOTES RECEIVED BY SOCIALIST CANDIDATE			% CHANGE 1916–1920
	1916	1918	1920	
Eastern Counties				
Bryan	915 (R)	109 (G)	404 (R)	−56
Johnston	778 (R)	66 (G)	392 (P)	−50
Marshall	698 (R)	90 (G)	269 (P)	−61
Murray	377 (R)	20 (G)	119 (P)	−68
Western Counties				
Beckham	986 (R)	150 (R)	679 (R)	−31
Dewey	890 (R)	304 (G)	590 (P)	−34
Roger Mills	627 (R)	207 (R)	431 (R)	−31
State Totals	46,979 (P)	7,433 (G)	25,698 (P)	−45

Source: Election Returns, Oklahoma State Archives, Oklahoma City, Oklahoma.

Note: Votes received by socialist candidates for governor or president are listed for state totals and for counties in which the Socialist Party did not field a candidate for representative.

R = representative
G = governor
P = president

Even more telling than the Party's anemic performance in the election was the relative absence of the organizing that had made it so dynamic in earlier years. Although some encampments were reported during the campaign season in 1920, the once-great network of county and local organizations was largely silent.[120] What remained was a small organization clustered around Ameringer's *Oklahoma Leader*. Having lost its rural base, the Party clung to life with help from various labor organizations.[121] By 1922 the Party that had once included in its ranks hundreds of thriving locals in the Sooner State could locate only seventy-two paid-up members.[122] The destruction of the Socialist Party of Oklahoma had finally been accomplished.

CHAPTER 8

Uncertain Legacy

Visible Failures and Hidden Achievements

While the repression of the war years was marvelously effective in destroying the Socialist Party of Oklahoma, it did nothing to lessen the inequities that made the gospel of socialism so attractive to Oklahoma farmers. As a result, thousands of voters who had supported socialist candidates prior to 1917 were left politically homeless after the war—convinced that only through political activism could they achieve the reforms they demanded, yet alienated from the remaining electoral choices.[1]

The state's progressive forces rushed to fill this void in 1921 with the formation of a new political coalition, the Farmer-Labor Reconstruction League. Consciously harkening back to the issues present at statehood and related to the creation of the Congress for Progressive Political Action on the national level, the League called for government ownership of public utilities, railroads, banks, and warehouses and favored guaranteed minimum prices for agricultural commodities. The movement's organizers proposed that candidates sympathetic with this agenda run as Democrats in the 1922 primaries, and they nominated Oklahoma City Mayor Jack Walton to head the ticket as their candidate for governor. The results of the primary elections surprised even those who had been most optimistic about the strength of the new coalition. Walton won the Democratic Party's nomination, along with four League candidates for other state offices and thirty for seats in the state legislature. Walton and the thirty legislative candidates went on to win in November, a stunning achievement for a political organization scarcely a year old.[2]

The connection between the demise of the Socialist Party of Oklahoma and the emerging Farmer-Labor Reconstruction League was so obvious that the League's critics dismissed the latter organization as a "socialist pawn." While this charge was an exaggeration, former socialists did play an active role in the League's success, and numerous "unrepentant socialist leaders" assisted in the birth of this new political coalition.[3] Indeed, John Hagel, the socialist editor of the *Oklahoma Leader*, wrote most of the League's platform, and at the nominating convention that chose Walton, those delegates who had been socialists exerted an influence "far out of proportion to their numbers."[4] During the campaign, former Socialist Party activists, such as Pat Nagle, Dan Hogan, Oscar Ameringer, and John Hagel, contributed their considerable skills to electing Walton.[5]

Of even more help to the League in 1922 were the thousands of former socialists who saw "Our Jack" as the only reasonable choice in the election. Just as the capture of the Farmers' Union by large landowners in 1907 was followed by a movement into the Socialist Party, the demise of the socialist movement called for another political migration, this time into the Farmer-Labor Reconstruction League. This kind of political uncertainty attested to the bitter reality of postwar politics.[6] The alienation of working farmers spawned a new political reality to which the Democratic Party in the lower Great Plains and the southern cotton belt was temporarily unable to respond. In the void left by the demise of the Socialist Party and the Democrats' inability to offer a progressive alternative to the Republican Party, the Farmer-Labor Reconstruction League represented the only remaining political option for most activists. In this sense, the momentum that swept Walton into the governor's mansion was one legacy of Oklahoma socialism.

But as a movement, the Socialist Party did not survive the war. The democratic ideal nurtured in the Indiahoma Farmers' Union and the Socialist Party of Oklahoma failed to become adequately instilled in the Farmer-Labor Reconstruction League. The critical mass of experienced activists necessary to ensure that the organization would remain uncompromising in its commitment to democratic reform simply did not exist within its ranks. Far too many of those who possessed such a democratic vision had been evicted from the political process by the trauma of the politics of crisis.

I

As thousands of Oklahoma farmers struggled to find a political home in an environment hostile to their interests, they unwittingly provided us with a rare glimpse of the dynamic of power in American society. Rarely in our history have the lines of political engagement been so clearly drawn between forces committed to the defense of laissez-faire capitalism and those working to replace it with a more equitable economic system. The success of the Socialist Party of Oklahoma forced the defenders of capitalism to adopt a sense of urgency not generally present in the American political dialogue. In such a charged atmosphere the trappings of power, normally submerged beneath a veneer of civility, exploded onto the surface with brutal clarity.

Of course, the repression suffered by the Socialist Party during the war years represented the clearest example of this dynamic. But presenting the demise of the Socialist Party of Oklahoma solely as a function of wartime hysteria, as an isolated instance when the defenders of the status quo used extralegal means to preserve their power, oversimplifies the political climate in which Oklahoma socialists operated. What happened between 1917 and 1920 represented only a more extreme—and thus more visible— manifestation of a broader reality suffusing the whole of American politics. For all of the rhetoric portraying the political process in the United States as a series of free, democratic choices between proponents of disparate ideological positions, the fact is that an enormous advantage is automatically accorded to those who work to obstruct fundamental alterations in the system.

The Oklahoma Socialist Party, which represented forces favoring substantive change, necessarily worked from a disadvantaged position, even during periods of relative calm far removed from the repression and hysteria of the war years. As Oklahoma socialists learned at every turn, countless barriers warped their relations with the innumerable businessmen, politicians, editors, and civil servants in the state, ensuring that the socialist movement would ultimately fail. Despite their sophistication and remarkable success, Oklahoma socialists were in the end unable to counteract the vastly superior resources of the opposition.

This generalization becomes more precise when infused with concrete historical evidence of the sort generated by the Oklahoma reform movement. For purposes of illustration, it is useful to review one specific incident: the Oklahoma socialists' attempt in 1916 to use the initiative provision of the state constitution to enact their Fair Election Law. The first barrier faced by the Socialist Party in this effort was the constitution's stipulation that sponsors of proposed initiatives collect the signatures of 50,000 voters in order to gain a place on the ballot. Since this number virtually equaled the total votes received by the socialist gubernatorial candidate in the most recent statewide election, the task was daunting. Nevertheless, through the mobilization of its political organization, the Socialist Party succeeded in collecting the necessary signatures—only to encounter an even more formidable barrier on election day. By misusing their authority as the superintendents of the electoral process, state and local Democratic officials worked to ensure the measure's defeat. The most popular tactic involved the distribution of ballots; voters in traditionally strong socialist precincts discovered that large segments of the electorate were not allowed to vote because of a mysterious shortage of ballots, while those in areas of less socialist activity encountered a consistent oversupply.[7]

Despite this practice, the socialists emerged triumphant, and the Fair Election Law received the support of the majority of the voters on election day. This victory forced Democratic leaders to resort to even less subtle tactics to defeat the measure. Relying on their majority status on the state election board, they changed the rules governing the counting of the ballots *post facto*, thereby overturning the socialist victory. For all of its organizational strength, the Socialist Party of Oklahoma could not reverse the manipulations of the election board, and the Fair Election Law, which should have been the socialists' greatest triumph, was defeated.

This incident makes clear a central lesson regarding the dynamic of power. As socialists in Oklahoma became increasingly sophisticated in their attacks on the prevailing institutions of capitalism, mobilizing an ever-increasing constituency in that effort, they ultimately succeeded only in laying bare additional layers of the elaborate system of defense that was available to the protectors of tradition. The resulting lesson comes as something of a paradox: Oklahoma socialists were able to glimpse with unprecedented clarity the enormous breadth of the forces arrayed against them only because of the depth of support that they themselves engendered.

The hysteria and repression that destroyed the Socialist Party of Oklahoma after 1917 must be seen within this larger context. Although the political debate in Oklahoma between 1917 and 1920 reached a shrill pitch seldom matched before or since, it falls well within the Oklahoma socialists' larger experience. In the Sooner State, the Party's enemies proved time and again their absolute commitment to the goal of preventing socialists from sharing governmental power. When the crisis of American involvement in the European war presented the ultimate opportunity to achieve this end, the state's political leaders had already demonstrated their opportunism. Yet their prior performance indicates that had the war not made available the weapon of direct repression, an only slightly less severe tactic would have been used to ensure the failure of the Socialist Party of Oklahoma.

II

The commitment of Democratic and Republican leaders to defeating socialism makes the success of the Oklahoma Socialist Party all the more remarkable. Indeed, returning to the question posed at the outset of this work, it is now possible to see more clearly how activists in the Sooner State were able to build the nation's most successful socialist movement. At the heart of the explanation lies one relatively simple generalization: The achievements of the socialist movement in the Sooner State were largely the result of regional reformers' skill in movement building, gained through their participation in the Indiahoma Farmers' Union and, indirectly, the Farmers Alliance.

In practical terms, this skill helped Oklahoma socialists gain remarkable sophistication in their understanding of the workings of the existing agricultural system. This insight set Oklahoma Party members apart from their comrades elsewhere in the United States. Here, we begin to discern the importance of the Indiahoma Farmers' Union to the Oklahoma socialist experience, for it was in the Union that Oklahoma activists received their education in the workings of agrarian capitalism. Through trial and error, Farmers' Union members built upon the inherited lessons of the Populist movement to devise a strategy for attacking the objectionable aspects of agrarian finance, thereby learning the lessons of movement building as well. At the heart of the Union's program was crop withholding, an inventive tactic in which farmers used their solidarity as producers to break down the conditions under which they received artificially low prices for their crops. By consolidating the victories achieved through crop withholding, Union members planned to gradually begin challenging the commercial agricultural system in more fundamental ways.

The clearing house plan allowed farmers to engage in a more ambitious tactic than crop withholding while still concentrating on reforming the selling relationship; as such, it represented the first important step in the implementing of a more inclusive and sophisticated vision of how the economic system should work. Future tactics would have included Union cotton schools to train farmers in the grading of cotton—thereby enabling them to participate on a more equal basis in selling their crop—and ultimately, cooperative stores to more directly challenge the power of the rural furnishing merchants. At the heart of this vision was a critical insight, which could be internalized only through practical experience; the lessons of the Alliance taught members of the Farmers' Union that they could hope to succeed only by mastering one tactic before moving to the next level of complexity.

As Union members moved into the Socialist Party after 1907, they brought these lessons with them, representing in the most concrete terms the process interpreters refer to, usually in the abstract, as "class consciousness." In this case, the transferring of the lessons of democratic activism from one movement to the next had enormous implications. It represented the joining of two previously separate traditions in the history of the American left. To the socialists' long tradition of political activism the Socialist Party in Oklahoma could now add the legacy of two generations of experience in cooperative economic organizing, which came in the form of the life experiences of those members who had been active in the Farmers' Union. As the recipient of this all-too-infrequent dynamic in American history, the Socialist Party of Oklahoma now had an unparalleled opportunity; its members possessed the skills to attack with equal intensity both the political and economic institutions of the existing system.

One central characteristic of the socialist movement, however, threatened to prevent the Party from realizing this potential. Those Party members schooled in the Farmers' Union tradition of cooperative economics understood immediately that the organization could hope to succeed only if it was willing to leave behind certain traditional Marxist preconceptions on agrarian issues. The qualitative difference between these two traditions on such issues was intimidating. The debate on agricultural issues within the Farmers' Union began with Jefferson's notion that land ownership was the centerpiece of democracy. Building on that premise, the dialogue included concrete discussions of problems such as the crop lien, the exploitive power of the furnishing merchant, and the role of street buyers in selling the farmers' crops. Socialists, on the other hand, were still quarreling in 1907 over the elemental questions of whether smallholders could belong to the Party and whether committed socialists could legitimately include land ownership in their demands.

This central contradiction between the Jeffersonian legacy of the Farmers' Union and the inherited Marxist practices of American socialists forced Oklahoma Party members to redefine the socialist position on agrarian issues. It is a process that has been outlined in some detail in this work. The response of Oklahoma socialists to this dilemma after 1907, in fact, represents the single most important manifestation of the effect of the Farmers' Union on the Socialist Party of Oklahoma. Without repeating the specifics of this critical ideological debate, it is important to appreciate the magnitude of Oklahoma socialists' achievement.

In the face of the accepted Marxist orthodoxy that agrarian landowners were in reality small businessmen who forfeited their membership in the proletariat, Oklahoma socialists proposed their own theoretical interpretation of the American reality: Those who performed the labor of farming, whether or not they owned the land they worked, were legitimate members of the working class. Confronted with the closely related Marxist concept that land collectivization was the only acceptable socialist solution to the agricultural crisis, Oklahoma socialists pointed out that collectivization—in this case the concentration of land into the hands of a few large landowners—was in actuality the *cause* of rural poverty. They argued persuasively that the solution must involve—not accelerating this process to a higher level of state collectivization as the Marxists proposed—but reversing it by placing land in the hands of those who worked it.

It is difficult to overemphasize the enormity and importance of this task. Oklahoma socialists, relative newcomers to American socialist politics, were asking veteran Party members to significantly modify a portion of the socialist ideological system that had come from Marx himself. This task was so sensitive, in fact, that even some contemporary interpreters are often reluctant to forgive Oklahoma socialists for committing what they see as ideological apostasy.[8]

Party members in Oklahoma succeeded in redefining some of the ideological precepts presumably controlling the day-to-day life of believing socialist reformers. The specific contributions of Oklahoma innovators not only brought the Party's agrarian program into harmony with the prevailing realities on the land, but it was much more democratic in application than state collectivization ever proved to be. Indeed, it is perhaps even more telling to note that the Oklahoma Party's solution to the land question in an industrializing world was much more democratic than the corporate collectivization that has come to dominate American agriculture.

It should be noted in passing that Marx's exclusion of smallholders from the working class as well as his aversion to land ownership resulted from the intense and penetrating analysis he conducted of European capitalism, a region where the legacy of feudalism tied rural landowners more directly to the bourgeoisie. However, American farmers, especially in the South, were products of a very different economic and social experience, one shaped in fundamental ways by the traumatic legacy of slavery and its progeny—tenancy and the crop lien system. In this very different agrarian world, all working farmers—tenants and smallholders alike—were legitimate members of the working class. Only farmers wealthy enough to hire wage labor had experientially removed themselves from the proletariat.[9] In the world of Oklahoma farmers, smallholders enjoyed none of the luxuries that were thought to accompany membership in the ruling class. Like tenants, most smallholders lived in a state of poverty caused by low crop prices and the high cost of credit. There simply was no justification for clinging to a theoretical concept that contrasted so dramatically with the reality of life in the Oklahoma countryside.

Nor did Oklahoma socialists see anything inappropriate in including in their program the demand that land be redistributed into the hands of working farmers. They were unambiguous about the fact that farmers could legitimately own only as much land as they could work. Thus, they argued, the Oklahoma socialist platform merely proposed that members of the rural working class own the means of agricultural production. Seen in this context, the Oklahoma socialists' position on land ownership was hardly as controversial as some within the national socialist movement portrayed it to be.[10]

In these ways, Oklahoma socialists conceptualized their response to capitalism in the United States in a way that rendered Marx's ideas more congruent with the particular experiences of American workers. By doing this, they broadened the ideological horizons of American socialists, allowing them to call upon the republican ideals of the American revolution as well as the class consciousness of Marxism. In the resulting symbiosis, both traditions were legitimized to create an ideological system that was peculiarly American, symbolically joining, as it were, Karl Marx with Thomas Jefferson.

III

In order to more fully understand how Oklahoma socialists drew upon the legacy of the Farmers' Union to create an expansive socialist movement in America, a second, closely related issue, merits additional discussion. Oklahoma Party members called upon their experience in the Farmers' Union in a more general way to ensure that the affairs of the Socialist Party of Oklahoma would be conducted in a democratic manner. The Farmers' Union possessed no canon of sacred ideological concepts that were above debate, and important issues such as the most appropriate minimum price for the next cotton crop or the wisdom of engaging in cooperative purchasing in coming years were thoroughly aired in the Union press. Organizational leaders did not deem certain views to be unworthy of consideration in advance of the debate. As their willingness to challenge even the ideas of Marx himself demonstrates, those socialists who remembered this practice demanded the same consideration in the Socialist Party. Furthermore, having participated in such events as the Tishomingo convention and the ongoing debate over the establishment of a separate Indian Territory Farmers' Union, they possessed the skills and confidence necessary to build this democratic practice of open dialog into the Oklahoma Socialist movement. Such an insight deepens our understanding of those aspects of the Socialist Party of Oklahoma that might otherwise seem idiosyncratic or, to some interpreters, misguided.

Those socialists who had been active in the Farmers' Union, for example, were disturbed by the ease with which conservatives in the Union had gradually centralized authority into the hands of the SEC, thereby controlling the Union for their narrow purposes. As socialists, those former Union members were especially vigilant lest a similar scenario unfold in the Socialist Party. In this context, the events of the socialist state convention of 1912, when the delegates rebuffed the "centralizers" associated with Victor Berger's Milwaukee organization, can be seen to possess a quiet consistency. The socialists' seemingly irrational fixation on the dangers presented by the *Oklahoma Pioneer* as the official Party newspaper should also be seen in this light. Having observed the conservatives' skillful use of the *Indiahoma Union Signal* to remove S. O. Daws from power and to further consolidate their authority, the socialists were unwilling to take the same risk with the *Pioneer*. Thus, their reactions were neither misguided nor irrational. They were merely democratic.

IV

The Socialist Party was well served by the combination of these attributes—the sophisticated understanding of the commercial agricultural system coupled with the confidence needed to demand accountability on the part of their leaders and their organization, both of which came to Oklahoma socialists only through their participation in the Indiahoma Farmers' Union. Indeed, this was an especially robust combination rarely present in American political life, whether in major parties or in insurgent movements. Oklahoma socialists saw more clearly than most other contemporary Americans the shortcomings of existing economic and political systems. They had the self-possession and insight to propose concrete and workable solutions. And, perhaps most importantly, they knew how to force their institution toward more democratic forms.

In this way, Oklahoma socialists succeeded in forging a party that presented the essential Marxist message of socialism in a form that made sense within inherited American traditions. The practical utility of this accomplishment was not limited to the Oklahoma Party's stand on the land question. It also influenced the way Party members responded to the received culture, the system of beliefs and practices that ordered their lives.[11] In the face of this system, Oklahoma socialists intuitively understood what many current scholars are only beginning to comprehend—the dominant culture is a double-edged sword which, depending upon its use, may either "dare the status quo or confirm it."[12] Agrarian Marxists in the Sooner State consistently and unapologetically availed themselves of the dominant culture to dare, rather than confirm, the existing system by employing it to make socialism acceptable to Oklahoma farmers.

That they embraced the values and traditions of evangelical Protestantism represents an additional manifestation of Oklahoma socialists' genius as activists. Just as they had molded the Marxist ideological tradition into a form true to the American agrarian experience, Party members transformed their inherited religious tradition into a unique kind of socially rooted Christianity. As a result, so closely did the contemporary language and message of religion mesh with those of the Socialist Party that it seemed natural for Oklahoma farmers seeped in the Christian tradition to join the Party.

Here, the Oklahoma success becomes most clearly unique. Nowhere else in the United States did socialist activists succeed in making the European doctrines of Marxism speak so unambiguously in American terms. As a result, virtually alone in the United States, socialists in Oklahoma were able to counteract the prevailing American notion that socialist political alternatives were inherently illegitimate. When leaders of the Democratic and Republican parties repeated the familiar charge that socialist ideas were beyond the pale in the American political system, socialists in Oklahoma could draw upon an especially effective rejoinder. Party members in the Sooner State pointed out in uniquely American ideological and cultural terms that they were fighting for nothing less than the democratic heritage central to the American experience. After all, their principal demands—the right to own the plot of land they worked and the right to a just portion of the fruits of their labor—were eminently reasonable and fell well within the mainstream of accepted American cultural traditions. As such, it was perfectly natural for socialists to marshal both their religious tradition and the legacy of the American past in support of their cause.

So it is instructive that Oklahoma socialists borrowed equally from the rhetorical and ideological traditions of the American Revolution, Christian doctrine, and Marxist political theory. With such diverse traditions, Oklahoma comrades framed the socialist debate in cultural and ideological terms that were authentically American. It was an achievement unmatched in the United States, one that explains the singular success of the Socialist Party of Oklahoma.

APPENDIX A

A Comment on the Success of Crop Withholding

Whether or not the crop withholding plan organized by the Farmers' Union actually resulted in higher prices is subject to debate. Certainly the initial assessment offered by farmers engaged in withholding was overwhelmingly positive. The statistical evidence seems just as clear; as table 12 indicates, cotton prices in the territories began to rise in 1903, at precisely the moment that farmers affiliated with the Indiahoma Farmers' Union began withholding cotton systematically.

As a result, Union members enthusiastically credited crop withholding for the increase in prices. As one correspondent put it, albeit with some hyperbole, "Had it not been for the Farmers' Union, cotton last season would have sold for five cents. Your organization saved the cotton market of the world by doing something which you should have done years ago."[1] Theodore Saloutos undoubtedly was swayed by such evidence when he argued in *Farmer Movements in the South* that crop withholding was responsible for considerable improvement in the lives of individual farmers. After the National Farmers' Union set the minimum price for the 1906–1907 cotton crop at eleven cents per pound, he pointed out, prices began an upward spiral from just over nine cents per pound in September of 1909 to twelve cents the following May.[2]

Some observers disagree, however, maintaining that the world cotton market was just too massive to have been affected by the actions of a few agricultural producers in the American South. The

TABLE 12. *Cotton Prices Received by Oklahoma Farmers, 1895–1920 (December 1, in cents per pound)*

Year	Price
1895	7.3
1896	6.2
1897	6.4
1898	5.8
1899	6.9
1900	8.7
1901	6.8
1902	6.7
1903	10.2
1904	8.5
1905	10.0
1906	9.5
1907	9.9
1908	8.0
1909	13.0
1910	13.3
1911	8.0
1912	11.3
1913	11.4
1914	6.5
1915	11.3
1916	19.0
1917	26.5
1918	25.5
1919	35.2
1920	10.5

Source: U. S. Departmentof Agriculture, Bureau of Agricultural Economics, "Prices of Farm Products Received by Producers," *USDA Statistical Bulletin*, no. 16 (1927): 222.

upturn in cotton prices at the time when the Union began withholding, these interpreters argue, was nothing more than a fortuitous accident. Indeed, a second look at the statistical evidence reveals that, at the very least, the picture is more complicated than supporters of withholding would have us believe. As the data in table 13

TABLE 13. *Cotton Prices in Southern States, 1900–1910 (Dec. 1 in cents per pound)*

	1900	1901	1902	1903	1904	1905	1906	1907	1908	1909	1910
Okla.	8.7	6.8	6.7	10.2	8.5	10.0	9.5	9.9	8.2	13.0	13.3
Tex.	8.9	6.8	7.3	10.3	8.7	10.5	9.5	10.2	8.5	13.6	14.0
Ala.	9.3	7.1	7.8	10.5	8.9	10.8	9.5	10.2	8.7	14.2	14.2
Ark.	9.0	6.9	7.0	10.4	8.8	11.1	9.5	10.3	8.8	14.0	14.4
Fla.	9.0	6.5	9.5	14.0	12.3	12.2	15.8	17.0	12.2	19.3	21.0
Ga.	9.5	7.2	8.0	10.7	9.4	10.9	9.8	10.6	8.7	14.2	14.2
La.	9.2	7.0	7.3	10.5	9.0	11.1	9.5	10.3	8.7	13.7	14.4
Miss.	9.4	7.2	8.0	10.6	8.9	11.1	9.5	10.5	8.8	14.3	14.4
N.C.	9.4	7.2	8.0	10.6	9.2	10.8	9.5	10.2	9.0	13.9	14.1
S.C.	9.5	7.3	8.0	10.6	9.4	11.0	9.7	10.5	8.8	14.1	14.2
Tenn.	9.0	7.1	7.8	10.3	9.0	10.6	9.5	10.3	9.0	13.6	14.1

Source: U.S. Department of Agriculture, Bureau of Agricultural Economics, "Prices of Farm Products Received by Producers," *USDA Statistical Bulletin*, no. 16 (1927): 222.

indicate, the general trend in cotton prices was remarkably consistent throughout the South, irrespective of the health or weakness of the Farmers' Union organization. In 1903, when farmers in Texas and the Indian and Oklahoma Territories began withholding their cotton, the Union was more firmly established there than anywhere else in the nation. Even so, prices rose just as sharply that year in other cotton-producing states—even those where the Farmers' Union was only beginning to make inroads—as in Texas and Oklahoma. Furthermore, prices in Oklahoma continued to be higher after 1907, when the Union collapsed in the Sooner State, than they had been prior to 1902. All of this leads to the conclusion that the rise and fall of cotton prices had little to do with the actions of farmers affiliated with the Farmers' Union.[3]

While this evidence obviously opens to question Union members' claims regarding the effectiveness of withholding, it should not necessarily result in the repudiation of the tactic. By itself, this data is insufficient to determine whether crop withholding caused an increase in cotton prices for early twentieth-century farmers. It should be remembered that regional price statistics like those presented in Tables 12 and 13 are averages. Of course, not all cotton farmers in Oklahoma received the price recorded by the Department of Agriculture for the month they sold their crops. It is entirely possible, indeed probable, that in a given region those who participated in the Farmers' Union crop withholding plan received better prices than those who did not.

Of course, the entire debate is to a certain extent tangential to the central concerns of this work. At issue here is not whether crop withholding caused the increase in prices, but whether or not Oklahoma Union members *believed* that holding their cotton resulted in higher prices. On this point, the evidence is much more conclusive. Irrespective of the quite legitimate misgivings of later interpreters (who are privy to evidence unavailable to Oklahoma cotton farmers), the fact is that Union members in the territories in 1903 were convinced that withholding worked. Until the disastrous withholding effort of 1907, by which time the nucleus of agrarian activism had moved out of the Union, nothing in their experience caused them to doubt the premise that collective marketing constituted the tactical foundation of their movement. Such a premise, in fact, helped recruit farmers to the movement, thus leading to their political education in the Farmers' Union and the Socialist Party.

APPENDIX B

Selected Listing of Prominent Oklahoma Socialist Ministers

Name	*Role in the Socialist Party (references in parentheses)*
Reddin Andrews	Organizer and lecturer (*Musings of the Old Kuss*, July 1916)
Sam Baldwin	Known as the "Socialist Poet-Preacher" (*Appeal to Reason*, 12 August 1911)
J. T. Beam	County organizer, Murray County (*New Century*, 16 February 1912)
H. I. Bryant	Candidate for representative, Dewey County, 1910, 1912 (*Oklahoma Pioneer*, 1 June 1910)
J. T. Cumbie	Candidate for U.S. Representative, 1907, 1912, 1914; candidate for governor, 1910; county organizer, Bryan County (*Durant Statesman*, 26 July 1907; *Sword of Truth*, 21 May 1913)
J. B. Dabney	"Preacher of Socialism," party lecturer, local chairman (*New Century*, 20 October 1911; *Oklahoma Pioneer*, 30 March 1910, 21 January 1911)
O. E. Enfield	Lecturer and organizer, candidate for governor
George G. Hamilton	Associate editor, *Social Democrat*

"Comrade Hollis"	County organizer, Washita County (*Oklahoma Pioneer*, 26 January 1910)
W. E. Huckins	Socialist lecturer (*Appeal to Reason*, 27 March 1909)
George W. Hutton	Editor, *Strong City Herald*
Leonard Johnson	Farmers' Union organizer and socialist organizer (*Durant Independent Farmer*, 6 July 1906; *Industrial Democrat*, 6 August 1910)
Granville Lowther	Socialist lecturer (*Common People*, 1 October 1903)
Thomas H. McLemore	Elected to Oklahoma State House of Representatives, 1914; county secretary, Beckham County (*Elk City News*, 14 February 1918; *Industrial Democrat*, 26 February 1910)
W. L. Thurman	Billed as "the best man to clean up on the capitalist-minded preachers" (*Social Democrat*, 8 October 1913)
E. R. Williams	Contributor to the *Appeal to Reason*, (*Appeal to Reason*, 3 February 1912)

Notes

PREFACE

1. James Green, *Grass-Roots Socialism: Radical Movements in the Southwest, 1895–1943* (Baton Rouge: Louisiana State University Press, 1978); Garin Burbank, *When Farmers Voted Red: The Gospel of Socialism in the Oklahoma Countryside, 1910–1924* (Westport, Conn.: Greenwood Press, 1976); John Thompson, *Closing the Frontier: Radical Responses in Oklahoma, 1899–1923* (Norman: University of Oklahoma Press, 1986).
2. Irving Howe, *Socialism and America* (New York: Harcourt, Brace, Jovanovich, 1985), 13.
3. Burbank, *When Farmers Voted Red*, 189. For virtually the same conclusion, see Thompson, *Closing the Frontier*, 139.
4. Green, *Grass-Roots Socialism*, 161.

INTRODUCTION

1. According to the *Appeal to Reason*, in 1907 the Oklahoma Socialist Party was the largest state branch in the nation in terms of dues paying membership as a proportion of the total population. New York and Illinois, the next largest branches, had socialist memberships only twice as large as Oklahoma's, but their populations were eight to ten times that of the Sooner State. See *Appeal to Reason*, 18 January 1908.

An extended discussion of the historiography of the Socialist Party of America is provided in the bibliographical essay.

2. See Worth Robert Miller, *Oklahoma Populism: A History of the People's Party in the Oklahoma Territory* (Norman: University of Oklahoma Press, 1987), 10–11; and Bruce Palmer, *"Man Over Money": The Southern Populist Critique of American Capitalism* (Chapel Hill: University of North Carolina Press, 1980), 14.

3. In his treatment of Oklahoma socialism, for example, John Thompson explains the rise of the party in terms of this prevailing model. "Oklahoma's socialist leaders," Thompson asserts in *Closing the Frontier*, "enjoyed remarkable success in trans-

forming impoverished farmers and tenants into leftists." Thus, Oklahoma farmers are depicted as passive forces, acted upon by organizational leaders in order to be made into socialists. Indeed, Thompson uses this very language, arguing on one occasion that "groups of organizers thoroughly canvassed the region '*making socialists.*'" These organizers were successful, Thompson continues, because of their remarkable talent in "translating their messages into a language which ignorant and often semi-literate tenants could understand." John Thompson, *Closing the Frontier: Radical Responses in Oklahoma, 1889–1923* (Norman: University of Oklahoma Press, 1986), 131, 141, emphasis added.

4. Throughout this work, Karl Marx, Thomas Jefferson, and Jesus Christ serve as convenient representatives of intellectual or ideological traditions that were important to the Oklahoma Socialist Party's success. For the purposes of this analysis, Marx represents the basic ideas of class and internationalism that defined early twentieth-century socialist movements; Jefferson refers to the republican ideals of the American Revolution; and Jesus, to the moral teachings of the Christian Gospel. In each case, Oklahoma socialists borrowed freely from the traditions these men represent. Party members subscribed enthusiastically to the Marxist theoretical underpinnings of the American Socialist Party (with the exception of the party's stand on agricultural issues, a distinction which will be discussed at length in chapter 4). From the Populist movement, Oklahoma socialists inherited a reverence for the Jeffersonian ideals of democracy and the importance of the yeoman farming class for the maintenance of the American democratic tradition. And from evangelical Protestantism, party members in the Sooner State drew upon the ideas and teachings of Jesus Christ.

In other words, Oklahoma socialists consciously borrowed from three of the most radical documents of all time: the Communist Manifesto, the Declaration of Independence, and the Sermon on the Mount.

CHAPTER 1

1. *Indiahoma Union Signal*, 14 November 1905.
2. Roger L. Ransom and Richard Sutch, *One Kind of Freedom: The Economic Consequences of Emancipation* (Cambridge: Cambridge University Press, 1977), xi.
3. Harold D. Woodman, *King Cotton and His Retainers: Financing and Marketing of the Cotton Crop of the South, 1800–1925* (Lexington: University of Kentucky Press, 1968), 346. Woodman lists the following rates of increase in per capita income from 1840 to 1900 in other states: Alabama: 17 percent; South Carolina: no increase; Tennessee: 30 percent.
4. Danney Goble, *Progressive Oklahoma: The Making of a New Kind of State* (Norman: University of Oklahoma Press, 1980), 156.
5. *Historical Statistics of the United States, Colonial Times to 1957: A Statistical Abstract Supplement* (Washington, D.C.: Government Printing Office, 1960).
6. *Sulphur New Century*, 27 June 1913.

7. Oscar Ameringer, *If You Don't Weaken: The Autobiography of Oscar Ameringer* (New York: Henry Holt, 1940), quoted in James R. Scales and Danney Goble, *Oklahoma Politics: A History* (Norman: University of Oklahoma Press, 1982), 67.

8. Ameringer, *If You Don't Weaken*, 232.

9. "A Picture of the Average Farmer," *Indiahoma Union Signal*, 21 November 1905.

10. Ibid. For additional insight into this process, see the series of articles written by *Appeal to Reason* correspondent John Kenneth Turner in 1914, especially "Turner Pillories Parasites of Cotton Producers," *Appeal to Reason*, 26 December 1914.

11. The following works describe the crop lien system in greater detail: C. Vann Woodward, *Origins of the New South, 1877–1913* (Baton Rouge: Louisiana State University Press, 1951), 179–85; Lawrence Goodwyn, *The Populist Moment: A Short History of the Agrarian Revolt in America* (New York: Oxford University Press, 1978), 20–27; and Ransom and Sutch, *One Kind of Freedom*, 126–70.

12. Arthur N. Moore and J. T. Sanders, "Credit Problems of Oklahoma Cotton Farmers," *Agricultural Experiment Station Bulletin*, no. 198 (October 1930): 32–34.

13. Ransom and Sutch, *One Kind of Freedom*, 128–31.

14. There is considerable scholarly debate, of course, over the terms of the agricultural crisis. In addition to the works cited above, see also Pete Daniel, *The Shadow of Slavery: Peonage in the South, 1901–1969* (New York: Oxford University Press, 1973); and Jonathan Wiener, "Class Structure and Economic Development in the American South," *American Historical Review* 84 (1979): 970–1006.

For additional interpretations, some of which differ significantly from mine, see the following: Joseph D. Reid, Jr., "Sharecropping as an Understandable Market Response," *Journal of Economic History* 33 (1973): 106–30; W. Brown and M. Reynolds, "Debt Peonage Re-examined," *Journal of Economic History* 33 (1973): 862–71; C. Goldin, "'N' Kinds of Freedom," *Explorations in Economic History* 16 (1979): 8–30; and P. Temin, "Freedom and Coercion: Notes on the Analysis of Debt Peonage in *One Kind of Freedom*," *Explorations in Economic History* (1979): 56–63.

15. *Appeal to Reason*, 19 December 1914.

16. This account of the process by which Oklahoma passed from Indian to white control is derived from the following sources: Goble, *Progressive Oklahoma*; Kenneth Marvin Hamilton, "Black Town Promotion and Development on the Middle Border, 1877–1914" (Ph.D. diss., Washington University, 1978); Worth Robert Miller, *Oklahoma Populism: A History of the People's Party in the Oklahoma Territory* (Norman: University of Oklahoma Press, 1987); and Scales and Goble, *Oklahoma Politics*.

17. This premise is central to the argument presented in John Thompson's *Closing the Frontier*.

18. Scales and Goble, *Oklahoma Politics*, 65–66.

CHAPTER 2

1. For a thoughtful overview of the varied and complex historiography of Populism, see Robert C. McMath, *American Populism: A Social History, 1877–1898*

(New York: Hill and Wang, 1993), 9–18, 214–16; and William F. Holmes, "Populism: In Search of Context," *Agrarian History* 64 (1990): 26–58. As McMath points out, the pioneering work of C. Vann Woodward—*Origins of the New South, 1877–1913* (Baton Rouge: Louisiana State University Press, 1951) and *Tom Watson: Agrarian Rebel* (New York: Macmillan, 1938)—provides the interpretive framework for virtually every subsequent study.

See especially Lawrence Goodwyn, *Democratic Promise: The Populist Movement in America* (New York: Oxford University Press, 1976); Lawrence Goodwyn, *The Populist Moment: A Short History of the Agrarian Revolt in America* (New York: Oxford University Press, 1978); Bruce Palmer, *"Man Over Money"* (Chapel Hill: University of North Carolina Press, 1980); Robert McMath, *Populist Vanguard: A History of the Southern Farmers' Alliance* (Chapel Hill: University of North Carolina Press, 1975); Robert McMath, *American Populism*; Norman Pollack, *The Just Polity: Populism, Law, and Human Welfare* (Urbana: University of Illinois Press, 1987); Norman Pollack, *The Humane Economy: Populism, Capitalism, and Democracy* (New Brunswick: Rutgers University Press, 1990); Peter H. Argersinger, *The Limits of Agrarian Radicalism: Western Populism and American Politics* (Lawrence: University Press of Kansas, 1995); and Gene Clanton, *Populism: The Humane Preference in America, 1890–1900* (Boston: Twayne Publishers, 1991).

The story of Oklahoma Populism is told by Worth Robert Miller in *Oklahoma Populism: A History of the People's Party in the Oklahoma Territory* (Norman: University of Oklahoma Press, 1987).

2. The insight and language regarding the Populists' cultural resources comes from Palmer, *"Man Over Money"*, 37–38. Lawrence Goodwyn's *Democratic Promise* describes how the experience gained in Alliance cooperatives radicalized Populists.

3. In her work on farmers in Lewis County, Washington, Marilyn P. Watkins illuminates particularly well how Populism provided the foundation for future agrarian movements. The "knowledge and hope" that Populism instilled "did not disintegrate in 1896 when the People's party collapsed," she writes. Farmers in western Washington built upon the Populists' "vision of democracy and independence" to keep their movement alive. See Marilyn P. Watkins, *Rural Democracy: Family Farmers and Politics in Western Washington, 1890–1925* (Ithaca, New York: Cornell University Press, 1995), 191.

4. An excellent source on the early years of the Farmers' Union is Robert Lee Hunt, *A History of Farmer Movements in the Southwest, 1873–1925* (College Station: Agricultural and Mechanical College of Texas, 1935).

5. By August of 1904, Sam Hampton was editing a regular column in the *Durant Weekly News* entitled the "Farmers Open Forum." *Durant Weekly News*, 12 August 1904.

6. *Indiahoma Union Signal*, 5 September 1905.

7. Hunt, *A History of Farmer Movements*, 76–81.

8. *Durant Independent Farmer*, 30 March 1905.

9. Goodwyn, *Democratic Promise*, 37, 491, 546.

10. Daws's address was printed in both the *Indiahoma Union Signal* (16 January 1906) and the *Durant Independent Farmer* (1 February 1906).

11. *Indiahoma Union Signal*, 26 December 1905.

12. To the extent that the Alliance and People's Party provided valuable experience in the workings of agrarian capitalism and the trials of movement building, the Populist movement is relevant to the Socialist Party that emerged in Oklahoma in the early twentieth century. However, in an institutional sense, the Populist contribution came only indirectly; the Farmers' Union provided the organizational link between the agrarian movement and socialism. As a result, it is the Indiahoma Farmers' Union, not the institutional manifestations of the Populist movement in the Oklahoma Territory, that are most relevant here. For the complete story of the latter phenomenon, see Miller, *Oklahoma Populism*.

Both Miller and James Green recognize the presence of populism in Oklahoma socialists' heritage, but they erroneously assume that the former led directly to the latter, thereby missing the middle step (the Farmers' Union) in the equation. The result is a flawed logic that ultimately diminishes the impact of the agrarian movement on the Socialist Party. To be specific, the most obvious conundrum caused by the failure to incorporate the Farmers' Union into their analysis is geographic. Populism flourished in the old Oklahoma Territory, especially near the Kansas border, whereas the Socialist Party's strength was greatest in the old Indian Territory, an area barely organized by Populists. Both Green and Miller attribute this to the fragility of the Populist/socialist connection. Green makes this assumption most readily, arguing that the low correlation between People's Party voting in the late nineteenth century and socialist electoral patterns in the early twentieth century suggests that Populists "were less important in planting the grass-roots seeds of socialism in the Southwest than most historians believe." (*Grass-Roots Socialism*, 12–29, quote from p. 29.) Miller comes to a similar conclusion, pointing out that in the areas that had been Populist strongholds in the 1890s, "socialists never came close" to matching People's Party successes. (*Oklahoma Populism*, 178.)

Of course, the experience of the Farmers' Union explains this geographic anomaly, rendering Green's (and to a lesser extent, Miller's) analysis faulty. The areas of the old Indian Territory where socialism flourished were precisely the same locations where the Farmers' Union was strongest.

13. See Miller, *Oklahoma Populism*, chaps. 3–10, for a detailed analysis of Oklahoma Populists' struggle with the fusion/midroad dilemma.

14. *Durant Independent Farmer*, 30 March 1905, 4 May 1905, and 13 June 1905. The conductor was charged with maintaining the Union's facilities and with supervising initiation ceremonies.

15. *Durant Independent Farmer*, 11 May 1905, 18 May 1905, and 22 June 1906.

16. *Durant Independent Farmer*, 30 March 1905 and 12 January 1905.

17. See Goodwyn, *The Populist Moment*, 35–41.

18. *Indiahoma Union Signal*, 27 June 1905.

19. Ibid., 23 January 1906.

20. *Durant Independent Farmer*, 3 May 1906.

21. Ibid., 29 June 1905.

22. The organizers of the Farmers' Union in Texas had only partially anticipated this problem, consciously limiting membership to those who were primarily involved in farming. The only exceptions were those from occupations that previous organizing experience had indicated could be recruited to whole-hearted affiliation with the farmers' cause: rural mechanics, rural school teachers, rural physicians, "ministers of the Gospel" in rural churches, and rural newspaper editors. By enumerating eligibility by specific occupation, the Union overtly excluded from membership bankers, merchants, and major political figures. This provision made the Texas Farmers' Union different from other agricultural organizations, such as the Southern Cotton Association, whose ranks included bankers and merchants. Even so, the Union's restrictions were far from perfect in insulating the movement from external cooptive influences. Working farmers particularly feared that the organization could be overwhelmed by commercial interests and their self-described "farmer spokesmen." As a result, the Texas Union renewed debates after 1902 over the question of including even the few nonfarmers who were eligible for membership under the original constitution. The issue was decided at the fourth convention of the Texas Farmers' Union, held in Waco in August of 1905. After a full airing of the question, advocates of the interests of the rank and file convinced the membership of the danger, amending the constitution to exclude all nonfarmers from Union offices. See Hunt, *A History of Farmer Movements*, 62, 75; and Theodore Saloutos, *Agricultural Discontent in the Middle West, 1900–1939* (Madison: University of Wisconsin Press, 1951), 154–60.

23. *Durant Independent Farmer*, 9 February 1905.

24. Ibid., 5 July 1906.

25. Ibid., 29 June 1905.

26. Hunt, *A History of Farmer Movements*, 103–5; *Durant Independent Farmer*, 13 July 1905, 5 October 1905, 7 December 1905; U.S. Department of Agriculture, Bureau of Agricultural Economics, "Prices of Farm Products Received by Producers," *USDA Statistical Bulletin*, no. 16 (1927): 222.

Grain farmers participated as well, withholding over 800,000 bushels from their 1906 crop. *Marshall County Democrat*, 16 August 1907. See appendix A for additional discussion on crop withholding and crop prices.

27. For examples of this argument, see the *Durant Independent Farmer*, 12 January 1905 and 23 February 1905.

28. *Indiahoma Union Signal*, 26 May 1905.

29. Farmers' Union newspapers refused to refer directly to acreage reduction as an alternative, mentioning it only in the process of refuting it. In fact, virtually every argument that favored collective marketing and was published during this period explicitly rejected acreage reduction.

30. *Marshall County Democrat*, 23 August 1907.

31. Harold Woodman points out that the crop diversification argument was "in reality, a fantasy." This was especially true for tenant farmers, who constituted a sizeable segment of the farmers in the territories: "A tenant who owned nothing was being asked to grow a food crop for which he had neither seed nor land. And, presumably,

the landlord was expected to supply land to a tenant who was cutting back on his cash crop, the only means he had to pay his rent." Harold Woodman, *King Cotton and His Retainers: Financing and Marketing the Cotton Crop of the South, 1800–1925* (Lexington: University of Kentucky Press, 1968), 343.

32. *Indiahoma Union Signal*, 4 July 1904, 27 June 1905.
33. Ibid., 4 July 1905.
34. *Durant Independent Farmer*, 13 July 1905, emphasis in original.
35. Ibid.
36. Ibid.
37. Ibid., 6 July 1905.
38. Ibid., 13 July 1905.
39. Convention planners prepared accommodations for 1,500 in Tishomingo; roughly half of this number were expected to be convention delegates. Only about three hundred delegates actually attended, with the total attendance estimated at six hundred. *Durant Independent Farmer*, 27 July 1905.
40. Ibid.
41. *Indiahoma Union Signal*, 8 August 1905.
42. Ibid., 7 November 1905.
43. *Marshall County Democrat*, 16 August 1907; *Oklahoma Farmer*, 25 October 1905; *Indiahoma Union Signal*, 9 January 1906.
44. For additional detail on the demise of the Texas Exchange, see Goodwyn, *The Populist Moment*, 74–90. Daws was not the only Union leader to come to this conclusion. Another, the editor of an important Union newspaper, discouraged members from establishing cooperative stores in 1905: "It was on this rock that the Farmers' Alliance went to pieces, and if experience is worth anything it should teach us not to make the same mistake twice." *Durant Independent Farmer*, 12 October 1905.
45. *Indiahoma Union Signal*, 29 August 1905.
46. *Durant Independent Farmer*, 23 November 1905.
47. Ibid., 12 October 1905.
48. *Indiahoma Union Signal*, 13 February 1906; *Cheyenne Sunbeam*, 16 February 1906.
49. *Indiahoma Union Signal*, 8 March 1906.
50. Under Oklahoma law, incorporation was necessary in order for the clearing houses to be legal institutions. See "History of the Indiahoma Farmers' Union," Thomas W. Cheek Papers, Special Collections, Oklahoma State University Library, Stillwater, Oklahoma.
51. For a different interpretation, see Danney Goble's *Progressive Oklahoma*. Goble maintains that the clearing house was an attempt to "totally avoid the entire machinery of the market system by the direct exchange of [the farmers'] goods and services." As such, he argues, this tactic was actually more militant than cooperative stores because the latter were "intimate participants in the market system." Danney Goble, *Progressive Oklahoma: The Making of a New Kind of State* (Norman: University of Oklahoma, 1980), 162–63.
52. *Indiahoma Union Signal*, 6 February 1906.

53. Ibid., 13 February 1906.
54. Ibid.
55. *Indiahoma Union Signal*, 10 May 1906.

CHAPTER 3

1. This summary of the Farmers' Union coal purchasing plan and the response of mine owners is based on the account published in the *Indiahoma Union Signal*, 26 December 1905.
2. Ibid.
3. Ibid., 30 January 1906.
4. Ibid., 26 December 1905, 15 March 1906, 22 March 1906; *Durant Independent Farmer*, 28 December 1905.
5. *Indiahoma Union Signal*, 20 February 1906.
6. Ibid.
7. "Protest Supplement," *Indiahoma Union Signal*, 13 February 1906.
8. Ibid.
9. The publications in question were the *Farmers' Union Bulletin* and the *Farmers' Union Advocate*. *Indiahoma Union Signal*, 19 July 1906.

In yet another instance of harassment, occurring in May of 1906, the Post Office Department fined State Union Secretary J. W. Harrison twenty dollars for the improper use of printed matter rates. Harrison had sent broadsides advertising upcoming meetings at third-class rates to the local secretary in Guthrie. The Post Office ruled that since he had written "Please distribute these," on the back of one of the broadsides, Harrison had violated the rules governing the mailing of printed matter. *Indiahoma Union Signal*, 17 May 1906.

10. *Indiahoma Union Signal*, 3 May 1906, 17 May 1906.
11. Ibid., 20 February 1906.
12. In the 1 March 1906 edition of the *Indiahoma Union Signal*, for example, editors printed over one hundred letters of support, many of which included donations.
13. *Indiahoma Union Signal*, 28 June 1906, 19 July 1906.
14. Tracy Campbell, *The Politics of Despair: Power and Resistance in the Tobacco Wars* (Lexington: University Press of Kentucky, 1993), 72–74.
15. *Union Review*, 19 October 1907.
16. *Farmers' Union Advocate*, 27 February 1908.
17. Robert Lee Hunt, *A History of Farmer Movements in the Southwest, 1873–1925* (College Station: Agricultural and Mechanical College of Texas, 1935), 110.
18. Although in retrospect the decision to hold cotton for fifteen cents seemed particularly ill-timed in 1907, Theodore Saloutos points out in *Farmer Movements in the South* that at the time this figure was agreed upon, it did not seem at all unreasonable. "Cotton was selling for about 13.55 cents a pound," he notes, "and the prospects of climbing to a still higher level looked promising indeed." Theodore Saloutos, *Farmer Movements in the South, 1865–1933* (University of California, 1960), 197.

19. *Durant Independent Farmer*, 14 December 1905.
20. *Indiahoma Union Signal*, 22 August 1905.
21. *Durant Independent Farmer*, 31 May 1906, 7 June 1906, 5 July 1906.
22. See James R. Scales and Danney Goble, *Oklahoma Politics: A History* (Norman: University of Oklahoma Press, 1982), 3–19. A more sympathetic treatment of Murray is provided by Robert L. Dorman, who sees "Alfalfa Bill" as a tragic figure, torn between his commitment to the ideals of "agrarianism," which celebrated independence and yeoman democracy, and the competing impulse toward the accumulation of power. Robert L. Dorman, "The Tragical Agrarianism of Alfalfa Bill Murray, The Sage of Tishomingo," *Chronicles of Oklahoma* 66 (1988–1989): 240–67.
23. *Indiahoma Union Signal*, 19 December 1905.
24. Ibid.
25. *Indiahoma Union Signal*, 9 January 1906.
26. Ibid., 30 January 1906; *Durant Independent Farmer*, 1 February 1906.
27. *Union Review*, 17 March 1906.
28. *Durant Independent Farmer*, 29 March 1906. It is important to note that at this time the National Farmers' Union was embroiled in its own internal power struggle, in which conservatives were ultimately successful in wrestling control from the original Texas leaders. Murray's success in obtaining recognition for the Indian Territory Farmers' Union (recognition that was rescinded two months after it was granted) must be viewed within the context of this struggle. See *Durant Independent Farmer*, 31 May 1906.
29. *Indiahoma Union Signal*, 29 March 1906.
30. *Durant Independent Farmer*, 19 April 1906.
31. Of the more than 2,500 locals of the Indiahoma Farmers' Union in the Indian Territory, only 115 sent delegates to Shawnee. It should not be assumed, however, that this small attendance indicates that large numbers of locals were becoming loyal to the Indian Territory Farmers' Union. Had this been the case, Murray, who attended the convention, would have seen to it that these pro–Indian Territory locals were represented there. A more logical explanation for the small number of delegates is that the Indiahoma organization did not have the resources to pay the travel expenses of the delegates to this special convention. State funds were set aside to reimburse local delegates for travel expenses to regularly scheduled annual conventions, but there were no such funds for additional special conventions like this one. Those who attended, therefore, were either financed by their locals or paid their own expenses. See the *Indiahoma Union Signal*, 26 December 1905.
32. *Indiahoma Union Signal*, 19 April 1906.
33. Ibid., 19 May 1906; *Durant Independent Farmer*, 21 June 1906.
34. *Union Review*, 19 May 1906.
35. *Indiahoma Union Signal*, 20 September 1906.
36. In August of 1907, delegates to the annual convention of the Indiahoma Farmers' Union finally settled the matter by voting to consolidate the two organizations. *Indiahoma Union Signal*, 22 August 1907.

37. *Durant Independent Farmer*, 14 June 1906. According to Section 25 of the Farmers' Union Constitution, state leaders sent a new password quarterly to local and county organizations in good standing.

38. *Indiahoma Union Signal*, 6 September 1906.

39. *Durant Independent Farmer*, 7 June 1906. At this point, the Post Office had not yet reversed its ruling regarding the *Signal*.

40. The *Indiahoma Union Signal* was under Tobin's control and consistently opposed Daws in the debate. The *Durant Independent Farmer*, on the other hand, was equally consistent in its opposition to Tobin.

41. *Sayre Citizen*, 22 April 1910.

42. *Durant Independent Farmer*, 5 July 1906.

43. Ibid., 21 June 1906.

44. *Indiahoma Union Signal*, 14 June 1906.

45. *Durant Independent Farmer*, 28 July 1906.

46. See *Shawnee News*, 24 and 25 August 1906 for an account of the convention; and *Indiahoma Union Signal*, 20 September 1906 for a description of the event from Tobin's point of view.

47. *Indiahoma Union Signal*, 11 October 1906.

48. Indiahoma Farmers' Union Constitution, *Indiahoma Union Signal*, 7 March 1907.

49. *Indiahoma Union Signal*, 11 October 1906, 6 December 1906.

50. Ibid., 20 December 1906.

51. Ibid., 11 October 1906, 29 November 1906.

52. Daws expressed this warning in the pages of the *Durant Independent Farmer* (9 February 1905): "Old members of the Alliance remember that one of the chief causes of the downfall of that organization was the admission of politicians to its ranks, who, when on the inside endeavored to use the order for their personal benefit. The Farmers' Union will not make the same mistake."

53. *Indiahoma Union Signal*, 7 March 1907; Hunt, *A History of Farmer Movements*, 69; John A. Compton, *The National Farmers' Union: Ideology of a Pressure Group* (Lincoln: University of Nebraska Press, 1965), 77. See also the *Durant Independent Farmer*, 11 January 1906, for that publication's pledge to avoid "influencing the Union to the support of any party."

54. *Marshall County Democrat*, 26 July 1907.

55. *Shawnee News*, 21–23 August 1907. Russell, a member of the Farmers' Union Executive Committee, was also a Democratic Party candidate in 1907, running for state senator. *Indiahoma Union Signal*, 18 April 1907.

56. Accurate membership figures for the Union are not directly available, so I have arrived at these numbers through a variety of sources. In late December of 1905 the Union held a referendum vote in which 4,947 locals participated. Since the Farmers' Union Constitution specified that each local must have at least ten members to remain active, this vote reflected a membership of at least 49,500 farmers. By the conservative estimate that each local averaged fifteen members, it is reasonable to conclude that the Indiahoma Farmers' Union had at least seventy-four thousand members.

By October of 1906 membership had dropped considerably; the secretary treasurer reported that approximately twenty-one thousand members paid their dues that month. The following month, Farmers' Union state headquarters received only $306.29 in membership dues from locals in the two territories. With dues at twenty-five cents per month, the November total reflected a paid membership of just over twelve hundred. Finally, only three thousand members participated in the referendum taken in the last quarter of 1906 on the issue of amending the constitution to dissolve the offices of state organizer and state business agent. See the *Indiahoma Union Signal*, 9 January, 6 December, and 20 December 1906. The organization's constitution was printed in the *Indiahoma Union Signal*, 7 March 1907. See also Hunt, *A History of Farmer Movements*, 53.

The new, more moderate Farmers' Union moved in a different direction and appealed to a different constituency. By 1908, Union membership rolls in Oklahoma had increased to almost thirteen thousand. Even so, this was a fraction of the Union's strength in 1905–1906, and there is little reason to assume that the working farmers who were the core of the Union's earlier strength ever returned in large numbers to the organization. For membership data after 1907, see Robert L. Tontz, "Memberships of General Farmers' Organizations, United States, 1874–1960," *Agricultural History* 38 (1964): 147–48, 155.

57. John Thompson recognizes this dynamic, pointing out that the Oklahoma Socialist Party's growth occurred "immediately after the Farmers' Union ceased to represent the more radical ideas of poor farmers and laborers." John Thompson, *Closing the Frontier: Radical Responses in Oklahoma, 1889–1923* (Norman: University of Oklahoma Press, 1986), 127.

CHAPTER 4

1. William H. Murray, now the speaker of the state legislature, raised the ire of labor leaders by ignoring their advice on key political appointments and legislation. See Suzanne Jones Crawford and Lynn R. Musslewhite, "Progressive Reform and Oklahoma Democrats: Kate Bernard versus Bill Murray," *Historian* 53 (1991): 487.

2. James R. Scales and Danney Goble, *Oklahoma Politics: A History* (Norman: University of Oklahoma Press, 1982), 44–45.

3. In 1907 Democratic leaders had perfected the strategy of linking the general election to the Oklahoma Constitution. That year, Democratic candidates won overwhelmingly, following the lead of presidential candidate William Jennings Bryan, who lauded the state constitution as "the most progressive ever written." Republican William Howard Taft, on the other hand, criticized the document as being "excessively complex and confusing." See Scales and Goble, *Oklahoma Politics*, 30–32.

For correspondence directly related to Democratic leaders' strategy in 1908, see R. L. Williams to J. B. Thompson, 4 September 1908 and 22 September 1908, R. L. Williams Collection, Oklahoma Historical Society, Oklahoma City, Oklahoma.

4. Following his removal from the Farmers' Union, Daws had reportedly been offered $5,000 to enter the gubernatorial race in 1907 as the independent candidate, a proposition which he declined, since it involved running against the Democratic nominee. Grateful party leaders quickly rewarded Daws by appointing him to the spot of state librarian. Edward Everette Dale and James D. Morrison, *Pioneer Judge: The Life of Robert Lee Williams* (Cedar Rapids, Iowa: The Torch Press, 1958), 187. See also the *Union Review*, 6 December 1907; and *Oklahoma Libraries, 1900–1937: A History and Handbook* (Oklahoma City: Oklahoma Library Commission, 1937), 147.

5. See, for example, S. O. Daws, "Let Us Alone," pamphlet, 1908, Western History Collections, University of Oklahoma, Norman, Oklahoma.

6. See *Union Review*, 27 March, 15 May, 21 July 1908; *Farmers Union Advocate*, 5 March 1908; and Mary Hays Marable and Elaine Boylan, *A Handbook of Oklahoma Writers* (Norman: University of Oklahoma Press, 1939). For additional information on Daws's life, see his obituary in the *Daily Oklahoman*, 25 March 1916.

7. Printed Proceedings, Thirteenth Annual Convention (1916), Oklahoma State Federation of Labor Collection, Western History Collections, University of Oklahoma, Norman, Oklahoma.

8. James Green unwittingly affirms this characteristic, pointing out that one of State Secretary Otto Branstetter's challenges in 1906 was to bring "some of the old 'Pops' under party discipline." James Green, *Grass-Roots Socialism: Radical Movements in the Southwest* (Baton Rouge: Louisiana State University Press, 1978), 39.

9. Green, *Grass-Roots Socialism*, 13–14.

10. *Appeal to Reason*, 27 January 1900. The counties represented were Pottawatomie, Lincoln, Oklahoma, Noble, Logan, Kay, Grant, Kingfisher, Canadian, and Blaine.

11. *Appeal to Reason*, 30 May 1903. Among the organizers sent to the Indian Territory were John C. Chase, George Bigelow, Luella Kraybill, and Kate Richards O'Hare.

12. Meredith, "A History of the Socialist Party in Oklahoma" (Ph.D. diss., University of Oklahoma, 1969), 47–48; *Appeal to Reason*, 27 May 1905.

13. Indeed, this relationship must have been much like that experienced by urban socialist workers, who belonged to both their union and socialist locals.

14. *Durant Independent Farmer*, 10 May 1906.

15. *Indiahoma Union Signal*, 4 July 1905. See also the comments of a Farmers' Union organizer in the *Durant Independent Farmer*, 2 February 1905: "In the language of Karl Marx: 'Workers of the world, unite; you have nothing to lose but your chains; you have a world to gain.'"

16. *Appeal to Reason*, 21 January 1905. Among the speakers listed by a socialist newspaper in 1910 as being available for "county work, conventions, picnic, etc." were former Union organizers G. W. (Pap) Davis and Leonard Johnson. See the *Industrial Democrat*, 7 May 1910.

17. *New Century*, 14 March 1913.

18. *Oklahoma Socialist*, 20 June 1901, quoted in Meredith, "A History of the Socialist Party in Oklahoma," 25.

19. Seymour Martin Lipset, *Agrarian Socialism: The Cooperative Commonwealth Federation in Saskatchewan, A Study in Political Sociology* (Berkeley and Los Angeles: University of California Press, 1971), 27. Two years earlier, Victor Berger had proposed a series of demands for farmers which were more amenable to agrarian socialists. His proposal, however, was defeated in referendum vote by members of the Social Democratic Party. Donald B. Marti, "Answering the Agrarian Question: Socialists, Farmers, and Algie Martin Simons," *Agricultural History* 65 (1991): 56, 59.

20. Howard H. Quint, *The Forging of American Socialism: Origins of the Modern Movement* (New York: Bobbs-Merrill, 1964), 322–23.

21. John Graham, ed., *"Yours for the Revolution": The Appeal to Reason, 1895–1922* (Lincoln: University of Nebraska Press, 1990), 135–36; Marti, "Answering the Agrarian Question," 66.

22. The platform listed "small farmers" as one of the "other classes" (in addition to the working class) that would benefit under socialism. See Donald Bruce Johnson, comp., *National Party Platforms*, vol. 1, *1840–1956* (Urbana: University of Illinois Press, 1978), 164.

23. Marti, "Answering the Agrarian Question," 61–65; Kent Kreuter and Gretchen Kreuter, *An American Dissenter: The Life of Algie Martin Simons, 1870–1950* (Lexington: University of Kentucky Press, 1969), 59–60, 122–23.

24. Kreuter and Kreuter, *An American Dissenter*, 125–26.

25. *New Century*, 20 August 1912.

26. See Worth Robert Miller, *Oklahoma Populism: A History of the People's Party in the Oklahoma Territory* (Norman: University of Oklahoma Press, 1987), 185.

27. *Oklahoma Pioneer*, 26 September 1910.

28. Meredith, "A History of the Socialist Party in Oklahoma," 35.

29. The platform was printed in the *Oklahoma Pioneer*, 12 January 1910.

30. Ameringer, *If You Don't Weaken*, quoted in Graham, *"Yours for the Revolution"*, 133.

31. Platform of the Socialist Party of Oklahoma, 1912, State and Local File (Oklahoma), Socialist Party Papers, Manuscript Department, Perkins Library, Duke University, Durham, North Carolina. A similar, though less forceful, position was adopted at the national convention of the Socialist Party in 1912. See Kreuter and Kreuter, *An American Dissenter*, 134–35; and Marti, "Answering the Agrarian Question," 68.

32. The national party's position on land ownership, by comparison with the Oklahoma party's stand, was still only mildly supportive of the needs of working farmers. Instead of pledging to return land to the hands of working farmers, the American party called for the "collective ownership of land wherever practicable, and in cases where such ownership is impracticable, the appropriation by taxation of the annual rental value of all land held for speculation or exploitation." Johnson, *National Party Platforms*, 189.

33. *Appeal to Reason*, 6 January 1917.

34. *New Century*, 14 March 1913.

35. Ibid., 27 June 1913.

36. For the Renters' Union Demands and Constitution, see the *Oklahoma Pioneer*, 9 February 1910, 6 March 1910, 30 March 1910.

37. Despite the Renters' Union's obvious ties with socialism, membership in the Socialist Party was not a prerequisite; the organization's constitution stated that all who engaged in the labor of farming, "regardless of their politics," would be welcome. *Sword of Truth*, 5 March 1913.

38. *New Century*, 5 January 1912, 27 December 1912, 28 March 1913, 11 April 1913. James Green presents a different interpretation of the Renters' Union, arguing that this "labor union for land renters" was one of the few examples of proletarian consciousness in the Oklahoma movement. Instead of acknowledging the contributions of the Farmers' Union, Green argues that the Renters' Union's tactics were modeled on organized labor. John Thompson, on the other hand, portrays the Union as a "quasi-socialist" organization that stopped short of espousing a "comprehensive Marxist program." See Green, *Grass-Roots Socialism*, 81, 161; and John Thompson, *Closing the Frontier: Radical Responses in Oklahoma, 1899–1923* (Norman: University of Oklahoma Press, 1986), 150–51.

39. *Oklahoma Pioneer*, 22 June 1910. See also James J. Lorence, "The Milwaukee Connection: The Urban-Rural Link in Wisconsin Socialism, 1910–1920," *Milwaukee History* 3 (1980): 102–11.

40. *Industrial Democrat*, 1 January 1910.

41. Ibid., 15 January 1910. For more on Ameringer's background, see his autobiography, *If You Don't Weaken* (New York: Henry Holt, 1940).

42. *Industrial Democrat*, 15 January 1910. For various contemporary interpretations of the effects of the amendment, see the *Industrial Democrat*, 2 April 1910; *Oklahoma Pioneer*, 27 April 1910, 8 June 1910.

43. *Industrial Democrat*, 15 January 1910.

44. Ibid.

45. *Oklahoma Pioneer*, 25 May 1910.

46. *Industrial Democrat*, 7 May 1910.

47. Ibid., 15 January 1910. For additional examples of this point of view, see the *Industrial Democrat*, 21 May 1910, 28 May 1910, 20 August 1910.

48. *Oklahoma Pioneer*, 27 April 1910, 11 May 1910.

49. See the *Oklahoma Pioneer*, 18 May 1910.

50. Ibid., 25 May 1910. There is considerable evidence that this action had the direct support of state party leaders. The Oklahoma City local was traditionally openly supportive of the state executive committee. In addition, the specific charge on which the three were expelled was the open criticism of State Secretary Branstetter.

51. The *Oklahoma Pioneer*, 15 June 1910, reports the results of the special election on the railroad amendment. See the *Oklahoma Pioneer*, 23 February 1910 and 6 April 1910 for the minutes of the state executive committee meetings at which the question of publishing the *Pioneer* was discussed.

52. Minutes of the SEC meeting are printed in the *Oklahoma Pioneer*, 25 May 1910.

53. *New Century*, 10 February 1911; *Oklahoma Pioneer*, 11 February 1911. The vote was 420 in favor, 868 opposed.
54. *Oklahoma Pioneer*, 4 March 1911, 14 October 1911.
55. Ibid., 18 November 1911, 29 June 1912, October 1912. (In October of 1912 the *Pioneer* changed from a weekly to a monthly.)
56. Ibid., 14 January 1911.
57. Ibid., 1 June 1910; *Industrial Democrat*, 1 January 1910.
58. Strictly speaking, this assessment differed slightly from dues in that it was to be paid by the party locals, rather than individual members. Locals could raise the money in any way they saw fit. *Oklahoma Pioneer*, 14 January 1911.
59. Ibid., 18 February 1911.
60. Ibid., 28 October 1911.
61. Nagle's article appeared in the *Oklahoma Pioneer*, 15 June 1912.
62. *Oklahoma Pioneer*, 18 March 1912, 3 May 1912.
63. *New Century*, 15 November 1912.
64. *Beckham County Advocate*, 15 May 1913.
65. The proposed changes were first revealed in a letter by H. M. Sinclair published in the *Oklahoma Pioneer*. They were later introduced in the form of amendments by Local McAlester, Sinclair's local. *Oklahoma Pioneer*, 14 October 1911.
66. Ibid., 23 December 1911.
67. Ibid., 6 January 1912.
68. *New Century*, 12 January 1912.
69. Ibid., 8 November 1912. For more on "Red Tom" Hickey, especially his later life, see Robert W. Clark, "Thomas A. Hickey: Texas Socialist and Oilman," *West Texas Association Year Book* 66 (1990): 129–38.
70. *New Century*, 3 January 1913. Branstetter, a Socialist Party functionary, had been sent to Oklahoma by national socialist leaders for the purpose of leading the state party. His three years as state secretary coincided with the time of his residence in the Sooner State. See the "Book of Pictures of Prominent Socialists, 1918," Socialist Party Papers.
71. *New Century*, 14 February 1913.
72. Ibid., 13 June 1913.
73. James Green discusses the struggle over centralization in *Grass-Roots Socialism*. However, his failure to incorporate the Farmers' Union into his analysis makes it difficult to make sense of the incident. Green attempts to explain the struggle over centralization in terms of ideology: the centralizers supported the "gradualist policies" of the Socialist Party of America's National Executive Committee, while the decentralizers often took more "radical" stands and were "sincere friends of the IWW." But this way of conceptualizing the dispute is ultimately unsatisfying for Green, since elsewhere in *Grass-Roots Socialism* the decentralizers are depicted as undisciplined, individualistic party members who made life difficult for party leaders. He resolves this internal contradiction by arguing that the decentralizers were inconsistent: "The southwestern Reds identified themselves with the radical wing of the party, but in

practice their politics often deviated from 'orthodox' left-wing positions." See Green, *Grass-Roots Socialism*, 116–19. Of course, it was their experience in the Farmer's Union, not their ideological idiosyncrasies, that made many Oklahoma Socialists wary of centralized party authority.

CHAPTER 5

1. Although the use of religion by Oklahoma Socialists is, for the purposes of thematic clarity, considered separately from the debates on the land question and local organizational autonomy, no such separation occurred in the movement itself.

2. The presence of religion in Oklahoma socialism was so prominent that it can scarcely be ignored by scholars writing about the movement, and virtually every one has commented on this feature of the party. Ellen Rosen, for example, describes socialist organizers who saw themselves as "secular preachers of a new religion" and whose message was "deeply imbedded in rural culture and folk religion." See Ellen I. Rosen, "Peasant Socialism in America? The Socialist Party in Oklahoma Before the First World War" (Ph.D. diss., City University of New York, 1975), 253. Irving Howe credits religion with helping Oklahoma Socialists create "an inner world in which they would feel valued and could express the desires that moved them." See Irving Howe, *Socialism and America* (New York: Harcourt, Brace, Jovanovich, 1985), 12. Howard Meredith points to the presence of religion in Oklahoma socialism as giving the movement its "peculiar flavor." See Howard Meredith, "Oscar Ameringer and the Concept of Agrarian Socialism," *Chronicles of Oklahoma* 45 (1967): 77–83. See also Robert H. Craig, *Religion and Radical Politics: An Alternative Christian Tradition in America* (Philadelphia: Temple University Press, 1992), especially 108–110.

While these interpreters deal with religion in the movement only fleetingly, Garin Burbank and James Green devote more energy to understanding its role. Both, however, come to interpretive conclusions that tend to diminish the importance of religion to the success of the Socialist Party of Oklahoma.

After describing the use of religious language and imagery by Oklahoma Socialists, Burbank concludes that there were "two socialisms circulating under the auspices of the Oklahoma party." On the one hand, the "imported [socialist] orthodoxy" advocated a "completely secular" version of socialism that "addressed exclusively the major 'industrial and political' issues." Opposed to this version, Burbank argues, was the "indigenous" socialism of the Oklahoma countryside, whose religious nature amounted to "an unschooled variant of the social gospel." These descriptions leave little doubt as to Burbank's opinion on the matter: The secular, imported version of the Socialist Party was the genuine article, while the indigenous religious variant that all too often held sway in Oklahoma was illegitimate. Thus, although Oklahoma Socialists were at times able to use religion to communicate more effectively with their rural constituency, the long-term effects of the party's use of religion were largely negative. Burbank argues that the party's religious bent caused it to espouse such "nonsocialist" causes as temperance, anti-Catholicism, and creationism. Even more importantly, he maintains, the energy of Sooner socialists was wasted on meaningless religious arguments. "Like the mingling waters at the confluence of a smaller with a larger stream," he writes, "the ideas of socialism flowed into, and were absorbed by, the roiling currents of evangelical emotion." See Garin Burbank, *When Farmers Voted Red: The Gospel of Socialism in the Oklahoma Countryside, 1910–1924* (Westport, Conn.: Greenwood Press, 1976), especially chap. 2, "The Gospel According to Local Socialists."

James R. Green is more positive in his assessment of the impact of religion on the movement. His discussion in *Grass-Roots Socialism* of the class nature of Oklahoma socialists' fundamentalist Christianity is pathbreaking and provides much of the foundation for the argument that will be presented in this chapter. He incorporates E. J. Hobsbawm's insights into the Oklahoma movement in a way that recognizes the presence of religion in the party. Even so, Green's central presumption, that Oklahoma party members' adoption of the "proletarian" values of the urban-based national socialist movement was a prerequisite for success, diminishes religion as a substantive force in the movement. He argues that while the religious tenor of Oklahoma socialism may not have been destructive (as Burbank maintains), relying on religious arguments was a decidedly "unproletarian"—and therefore ineffective—way of furthering the socialist cause. James Green, *Grass-Roots Socialism: Radical Movements in the Southwest* (Baton Rouge: Louisiana State University Press, 1978), esp. 168–75.

This aspect of Green's argument is neatly summarized by Nick Salvatore through a series of rhetorical questions meant to challenge the conclusions of *Grass-Roots Socialism*: "In the actual historical experience were these themes [class-based Marxism and religious fundamentalism] contrary to and exclusive of each other? Could an engaged socialist be religious in some important sense, take pride in the religious underpinnings of a democratic tradition with roots in Populism and before—and still embrace a class analysis? Or did a commitment to socialism by definition require disdain for the religious impulse?" See Nick Salvatore, "Americans as Radicals," *Radical History Review* 24 (Fall 1980): 142–52 (quote from p. 148).

3. The stark secularism of socialist politics can be traced in part to Marx himself, who saw religion as a force that inhibited class consciousness, thereby helping to preserve the rule of the bourgeoisie. As he put it, religion represented "the sigh of the oppressed creature, the sentiment of a heartless world, and the soul of soulless conditions." "It is," Marx continued in his most famous pronouncement on the subject, "the opium of the people." See Karl Marx, introduction to "Contribution to the Critique of Hegel's *Philosophy of Right*," in *The Marx-Engels Reader*, ed. Robert C. Tucker (New York: W. W. Norton and Company, 1972), 12.

For useful summaries of Marx's views on religion, see John Joseph Marsden, *Marxian and Christian Utopianism: Toward a Socialist Political Theology* (New York: Monthly Review Press, 1991), 166–67; and David McLellan, *Marxism and Religion: A Description and Assessment of the Marxist Critique of Christianity* (New York: Harper and Row, 1987), 2–5.

For commentary on many scholars' latent distrust of religion as a force in American society, see Paul Merkley's discussion of what he calls the "secularization hypothesis" in "Religion and the Political Prosperity of America: An Historian's Reflections on Recent Publications in Religious Studies," *Canadian Journal of History* 26 (1991): 277–91.

4. As Garry Wills puts it, "every time religiosity catches the attention of intellectuals, it is as if a shooting star had appeared in the sky." See Wills, *Under God: Religion and American Politics* (New York: Simon and Schuster, 1990), 15.

5. *Strong City Herald*, 27 June 1917, 15 July 1917.

6. Ibid., 15 July 1917.

7. *Durant Statesman*, 26 July 1907.

8. *New Century*, 3 February 1911, 30 June 1911.

9. *Durant Independent Farmer*, 16 March 1906.

10. *Oklahoma Pioneer*, 27 April 1912.

11. *Common People*, 17 January 1904.

12. *Sword of Truth*, 13 November 1912.

13. The verses were Luke 1:53 ("He hath filled the hungry with good things; and the rich he hath send away empty.") and John 8:32 ("And ye shall know the truth, and the truth shall make you free.") *Sword of Truth*, 23 July 1913.

14. *New Century*, 6 January 1911, quoted in Burbank, *When Farmers Voted Red*, 23.

15. *Appeal to Reason*, 23 May 1903.

16. *Sword of Truth*, 5 March 1913, quoted in Burbank, *When Farmers Voted Red*, 19–20.

17. *New Century*, 12 July 1912.

18. *Strong City Herald*, 27 September 1917.

19. *Boswell Submarine*, 14 November 1913.

20. *Ellis County Advocate*, 23 May 1918.

21. See the *Beckham County Advocate*, 27 November 1913; *Appeal to Reason*, 21 December 1895; *New Century*, 25 April 1913; *Ellis County Advocate*, 15 May 1919.

22. *Beckham County Advocate*, 27 November 1913.

23. *New Century*, 6 February 1912. Union members often made the same point. According to one labor organizer, "The Carpenter of Nazareth gave us our charter and by-laws." *Labor Signal*, 20 June 1902.

24. *Oklahoma Socialist*, 3 July 1902.

25. *Sayre Citizen*, 18 February 1910. Sam Hampton, the Farmers' Union organizer, made the same argument about unions. Hampton wrote that "Jesus Christ was a member of the first Union, and it had one scab in it." Quoted in Hunt, p. 85.

26. *New Century*, 22 March 1912.

27. *Strong City Herald*, 13 September 1917.

28. Two historians make just this point regarding the Farmers Alliance. See Robert C. McMath, "Populist Base Communities: The Evangelical Roots of Farm Protest in Texas," *Locus* 1 (Fall 1988): 53–63; and Peter H. Argersinger, "Pentecostal Politics in Kansas: Religion, the Farmers' Alliance and the Gospel of Populism," *Kansas Quarterly* 1 (1969):24–35. Argersinger argues that local suballiances "functioned on the local level as religious substitutes for the absent or detached churches" and that

"[s]tructurally and functionally, the Farmers' Alliance resembled the church in Kansas."

Another scholar sees the connection between Populism and the Second Great Awakening. In *The Democratization of American Christianity*, Nathan O. Hatch characterizes this early nineteenth-century religious revival as "religious populism," which reflected "the passions of ordinary people and the charisma of democratic movement-builders." See Nathan O. Hatch, *The Democratization of American Christianity* (New Haven: Yale University Press, 1989), 4–5.

29. *Boswell Submarine*, 28 August 1914, quoted in Burbank, *When Farmers Voted Red*, 19.

30. *Appeal to Reason*, 11 July 1903.

31. *Strong City Herald*, 14 March 1918.

32. While Clark's comments were largely ignored by socialist newspaper editors in Oklahoma, they were widely reported in the anti-socialist press. See, for example, the *Marshall County News-Democrat*, 29 June 1916; and the *Socialist Antidote*, 15 June 1916.

33. Dwight Spencer to Hon. Wilburn Cartwright, 12 March 1918, Wilburn Cartwright Collection, Carl Albert Center Archives, University of Oklahoma. Spencer was an active socialist, serving as secretary of his local and county organizations. See *Industrial Democrat*, 26 February 1910; *Oklahoma Pioneer*, 13 April 1910.

34. Catherine R. Harris, "Religion and the American Socialist Movement," in *Marxism and Christianity: A Symposium*, ed. Herbert Aptheker (New York: Humanities Press, 1968), 225–26.

35. *Oklahoma Pioneer*, 14 October 1911.

36. *Boswell Submarine*, 2 January 1914.

37. *Appeal to Reason*, 6 January 1917.

38. The party member was referring to Hughes County in southeastern Oklahoma. Burbank, *When Farmers Voted Red*, 24–25.

39. *New Century*, 6 February 1912.

40. *Christian Socialist Fellowship Bulletin*, April 1913, Thomas W. Woodrow Collection, Western History Collections, University of Oklahoma, Norman, Oklahoma. See also the *Industrial Democrat*, 24 September 1910; *Appeal to Reason*, 7 October 1911.

41. *Industrial Democrat*, 19 February 1910.

42. Minutes of the 1911 Annual State Convention, Pentecostal-Holiness Church, Oklahoma Conference Headquarters, Oklahoma City, Oklahoma. This fascinating evidence points to a crucial question: How widespread was the phenomenon of socialist ministers and members within the Pentecostal-Holiness community? While the convention's action suggests that in the aggregate only a minority of ministers were practicing socialists, it provides no accurate measure of the phenomenon nor does it offer insight into the political leanings of the laity.

Surviving statistical and demographic evidence, such as precinct-level election results or local church records, are ineffective indicators of the link between religious and political affiliation. As a result, despite tantalizing evidence of a significant socialist presence in fundamentalist churches, it is impossible to provide a precise measure of this presence.

43. *Durant Statesman*, 26 July 1907; *Sword of Truth*, 21 May 1913.

44. Election Returns, Oklahoma State Archives, Oklahoma City, Oklahoma; *Strong City Herald*, 5 July 1917.

45. *Elk City News*, 14 February 1918; *Industrial Democrat*, 26 February 1910.

46. *Durant Independent Farmer*, 6 July 1906; *Industrial Democrat*, 6 August 1910. J. T. Beam, a socialist organizer in Murray County, followed a similar practice. The *New Century* listed the towns where he was scheduled to speak on an organizing tour in 1912, concluding, "Then he comes back to Palmer where he will preach Sunday." *New Century*, 16 February 1912.

47. *Strong City Herald*, 31 August 1916. Hutton was also the chairman of the Roger Mills County socialist organization in 1916. *Guide*, Socialist Party of Oklahoma "Red Card" and Political Organizations, Thomas W. Woodrow Collection.

48. *Beckham County Advocate*, 21 August 1913. For additional examples of ministers who contributed to the success of the Socialist Party, see appendix B, "Selected Listing of Prominent Oklahoma Socialist Ministers."

49. *Oklahoma Pioneer*, 30 December 1911, quoted in Donald Graham, "Red, White and Black: An Interpretation of Ethnic and Racial Attitudes of Agrarian Radicals in Texas and Oklahoma, 1880–1920" (master's thesis, University of Saskatchewan, 1973), 266–67.

50. *Roger Mills Sentinel*, 11 February 1915.

51. Ibid., 24 February 1916. For additional examples of this kind of attack on the Socialist Party, see the *Roger Mills Sentinel*, 2 December 1915, 15 August 1915; *Marshall County News-Democrat*, 8 June 1916.

52. *Sword of Truth*, 15 January 1913 (emphasis added).

53. *New Century*, 23 August 1912.

54. Ibid., 28 June 1912.

55. *Strong City Herald*, 5 April 1917.

56. H. Richard Niebuhr's *The Social Sources of Denominationalism* is the classic work in this regard, and deservedly so. Niebuhr uses the concept of church and sect to explain the class division within American Protestantism. Religious groups such as the Pentecostal and Holiness churches, according to this argument, were sects that split away from the mainline denominations, labeled *churches* in this theoretical system. The basic source of the sects' disenchantment was that the established church represented the more materially successful members of society, thereby failing to serve the needs of the working-class portion of its constituency. Thus, the operative factors behind the formation of groups like the Primitive Baptists and Pentecostals were social and class issues rather than theological differences. See H. Richard Niebuhr, *The Social Sources of Denominationalism* (New York: Henry Holt and Company, 1929; reprint ed., Cleveland: World Publishing Company, 1970), chaps. 2 and 3. See also Donald Mathews, *Religion in the Old South* (Chicago: University of Chicago Press, 1977), 242. For a different perspective on the church–sect analysis, see Philip R. Vandermeer, "Religion, Society, and Politics: A Classification of American Religious Groups,"

Social Science History 5 (1981): 3–24. James Green also makes an important contribution to our understanding of this phenomenon in his work, *Grass-Roots Socialism*. Indeed, I am indebted to Green for introducing me to Niebuhr's work.

57. *New Century*, 25 April 1913, 30 May 1913. For additional examples of socialist attacks on established denominations, see O. E. Enfield's poems on the Methodist and Campbellite churches. Entitled, "Faith and Fried Chicken" and "Ever See a Campbellite," the poems appeared in the *Ellis County Advocate*, 30 January 1919 and 6 February 1919.

58. *Appeal to Reason*, 21 October 1895.

59. *New Century*, 9 May 1913.

60. In drawing this distinction, the use of the term, *fundamentalism* becomes somewhat problematic. The "quest for Christian perfection" (in Timothy L. Smith's words), which led to belief in the baptism of the Spirit, actually set Pentecostals apart from other fundamentalists. However, even R. Laurence Moore, one of the preeminent scholars in this field, minimizes the distinction between Pentecostalism and fundamentalism. For our purposes the salient difference was between mainline Protestantism (Methodists, Southern Baptists, Presbyterians) and what Niebuhr calls the "churches of the disinherited": Holiness, Primitive Baptists, Assemblies of God, and Pentecostals. In this context, it is appropriate to describe the latter as fundamentalists.

See R. Laurence Moore, *Religious Outsiders and the Making of Americans* (New York: Oxford University Press, 1986), 140–45; Timothy L. Smith, *Revivalism and Social Reform in Mid-Nineteenth Century America* (New York: Abingdon Press, 1957); and Edith L. Blumhofer, *Restoring the Faith: The Assemblies of God, Pentecostalism, and American Culture* (Urbana: University of Illinois Press, 1993).

61. It is important to note that this feature of the Oklahoma movement was distinct from the larger religious development known as the Social Gospel. Clearly part of the Progressive tradition, Social Gospel leaders like Walter Rauschenbusch had little in common with fundamentalist socialist ministers in Oklahoma. The relationship between fundamentalist Christian socialists and the Social Gospel, therefore, parallels that between socialism and Progressivism. As a result, it is no more appropriate to link Oklahoma minister and socialist organizer Enfield with Rauschenbusch than it is to think of Eugene Debs and Woodrow Wilson as part of the same movement.

For additional insight on the Social Gospel, see Donald K. Gorrell, *The Age of Social Responsibility: The Social Gospel in the Progressive Era, 1900–1920* (Macon, Ga.: Mercer University Press, 1988); Robert T. Handy, ed., *The Social Gospel in America: Gladden, Ely, Rauschenbusch* (New York: Oxford University Press, 1966); Robert H. Craig, *Religion and Radical Politics: An Alternative Christian Tradition in the United States* (Philadelphia: Temple University Press, 1992); Ronald C. White, Jr., and C. Howard Hopkins, *The Social Gospel: Religion and Reform in Changing America* (Philadelphia: Temple University Press, 1976); and Henry F. May, *Protestant Churches and Industrial America* (New York: Harper and Row, 1949).

62. *Beckham County Advocate*, 28 August 1913.

63. *Oklahoma Socialist*, 21 August 1902.

64. *New Century*, 26 April 1912. See also *Strong City Herald*, 4 January 1917; *Oklahoma Pioneer*, 4 February 1911.

65. *New Century*, 6 February 1912. With equal conviction, another confided that he "converted to Socialism by reading the Bible, history and by reasoning." *Who's Who in Socialist America* (Girard, Kans.: *Appeal to Reason*, 1914), 107.

66. *New Century*, 26 April 1911.

67. Ibid., 5 April 1912.

68. *Oklahoma Socialist*, 31 July 1902.

69. *Boswell Submarine*, 28 November 1913.

70. *Beckham County Advocate*, 25 September 1913.

71. Herbert Gutman made this argument for an urban constituency in his article, "Protestantism and the American Labor Movement," maintaining that Protestant Christianity helped provide workers in the Gilded Age with the tools to oppose industrialization. In his words, Protestantism "justified labor organization and agitation, encouraged workers to challenge industrial power, and compelled criticism of 'natural' economic laws, the crude optimism of social Darwinism, and even the conformist Christianity of most respectable clergymen." Herbert G. Gutman, "Protestantism and the American Labor Movement: The Christian Spirit in the Gilded Age," *American Historical Review* 72 (1966–1967): 74–101 (quote from p. 81). See also Jean B. Quandt, "Religion and Social Thought: The Secularization of Postmillennialism," *American Quarterly* 25 (1973): 390–409.

Thus, in the words of David DeLeon, "religious ferment was a yeast capable of unexpected results." See David DeLeon, *The American as Anarchist: Reflections on Indigenous Radicalism* (Baltimore: Johns Hopkins University Press, 1978), 20. In similar fashion, Nathan Hatch points to the "profoundly democratic spirit" of fundamentalist Christianity, which "empowered ordinary people by taking their deepest spiritual impulses at face value rather than subjecting them to the scrutiny of orthodox doctrine and the frowns of respectable clergymen." See Nathan Hatch, *The Democratization of American Christianity*, 9–10.

72. *Appeal to Reason*, 7 March 1896; *Strong City Herald*, 31 August 1916.

73. *Beckham County Advocate*, 7 August 1913.

74. *Boswell Submarine*, 26 December 1913.

75. *New Century*, 21 March 1913. See also *Sword of Truth*, 26 March 1913 for a similar argument. In this case, a socialist minister named H. H. Clark preached that the church should oppose, not just usury, but "Profit and Special Privilege."

76. *Industrial Democrat*, 3 September 1910.

77. *Oklahoma Socialist*, 3 July 1902.

78. *Sayre Social Democrat*, 28 February 1912.

79. *Beckham County Advocate*, 27 November 1913.

80. Thomas W. Woodrow Collection.

81. *New Century*, 7 March 1913.

82. Ibid.

83. Ibid., 30 May 1913.

CHAPTER 6

1. According to the United States Census taken in 1910, the total population of Oklahoma was 1,657,155; of that number, 1,022,000 lived on farms.
2. According to the Census of 1910, 55 percent of farmers in Oklahoma were tenants. Of the remaining 45 percent who owned their farms, only slightly more than half were free of mortgage debt. As a result, only one in four farmers in the state worked land that they owned and that was free of debt.
3. James R. Scales and Danney Goble, *Oklahoma Politics: A History* (Norman: University of Oklahoma Press, 1982), 74. Garin Burbank demonstrates that Williams was quite typical of Democratic Party leaders. According to Burbank, 61 percent of the Democratic Party's leaders were bankers, lawyers, merchants, or "farmers" (a category defined loosely enough to include large landowners like Williams). Garin Burbank, *When Farmers Voted Red: The Gospel of Socialism in the Oklahoma Countryside, 1910–1924* (Westport, Conn.: Greenwood Press, 1976), 92.
4. Patrick Nagle Typescript, Oklahoma Historical Society, Oklahoma City, Oklahoma.
5. *Sword of Truth*, 1 January 1913.
6. *Strong City Herald*, 12 October 1916.
7. *Harlow's Weekly*, 26 October 1912.
8. Socialist Campaign Book, 1916, Socialist Party Papers, Manuscript Department, Perkins Library, Duke University, Durham, North Carolina.
9. *Tenant Farmer*, September 1912.
10. Socialist Campaign Book, 1916, Socialist Party Papers.
11. "State Platform," Socialist Party of Oklahoma, 1912, Socialist Party Papers.
12. N. Creekmuir to R. L. Williams, 14 July 1914, R. L. Williams Collection, Manuscript Division, Oklahoma Historical Society, Oklahoma City, Oklahoma.
13. *Harlow's Weekly*, 4 October 1916.
14. Ibid., 16 August 1916.
15. *Appeal to Reason*, 20 November 1909.
16. *Appeal to Reason*, 21 February 1904; Howard Meredith, "A History of the Socialist Party in Oklahoma" (Ph.D. diss., University of Oklahoma, 1969), 73.
17. *Appeal to Reason*, 30 June 1906.
18. Untitled typescript, 25 December 1909, in the Barde Collection, Manuscript Division, Oklahoma Historical Society, Oklahoma City, Oklahoma.
19. Complaint filed with the State Election Board, 13 August 1910, Oklahoma State Archives, Oklahoma City, Oklahoma.
20. George L. Bowman to Will Linn, 8 August 1908, Governors' Papers (Haskell), Oklahoma State Archives, Oklahoma City, Oklahoma; *Oklahoma Pioneer*, 13 August 1910, 20 August 1910.
21. *New Century*, 19 July 1912.
22. R. E. Dooley to John M. Work, 21 November 1912, Socialist Party Papers.
23. *New Century*, 17 January 1913.

24. Meredith, "A History of the Socialist Party in Oklahoma," 151.
25. Will T. Geers to R. L. Williams, 18 November 1916, R. L. Williams Collection.
26. Scales and Goble, *Oklahoma Politics*, 46–47.
27. Indeed, it seems that the practice was largely responsible for the Democratic gubernatorial victory in 1910. The Democratic candidate's margin of victory that year was less than 21,000, well below the estimated 27,000 blacks who were deprived of the right to vote in the election. See the undated, untitled typescript in the Barde Collection.
28. Donald Graham, "Red, White and Black: An Interpretation of Ethnic and Racial Attitudes of Agrarian Radicals in Texas and Oklahoma, 1880–1920" (master's thesis, University of Saskatchewan, 1973), 359.
29. The timing was hardly accidental. Democrats chose the primary elections in order to guarantee that the literacy test and grandfather clause would be in effect in time for the general elections in November.
30. *Marshall County News-Democrat*, 1 July 1910.
31. "The 'Grandfather' Amendment," n.d., in the Green McCurtain Collection, Western History Collections, University of Oklahoma, Norman, Oklahoma.
32. *Industrial Democrat*, 25 June 1910.
33. Ibid., 25 June 1910.
34. *Oklahoma Pioneer*, 1 June 1910.
35. Ibid., 9 February 1910.
36. For an example of GOP opposition to the measure, see the *Sweetwater Breeze*, 21 July 1910.
37. The Democratic-controlled state legislature had quietly given election officials the authority to change the ballot in this way in legislation passed the previous March. *Harlow's Weekly*, 25 April 1914; Graham, "Red, White and Black," 277–78.
38. Indeed, some scholars have concluded that more than twenty thousand of the affirmative votes on the measure came in the form of blank ballots. Scales and Goble have calculated that 241,665 total votes were recorded on the literacy test and grandfather clause, while only 221,301 votes were cast for candidates in the primaries. Scales and Goble, *Oklahoma Politics*, 7. See also *Harlow's Weekly* (19 February 1916), a Democratic publication, which concludes that, were it not for the manipulation of the ballot, the provision would never have carried.
39. *Directory and Manual of the State of Oklahoma* (Oklahoma City: State Election Board, 1961), 242.
40. Graham, "Red, White and Black," 282–84; *Oklahoma Pioneer*, 29 October 1910. This decision was written by Judge R. L. Williams, who four years later would become the Democratic Party's candidate for Governor.
41. Donald Kenneth Pickens, "The Principles of Oklahoma Socialism, 1900–1918" (master's thesis, University of Oklahoma, 1957), 66–68; *Roger Mills Sentinel*, 24 June 1915.
42. Quoted in Graham, "Red, White and Black," 221–22. Stallard's statement reflected the Farmers' Union's official policy of strict racial segregation.

43. *Oklahoma Pioneer*, 30 March, 1912, cited in Graham, "Red, White and Black," 225.
44. *Oklahoma Pioneer*, 6 April 1910.
45. *New Century*, 31 May 1912.
46. *Otter Valley Socialist*, 14 July 1916, quoted in Graham, "Red, White and Black," 238–39.
47. *Kiowa Breeze*, 18 January 1907.
48. *New Century*, 31 May 1912, 20 December 1912, 24 January 1913.
49. *Beckham County Advocate*, 28 August 1913.
50. *Ellis County Socialist*, 13 July 1916, quoted in Graham, "Red, White and Black," 238. See also Wood Hubbard's poem, "The 'Pedigree' of the Democrat Party," *Ellis County Advocate*, 21 and 28 August 1919.
51. *Marshall County Democrat*, 23 August 1907; Nudie E. Williams, "They Fought for Votes: The White Politicians and the Black Editor," *Chronicles of Oklahoma* 64 (1986): 21–24.
52. "Negroes Favor the Socialist Party," Broadside, Socialist Party Papers; *Appeal to Reason*, 5 November 1910.
53. Platform of the Socialist Party of Oklahoma, 1912, Socialist Party Papers.
54. This is the position taken by most interpreters who have examined carefully the Oklahoma Party's relationship with blacks. See, for example, James Green, *Grass-Roots Socialism: Radical Movements in the Southwest* (Baton Rouge: Louisiana State University Press, 1978), 96–106; Graham, "Red, White, and Black"; H. L. Meredith, "Agrarian Socialism and the Negro in Oklahoma, 1900–1918," *Labor History* 11 (1970): 277–84; and Philip S. Foner, *American Socialism and Black Americans: From the Age of Jackson to World War II* (Westport, Conn.: Greenwood Press, 1977), 220–37.

The most important dissenter from this position is Garin Burbank, who sees the party's progressive stand on race as an anomaly, the product of outside influences. Despite the party's opposition to the disfranchisement of blacks, Burbank questions the extent to which it "significantly altered the traditional attitudes and social mores of white Southerners in Oklahoma." See Burbank, *When Farmers Voted Red*, 87.

For an important commentary on the national Socialist Party and blacks, see R. Laurence Moore, "Flawed Fraternity: American Socialist Response to the Negro, 1901–1912," *Historian* 32 (1969): 1–18; and Sally M. Miller, *Race, Ethnicity, and Gender in Early Twentieth-Century American Socialism* (New York: Garland Press, 1996).

55. *Harlow's Weekly*, 19 August 1916.
56. See, for example, *Roger Mills Sentinel*, 10 November 1910; *Durant Weekly News*, 31 March 1916; *Harlow's Weekly*, 10 June 1916; *Marshall County News-Democrat*, 29 June 1916; Otis T. Weaver to W. H. Murray, 3 September 1914 and W. L. Blessing to W. H. Murray, 28 September 1914, W. H. Murray Papers, Manuscript Division, Oklahoma Historical Society, Oklahoma City, Oklahoma.

Although socialists and Republicans at times found themselves taking similar positions on issues relating to the Democratic Party, neither the Socialist Party of

Oklahoma nor the Republican Party agreed to any formal arrangement that resembled fusion.

57. Foner, *American Socialism and Black Americans*, 230.
58. Graham, "Red, White and Black," 250–51.
59. *Appeal to Reason*, 16 May 1908.
60. *Harlow's Weekly*, 25 April 1914. It should be noted that membership figures are notoriously elastic. The figures cited here are not "paid up members," which tended to be fewer in number.
61. H. Wayne Morgan and Anne Hodges Morgan, *Oklahoma: A Bicentennial History* (New York: W. W. Norton and Company, 1977), 96–97.
62. *Sword of Truth*, 27 August 1913.
63. *Industrial Democrat*, 13 August 1910.
64. "Williamson Writes of His Trip," *New Century*, 22 March 1912.
65. *Appeal to Reason*, 6 April 1912.
66. *Boswell Submarine*, 9 January 1914.
67. *Appeal to Reason*, 21 February 1914.
68. *Harlow's Weekly*, 20 June 1914.
69. *Boswell Submarine*, 28 November 1913.
70. "Articles Adopted at the Socialist Party of Oklahoma State Convention," December 29–31, 1913, Socialist Party Papers.
71. *Harlow's Weekly*, 28 February 1914.
72. Ibid., 17 October 1914. To place this in perspective, less than a decade earlier, farmers affiliated with the Indiahoma Farmers' Union were receiving as much as eleven cents per pound for their cotton.
73. *Directory and Manual of the State of Oklahoma*.
74. State and Local Files (Oklahoma), Socialist Party Papers; *Directory and Manual of the State of Oklahoma*, 48.
75. *Harlow's Weekly*, 15 January 1916.
76. "Proceedings of the Socialist State Convention of Oklahoma, 1915," Oklahoma Historical Society.
77. "Socialist Party of Oklahoma 'Red Card' and Political Organizations, 1916," in Thomas W. Woodrow Collection, Western History Collections, University of Oklahoma, Norman, Oklahoma. This publication lists the officers of every socialist local and the socialist chairmen of every voting precinct in the state.
78. *Appeal to Reason*, 13 March 1915.
79. For a comprehensive study of the conduct of the five socialists elected in 1914 to the state House of Representatives, see Von Russell Creel, "Socialists in the House: The Oklahoma Experience," *Chronicles of Oklahoma* 70 (1992–1993): 144–83, 258–301.
80. *Roger Mills Sentinel*, 28 January 1915; *Harlow's Weekly*, 13 February 1915.
81. *Roger Mills Sentinel*, 6 June 1916.
82. *Harlow's Weekly*, 2 October 1915.
83. Ibid., 1 November 1916.
84. C. A. Melton to R. L. Williams, 27 November 1911, R. L. Williams Collection.

85. Ed L. Spears to R. L. Williams, 22 January 1916, R. L. Williams Collection. Specifically, Spears proposed that District 7, where the socialists were strongest, be merged with the weak socialist precincts in Durant.

86. Roy Hoffman to R. L. Williams, 4 November 1914, R. L. Williams Collection.

87. Overtly antisocialist articles were printed on the front page of each of the following issues of the *Roger Mills Sentinel*: 31 December 1914; 28 January 1915; 4, 11, and 18 February 1915; 4 March 1915; 6 May 1915; 17 June 1915; 1 July 1915; 5 August 1915; 29 October 1915; 21 December 1915; 6 January 1916; 24 February 1916; 9,30 March 1916; 20 April 1916; 4,24 May 1916; 1 June 1916; 10 and 31 August 1916; 28 September 1916; 26 October 1916; 16 November 1916.

88. *Marshall County News-Democrat*, 23 September 1910, 8 June 1916, 15 June 1916, 6 July 1916.

89. Meredith, "History of the Socialist Party in Oklahoma," 133–34; *New Century*, 11 April 1913; *Socialist Antidote*, 15 November 1915.

90. For the text of the proposed Fair Election Law, see the State and Local File (Oklahoma), Socialist Party Papers.

91. *Sword of Truth*, 25 June 1913.

92. Scales and Goble, *Oklahoma Politics*, 83.

93. *Harlow's Weekly*, 20 November 1915.

94. *Roger Mills Sentinel*, 30 March 1916. As one interpreter points out, descendants of those serving as far back as the American Revolution were exempted from the literacy test under this provision. In this, the Democrats went beyond the original grandfather clause to impose "a great, great, great-grandfather clause." Creel, "Socialists in the House," 282.

As facile as this attempt to evade the Supreme Court was, it was positively sophisticated compared with an amendment proposed by State Representative Wilburn Cartwright of Coal County. Representative Cartwright's proposal was oxymoronic in its ambiguity: "No person shall be registered as an elector of this State, or be allowed to vote in any election herein, unless he be able to read and write any section of the Constitution of the State of Oklahoma; provided, that no person who has attained the age of thirty or more years at the time this law shall have taken effect shall be denied the right to register and vote because of his inability to read and write any section of the Constitution of Oklahoma." Undated Typescript, Wilburn Cartwright Collection, Carl Albert Congressional Research and Studies Center Congressional Archives, University of Oklahoma.

95. Graham, "Red, White and Black," 318–20. The measure was defeated by a margin of 42,000 votes in the primary election in 1916. Scales and Goble, *Oklahoma Politics*, 84.

96. *Harlow's Weekly*, 26 February 1916.

97. Creel, "Socialists in the House," 283–84.

98. In 1916 the registration period ran from April 30 until May 11. For future elections, the period was defined as the ten-day period ending ten days prior to election day.

99. J. T. Sanders, "The Economic and Social Aspects of Mobility of Oklahoma Farmers," *Agricultural Experiment Station Bulletin*, no. 195 (August 1929), 29.

100. *New Century*, 27 September 1912, 22 November 1912, 28 February 1913.
101. *Harlow's Weekly*, 2 October 1915.
102. Jack Moore to R. L. Williams, 29 September 1915; F. B. Semple to Williams, 29 September 1915; A. F. Manning to Williams, 29 September 1915 (all in the R. L. Williams Collection).
103. *Johnston County Capital-Democrat*, 4, 11, and 26 May 1916, 1 June 1916, cited in Burbank, "Agrarian Radicals and Their Opponents: Political Conflict in Southern Oklahoma, 1910–1924," *Journal of American History* 58 (1971): 11.
104. *Harlow's Weekly*, 20 May 1916, quoted in John Thompson, *Closing the Frontier*, 132.
105. *Strong City Herald*, 25 July 1918, 8 August 1918. This provision became effective in March of 1915.
106. *Harlow's Weekly*, 26 February 1916.
107. Ibid., 11 March 1916; Scales and Goble, *Oklahoma Politics*, 86. The amendment would make it unconstitutional for the state legislature to adopt the New Election Law, thereby rendering it useless.
108. *Harlow's Weekly*, 11 April 1916, 13 May 1916.
109. Richard A. Billup to R. L. Williams, 26 May 1916, R. L. Williams Collection.
110. O. J. Logan to R. L. Williams, 11 November 1916, R. L. Williams Collection.
111. *Harlow's Weekly*, 25 October 1916. It should be remembered that those precincts where socialist support was strongest often received an inadequate supply of ballots. Socialists had long contended that this was the Democrats' favorite ploy to reduce socialist voting.
112. It must be noted that the total vote of over 145,000 cast in favor of the socialist Fair Election Law overstated the level of socialist sentiment in Oklahoma. Besides socialists, most of the state's Republicans and not a few Democrats supported the measure. Indeed, at the state GOP convention in 1916, delegates adopted a resolution calling for Oklahoma Republicans to support the socialist election law on the grounds that it was "manifestly fair and just." See the *Appeal to Reason*, 18 April 1916.
113. The election figures used in this discussion of the Fair Election Law are from Graham's excellent treatment of the subject in "Red, White and Black." They also appear in *Harlow's Weekly*, 15 and 29 November 1916.
114. Some 304,000 ballots were issued, while 292,335 Oklahomans voted in the presidential election. Oliver Benson et al., *Oklahoma Votes, 1907–1962* (Norman: Bureau of Government Research, 1964). For the socialist reaction to the election and to the Democrats' actions, see also H. M. Sinclair, "Making Oklahoma Safe for Democracy," (Pamphlet, n.d.) in the Western History Collections, University of Oklahoma, Norman, Oklahoma.
115. Eugene Debs chose not to run for president in 1916, a decision that hurt the American Socialist Party badly in that election. In light of this, Oklahoma Socialists' performance in the election becomes even more remarkable.
116. *Harlow's Weekly*, 19 August 1916.

CHAPTER 7

1. James R. Scales and Danney Goble, *Oklahoma Politics: A History* (Norman: University of Oklahoma Press, 1982), 81.
2. The evidence in the McNabb case is derived from the following sources: Sherry Warrick, "Radical Labor in Oklahoma: The Working Class Union," *Chronicles of Oklahoma* 52 (1974): 180-81; Howard Meredith, "History of the Socialist Party in Oklahoma" (Ph.D. diss., University of Oklahoma, 1969), 168; and Garin Burbank, *When Farmers Voted Red: The Gospel of Socialism in the Oklahoma Countryside, 1910-1924* (Westport, Conn.: Greenwood Press, 1976), 141.
3. *New Century*, 28 February 1913; Edward Everette Dale and James D. Morrison, *Pioneer Judge: The Life of Robert Lee Williams* (Cedar Rapids, Iowa: The Torch Press, 1958), 249.
4. *Harlow's Weekly*, 26 February 1916.
5. Country leaders were ultimately successful in punishing McNabb. In April of 1918, disbarment proceedings were again initiated, this time successfully, for his alleged defrauding of a black client. *Strong City Herald*, 25 April 1918.
6. Hugh Johnson to Fred Gum, 1 May 1916, R. L. Williams Collection, Oklahoma Historical Society, Oklahoma City, Oklahoma.
7. J. B. Allen to Fred S. Gum, 10 May 1916; Fred S. Gum to R. L. Williams, 16 May 1916; R. L. Williams Collection.
8. *Harlow's Weekly*, 27 September 1916.
9. Ibid., 12 February 1916. Perhaps the most remarkable manifestation of antibanking sentiment among Oklahoma farmers involved the colorful and legendary Al Jennings. A convicted bank robber, Jennings ran for governor in 1914 and collected almost twenty-two thousand votes (24 percent) in the Democratic primary. See *Harlow's Weekly*, 26 October 1912, 15 August 1914.
10. T. G. McMahan to R. L. Williams, 3 November 1916, R. L. Williams Collection.
11. *Durant Weekly News*, 16 October 1914.
12. *Strong City Herald*, 15 November 1917.
13. Warrick, "Radical Labor in Oklahoma," 186.
14. A. W. Sanders to R. L. Williams, 19 May 1916, R. L. Williams Collection. See also Warrick, "Radical Labor in Oklahoma," 185.
15. Meredith, "History of the Socialist Party in Oklahoma," 153.
16. James Weinstein, *The Decline of Socialism in America, 1912-1925* (New York: Monthly Review Press, 1967), 121.
17. Quoted in Horace C. Peterson and Gilbert C. Fite, *Opponents of War, 1917-1918* (Madison: University of Wisconsin Press, 1957), 8-9.
18. *Harlow's Weekly*, 13 June 1917.
19. *Strong City Herald*, 22 March 1917.
20. Ibid., 15 March 1917.
21. Proceedings of the Socialist State Convention, 29-31 December 1914, quoted in Burbank, *When Farmers Voted Red*, 111.

22. *Strong City Herald*, 10 January 1918.
23. Ibid., 5 July 1917.
24. *Harlow's Weekly*, 13 June 1917.
25. William H. Murray, the architect of the Tishomingo convention and the separate Indian Territory organization during the height of the Farmers' Union, was in 1916 the U.S. Representative for the Fourth Congressional District. Murray had been a strong and vocal supporter of preparedness, a position which cost him his job. He was defeated in the Democratic primary in 1916 by a candidate who centered his campaign around opposition to the war. Scales and Goble, *Oklahoma Politics*, 85.
26. *Elk City News-Democrat*, 12 April 1917.
27. M. B. Cooley to R. L. Williams, 29 May 1917, R. L. Williams Collection. For a description of similar fears about Major County, see also Tom E. Willis to R. L. Williams, 6 August 1917, R. L. Williams Collection.
28. *Harlow's Weekly*, 27 June 1917.
29. *Elk City News-Democrat*, 7 June 1917; *Beckham County Democrat*, 7 June 1917; *Marietta Monitor*, 8 June 1917; *Strong City Herald*, 7 June 1917. The newspapers reported only six arrests made on June 5 in connection with conscription registration. Among those arrested were W. M. Williams, L. M. Stephens, J. H. Spence, and H. H. Munson.
30. *Strong City Herald*, 14 June 1917. The actual number of those registering was 111,986, with 80,139 claiming exemptions.
31. Louis C. Brown to R. L. Williams, 14 July 1917, R. L. Williams Collection.
32. *Beckham County Democrat*, 14 June 1917.
33. Michael Morton, "No Time to Quibble: The Jones Conspiracy Trial of 1917," *Chronicles of Oklahoma* 59 (1981–1982): 229.
34. Charles C. Bush, "The Green Corn Rebellion" (master's thesis, University of Oklahoma, 1932); Virginia Pope, "The Green Corn Rebellion: A Case Study in Newspaper Self-Censorship" (master's thesis, Oklahoma A and M University, 1940); James Green, *Grass-Roots Socialism: Radical Movements in the Southwest* (Baton Rouge: Louisiana State University Press, 1978), 358–65; Burbank, *When Farmers Voted Red*, 135–56.
35. Bush, "The Green Corn Rebellion," 44.
36. Ibid., p. 58.
37. *Harlow's Weekly*, 8 August 1917; Bush, "The Green Corn Rebellion," 50.
38. *Strong City Herald*, 23 August 1917, emphasis added. The fact that Socialist Party leader Pat Nagle had served as defense counsel for three members of the WCU in 1916 probably helped seal the Party's fate as co-conspirators in the Rebellion in the minds of Democratic leaders. See *Harlow's Weekly*, 27 September 1916.
39. R. L. Williams to Chief of Ordinance, Washington, D.C., 9 August 1917, R. L. Williams Collection.
40. *Harlow's Weekly*, 15 August 1917.
41. See Bush, "The Green Corn Rebellion," appendix A, for a comprehensive listing of those arrested. For a comprehensive listing of county and local socialist leaders, see "Socialist Party of Oklahoma 'Red Card' and Political Organizations,

1916," Thomas W. Woodrow Collection, Western History Collections, University of Oklahoma, Norman, Oklahoma.

42. Nell Irvin Painter points to this aspect of the red scares of 1886 and 1919, which, she argues, "intentionally crippled the organizations that challenged the hierarchy; red scares were eerily effective at enforcing identity of interest as seen from the top." Nell Irvin Painter, *Standing at Armageddon: The United States, 1877–1919* (New York: W. W. Norton and Company, 1987), 388–89.

43. *Beckham County Democrat*, 7 June 1917.

44. *Roger Mills Sentinel*, 3 May 1917. See also *Beckham County Democrat*, 26 April 1917.

45. *Beckham County Democrat*, 9 August 1917, capitalization in original.

46. Ibid., 15 November 1917.

47. Ibid., 11 April 1918.

48. *Harlow's Weekly*, 13 June 1917.

49. Carl Albert, with Danney Goble, *Little Giant: The Life and Times of Speaker Carl Albert* (Norman: University of Oklahoma Press, 1990), 46–48.

50. *Strong City Herald*, 22 March 1917.

51. Peterson and Fite, *Opponents of War*, 199. This work provides excellent detail on the hysteria that prevailed throughout the nation during World War I.

52. National Civil Liberties Bureau, "War-Time Prosecutions and Mob Violence," 1919, pp. 8–9, in Socialist Party Papers, Manuscript Department, Perkins Library, Duke University, Durham, North Carolina.

53. *Madill Record*, 28 March 1918.

54. Military Intelligence Division, U.S. Army, Reports compiled in *U.S. Military Intelligence Reports: Surveillance of Radicals in the United States*, Randolph Boem, ed. (Frederick, Md.: University Publications of America, 1984), 10 November 1917 (microfilm, reel 6, frame 00266).

55. Peterson and Fite, *Opponents of War*, 171–73.

56. *Madill Record*, 20 November 1917.

57. For additional explorations into the Wilson Administration's efforts to promote the war effort at home, see David M. Kennedy, *Over Here: The First World War and American Society* (New York: Oxford University Press, 1980); and Robert H. Ferrell, *Woodrow Wilson and World War I, 1917–1921* (New York: Harper and Row, 1985).

58. O. A. Hilton, "The Oklahoma Council of Defense and the First World War," *Chronicles of Oklahoma* 20 (1942): 23.

59. Hilton, "Oklahoma Council of Defense," 19–20; James H. Fowler, "Tar and Feather Patriotism: The Suppression of Dissent in Oklahoma During World War One," *Chronicles of Oklahoma* 56 (1978–1979): 414, 427; Chester Westfall to Clayton H. Hyde, Clayton H. Hyde Collection, Western History Collections, University of Oklahoma, Norman, Oklahoma.

60. Fowler, "Tar and Feather Patriotism," 416; Hilton, "The Oklahoma Council of Defense and the First World War," 22. See *Strong City Herald*, 2 August 1917, for a listing of the executive committees of most of the county councils.

61. Fowler, "Tar and Feather Patriotism," 414–15.

62. *Daily Oklahoman*, 14 April 1918, quoted in James Arthur Robinson, "Loyalty Investigations and Legislation in Oklahoma" (master's thesis, University of Oklahoma, 1955), 7.

63. Oklahoma State Council of Defense, General Bulletin Number 8, 11 October 1917, in Sam Williams Collection, Western History Collections, University of Oklahoma, Norman, Oklahoma.

64. Sam Williams to R. L. Williams, 22 February 1918, Sam Williams Collection. The writer suggested, for example, that the government seize the land of those who failed to adequately support the war effort.

65. Sam Williams to George W. Barnes, 2 April 1918, Sam Williams Collection.

66. Sam Williams to J. M. Aydelotte, 21 May 1918; J. F. Brooks to Sam Williams, 1 July 1918; Sam Williams to Perry C. Burkes, 29 June 1918 (all in Sam Williams Collection).

67. *Sooners in the War* (Oklahoma City: Oklahoma Council of Defense, 1919), 10.

68. J. P. Ensey to Sam Williams, 28 June 1918, Sam Williams Collection.

69. G. W. Barnes to County Chairmen, 13 June 1918, Sam Williams Collection.

70. See Charles W. Smith, "The Selling of America in Oklahoma: The First and Second Liberty Bond Drives," *Chronicles of Oklahoma* 73 (1996): 438–53.

71. J. M. Aydelotte to Members of County Councils of Defense, 12 October 1917, C. H. Hyde Collection, Western History Collections, University of Oklahoma, Norman, Oklahoma.

72. G. W. Barnes to Sam Williams, 7 June 1918, Sam Williams Collection.

73. Sam Williams to J. W. Kelley, John Brady, and John Fourier, 11 July 1918, Sam Williams Collection.

74. G. M. England to Sam Williams, 29 June 1918, Sam Williams Collection.

75. National Civil Liberties Bureau, "War-Time Prosecutions and Mob Violence," 7, 10.

76. *Sooners in the War*, 9–10.

77. G. W. Barnes to James E. Graves, 6 June 1918, Sam Williams Collection.

78. Sam Williams to G. W. Barnes and Barnes to Williams, 29 June 1918 (telegrams), Sam Williams Collection.

79. *U.S. Military Intelligence Reports*, 8 July 1917 (Microfilm; reel 3, frame 00463–00464).

80. Sam Williams to Geo. W. Barnes, 10 July 1918, Sam Williams Collection.

81. House Committee on the Judiciary, *Report of the Committee on the Judiciary*, H.R. *291*, 65th Cong., 1st sess., *Congressional Record* (7 June 1917), 55:3301–6 (Espionage Act); Senate Conference Committee, *Report of the Conference Committee*, H.R. *8753*, 65th Cong., 2nd sess., *Congressional Record* (22 April 1918), 56:5414 (Sedition Act).

82. G. W. Barnes to Sam Williams, 25 June 1918, Sam Williams Collection.

83. *Sooners in the War*, 22, 60, 64 (quotes on p. 22).

84. Ibid., 58.

85. Ibid., 6.

86. *Ellis County Advocate*, 30 January 1919.

87. See, for example, M. C. Badgett to Sam Williams, 3 July 1918, J. I. Breckenridge to Sam Williams, 29 June 1918, Sam Williams to G. W. Barnes, 2 February 1918, in Sam Williams Collection, Western History Collections; R. B. Quinn to J. M. Aydelotte, 17 June 1918, Roy Gittinger Collection, Western History Collections, University of Oklahoma, Norman, Oklahoma.

88. *Musings of the Old Kuss*, July 1916.

89. *Hammon Advocate*, 9 August 1917.

90. George Fisher to R. L. Williams, 25 December 1917, J. B. Patton to R. L. Williams, 25 December 1917, R. L. Williams Collection. Both of these letters were attempts to convince the governor to drop the charges against Hicks. See also the plea made to the Governor by Hicks's wife: Mrs. W. M. Hicks to Gov. Williams, 27 December 1917, R. L. Williams Collection.

91. *Strong City Herald*, 7 February, 18 April 1918.

92. Robinson, "Loyalty Investigations," 6; *Strong City Herald*, 18 April 1918; *Sooners in the War*, 28.

93. *Letter from the Attorney General Listing Government Prosecutions Under the Espionage Act*, 67th Cong., 2nd sess., S. Doc. 159, 10. In 1919, Hicks's sentence was commuted to five years.

For a fascinating, firsthand account of the experiences of those who, like Hicks, served time at Leavenworth for their opposition to the war, see Ralph Chaplin, *Wobbly: The Rough-and-Tumble Story of an American Radical* (Chicago: University of Illinois Press, 1948).

94. *Strong City Herald*, 16 August 1917, 14 March 1918, and 18 June 1918.

95. *Ellis County Advocate*, 19 April 1919.

96. *Sooners in the War*, 25.

97. The number of active socialist locals in Oklahoma declined from 1,082 in 1916 to 471 in January of 1918. *Harlow's Weekly*, 21 January 1918; *Oklahoma Leader*, 15 November 1919.

98. *Harlow's Weekly*, 26 November 1920.

99. Ibid., 22 May 1918.

100. Ibid., 10 July 1918.

101. *Oklahoma Leader*, 22 August 1918.

102. *Strong City Herald*, 30 May 1918; *Harlow's Weekly*, 22 May 1918. Stallard's position coincided with those of some national socialist leaders who called for the reconsideration of the St. Louis Proclamation. One of the most prominent of these, Carl D. Thompson, made his position clear: "I cannot see how any consistent Socialist can stand on the St. Louis platform any longer. I, for one, cannot and shall not try to do so." *Strong City Herald*, 6 June 1918.

103. *Harlow's Weekly*, 4 September 1918.

104. *Ellis County Advocate*, 27 June 1918.

105. Ibid., 5 June 1919.

106. Ibid., 28 August 1919.

107. *Oklahoma Leader*, 22 August 1918.

108. Oscar Ameringer, *If You Don't Weaken*, (New York: Henry Holt, 1940), 236–37. This episode is also reported in Donald Kenneth Pickens, "The Principles and Programs of Oklahoma Socialism, 1900–1918" (master's thesis, University of Oklahoma, 1957), 85–86; Meredith, "History of the Socialist Party in Oklahoma," 196–97; and R. O. Joe Cassity, Jr., "The Political Career of Patrick S. Nagle: 'Champion of the Underdog,'" *Chronicles of Oklahoma* 64 (1986): 61.

109. *Oklahoma Leader*, 22 August 1918. In January of 1920, in fact, the Socialist Party of Oklahoma held its regularly scheduled annual convention. See the *Ellis County Advocate*, 5 February 1920.

110. *Strong City Herald*, 24 May 1917.

111. Ibid., 20 December 1917, 28 February 1918.

112. Ibid., 28 March 1918. For additional evidence of Stallard's pro-war sentiment, see *Strong City Herald*, 30 May 1918.

113. Ibid., 9 May 1918.

114. Ibid., 5 September 1918.

115. Ibid., 21 March 1918.

116. Ibid., 29 March 1917, 10 May 1917, 21 June 1917.

117. Ibid., 11 April 1918.

118. Ibid., 7 February 1918, 23 May 1918.

119. Green, *Grass-Roots Socialism*, 394–95.

120. In one of the few exceptions to this generalizations, a socialist newspaper reported that Kate Richards O'Hare, H. M. Sinclair, and J. L. Langston led an eight-day socialist tour in the fall of 1920. *Ellis County Advocate*, 2 September 1920.

121. *Oklahoma Leader*, 13, 27 March 1920.

122. David A. Shannon, *The Socialist Party of America: A History* (New York: Macmillan, 1955), 163.

CHAPTER 8

1. John Thompson, *Closing the Frontier: Radical Responses in Oklahoma, 1899–1923* (Norman: University of Oklahoma Press, 1986), 207–8; Gilbert C. Fite, "The Non-Partisan League in Oklahoma," *Chronicles of Oklahoma* 24 (1946): 146–57.

2. This summary of the formation of the Farmer-Labor Reconstruction League is taken from James R. Scales and Danney Goble, *Oklahoma Politics: A History* (Norman: University of Oklahoma Press, 1982), 111–17.

3. Scales and Goble, *Oklahoma Politics*, 112.

4. Gilbert Fite, "Oklahoma's Reconstruction League: An Experiment in Farmer-Labor Politics," *Journal of Southern History* 13 (1947): 543, 545.

5. Fite, "Oklahoma's Reconstruction League," 546; James Green, *Grass-Roots Socialism: Radical Movements in the Southwest* (Baton Rouge: Louisiana State University Press, 1978), 397–401.

6. The life of Agnes Cunningham, a radical folk singer and organizer, is instructive as a fascinating example of this dynamic at work in a single lifetime. Cunningham

was born in Blaine County in 1909 into a tenant family active in the Socialist Party of Oklahoma. After attending Commonwealth College, she became active in the 1930s in the Southern Tenant Farmers' Union (STFU) in her home state. She then joined the Red Dust Players, a drama group that helped organize on behalf of the United Cannery, Agricultural, Packing and Allied Workers of America (with which the STFU was affiliated), before moving out of Oklahoma in 1941. Cunningham went on to become part of the famed Almanac Singers and was active in the Communist Party in New York and Detroit. For an overview of her life, see Suzanne H. Schrems, "Radicalism and Song," *Chronicles of Oklahoma* 62 (1984): 190–206.

Additional evidence of the connection between Oklahoma socialism and a later insurgent movement, the STFU, can be found in H. L. Mitchell's autobiography, *Mean Things Happening in This Land*. The STFU's first constitution was modeled after the bylaws of the Oklahoma Renters Union, which had been sent to Arkansas organizers by Oklahoma Socialist Oscar Ameringer. In addition, J. R. Butler, one of the STFU's organizers, had been active in the Working Class Union. See Mitchell, *Mean Things Happening in This Land: The Life and Times of H. L. Mitchell, Cofounder of the Southern Tenant Farmers Union* (Montclair, N.J.: Allanheld, Osmun and Company, 1979), 48–49.

Other examples of Oklahoma Socialists who continued to be activists after the demise of the Party include Ira Finley, who in 1932 helped organize the Veterans of Industry of America, and Dr. Michael Shadid, a physician who in the 1930s established a cooperative that pioneered the concept of prepaid health plans. See Patrick E. McGinnis, *Oklahoma's Depression Radicals: Ira M. Finley and the Veterans of Industry of America* (New York: Peter Lang, 1991); and Michael A. Shadid, *Crusading Doctor: My Fight for Cooperative Medicine* (Norman: University of Oklahoma Press, 1991).

Finally, for a fascinating exploration into the intricacies of the ideological journey made by Oklahomans, many of whom were affected by their experience with the Socialist Party, see Roxanne Dunbar-Ortiz, "One or Two Things I Know about Us: 'Okies' in American Culture," *Radical History Review* 59 (1994): 5–34.

7. H. M. Sinclair summarizes the Party's specific charges against election officials in "Making Oklahoma Safe for the Democratic Party," Western History Collections, University of Oklahoma, Norman, Oklahoma.

8. At various points, Green, Burbank, and Thompson all question Oklahoma socialists' legitimacy, in large part because of the party's stand on land ownership. Green suggests that "the frontier farmer's isolation and his feelings of 'possessive individualism' toward the land prevented the development of proletarian class consciousness." As a result, he concludes, "the party's rural masses . . . expressed a consciousness that was more petty bourgeois than proletarian." (Green, *Grass-Roots Socialism*, 161.) Or, as Thompson puts it, "Undoubtedly, many leftists in Little Dixie did not understand Marxism" (*Closing the Frontier*, 140). For Burbank, "there is much evidence to suggest that [Oklahoma socialists] had not achieved the proletarian perspective exemplified in the nationwide agitations of Eugene Debs." Indeed, Burbank cannot conceive of landowning socialist farmers as legitimate socialists. "At

some point," he argues, "Socialists who held power and believed in socialism would have had to approach the small holders to propose an enlarged scale of production, along with cooperative operation and ownership." Garin Burbank, *When Farmers Voted Red: The Gospel of Socialism in the Oklahoma Countryside, 1910–1924* (Westport, Conn.: Greenwood Press, 1976), 34.

Paul Buhle offers a comment regarding a later historical period that is relevant to the Oklahoma socialist experience. "Marxism is as Marxism does," Buhle contends, "and the Latin American revolutionary who takes inspiration from Liberation Theology and economics from Marx and Lenin has as much claim to the mantle as Trotsky, Mao Zedong or Marx himself. Any other definition is the claim of an ideological holding company." Paul Buhle, *Marxism in the United States: Remapping the History of the American Left* (London: Verso, 1987), 16.

9. For additional detail regarding this debate, see the following works: Lawrence Goodwyn, "The Cooperative Commonwealth and Other Abstractions: In Search of a Democratic Premise," *Marxist Perspectives* 3 (1980): 8–42; James Green, "Populism, Socialism and the Promise of Democracy," *Radical History Review* 24 (June 1981): 7–40; and Donald B. Marti, "Answering the Agrarian Question: Socialists, Farmers, and Algie Martin Simons," *Agricultural History* 65 (1991): 53–69.

10. As John Graham argues, there is no contradiction in land ownership by socialist smallholders: "Socialist theory required social ownership of socially-operated means of production, not of every enterprise; nor did it deny choice in non-exploitive matters." See John Graham, ed., *"Yours for the Revolution": The Appeal to Reason, 1895–1922* (Lincoln: University of Nebraska Press, 1990), 136.

11. This concept is defined most clearly in the introduction to Lawrence Goodwyn's *The Populist Moment: A Short History of Agrarian Revolt in America* (New York: Oxford University Press, 1978). Bruce Laurie also provides excellent insight into the idea of received culture in *Artisans Into Workers: Labor in Nineteenth-Century America* (New York: Noonday Press, 1989), 74.

12. Laurie, *Artisans Into Workers*, 74.

APPENDIX A

1. *Durant Independent Farmer*, 27 December 1905. See also the 15 July 1905 and 5 October 1905 issues of the same publication.

2. Theodore Saloutos, *Farmer Movements in the South, 1865–1933* (Berkeley and Los Angeles: University of California Press, 1960), 197.

3. I am indebted to Lowell Dyson for this observation, which he made in response to an earlier draft of a portion of this work.

Bibliographical Essay

As scholars, we all stand on the shoulders of those who came before us. It is appropriate, therefore, to begin the discussion of sources specific to the study of Oklahoma socialism by acknowledging those scholars whose works—although not always directly relevant to the subject of this book—have nevertheless shaped it in fundamental ways. First, we all owe a debt to E. P. Thompson, who showed us in *The Making of the English Working Class* (New York: Pantheon Books, 1963) how to rescue those at the bottom of society from what he called the "enormous condescension of posterity." In addition, Herbert Gutman's breathtaking essays, collected most prominently in *Work, Culture, and Society in Industrializing America* (New York: Random House, 1977), brought a richness and complexity to American workers that had previously been invisible to interpreters. C. Vann Woodward's *Origins of the New South, 1877–1913* (Baton Rouge: Louisiana State University Press, 1951) remains the most graceful, honest narrative of the tortured history of the post–Civil War South. Also important are Lawrence Goodwyn, *Democratic Promise: The Populist Movement in America* (New York: Oxford University Press, 1976); John Gaventa, *Power and Powerlessness: Quiescence and Rebellion in an Appalachian Valley* (Urbana: University of Illinois Press, 1980); Theodore Rosengarten, *All God's Dangers: The Life of Nate Shaw* (New York: Random House, 1974); Sean Wilentz, *Chants Democratic: New York City and the Rise of the American Working Class, 1788–1850* (New York: Oxford

University Press, 1984); and David Montgomery, *Workers Control in America* (Cambridge: Cambridge University Press, 1979).

I. THE SOCIALIST PARTY

The Socialist Party of Oklahoma has received significant scholarly attention. Among the book-length works on the subject are James Green's *Grass-Roots Socialism: Radical Movements in the Southwest, 1895–1943* (Baton Rouge: Louisiana State University Press, 1978); Garin Burbank, *When Farmers Voted Red: The Gospel of Socialism in the Oklahoma Countryside, 1910–1924* (Westport, Conn.: Greenwood Press, 1976); and John Thompson, *Closing the Frontier: Radical Responses in Oklahoma, 1889–1923* (Norman: University of Oklahoma Press, 1986). For commentary on these works, see William C. Pratt, "Radicals, Farmers, and Historians: Some Recent Scholarship About Agrarian Radicalism in the Upper Midwest," *North Dakota History* 52, no. 4 (1984): 12–25. Several useful theses also advance our knowledge of Oklahoma socialism: Donald Graham, "Red, White and Black: An Interpretation of Ethnic and Racial Attitudes of Agrarian Radicals in Texas and Oklahoma, 1880–1920" (master's thesis, University of Saskatchewan, 1973); "A History of the Socialist Party in Oklahoma" (Ph.D. diss., University of Oklahoma, 1969) by Howard L. Meredith; Donald Kenneth Pickens, "The Principles and Programs of Oklahoma Socialism, 1900–1918," (master's thesis, University of Oklahoma, 1957); and Ellen I. Rosen, "Peasant Socialism in America? The Socialist Party in Oklahoma Before the First World War," (Ph.D. diss., City University of New York, 1975).

Oscar Ameringer's fascinating autobiography, *If You Don't Weaken*, (New York: Henry Holt, 1940) provides the perspective of one who worked and suffered through the rise and fall of Oklahoma socialism. Also helpful is another study of an Oklahoma socialist leader: R. O. Joe Cassity, Jr., "The Political Career of Patrick S. Nagle: 'Champion of the Underdog,'" *Chronicles of Oklahoma* 64

(1986):48–67. Von Russell Creel provides an exhaustive study of the successes and failures of socialists elected to the state house of representatives in 1914 in "Socialists in the House: The Oklahoma Experience," *Chronicles of Oklahoma* 70 (1992–1993): 144–83, 258–301. Finally, see also Roger Horne, "The Christian Socialism of Thomas W. Woodrow," *Chronicles of Oklahoma* 66 (1988): 240–67.

In addition to these secondary sources, my study of Oklahoma socialism is based on the dozens of local socialist newspapers that flourished in the state during the first two decades of the twentieth century. These are listed at the end of this essay and are available at the Oklahoma Historical Society in Oklahoma City. In addition, the *Appeal to Reason* provides valuable insight into events in Oklahoma. Because of the sheer volume of Oklahoma socialists, many of whom were subscribers, the *Appeal* published a special Oklahoma edition, replete with news and announcements from the Sooner State.

Although not a socialist publication, *Harlow's Weekly* is indispensable in understanding Oklahoma socialism. The mouthpiece of the progressive wing of the state's Democratic Party, this paper opens to the researcher the often urgent discussions among Democrats about how to combat the socialist threat.

The manuscript collections that I found most relevant to the Socialist Party of Oklahoma are the Socialist Party Papers at Perkins Library, Duke University (especially the Oklahoma State file) and the Bureau of Government Research Collection and the Thomas W. Woodrow Collection at the Western History Collections at the University of Oklahoma. The Governors' papers, especially those of Governor Robert L. Williams, at the Oklahoma Historical Society are also extremely valuable.

Of course, the larger topic of socialism in America has an extensive literature of its own. Among the most useful general works are James Weinstein, *The Decline of Socialism in America, 1912–1925* (New York: Monthly Review Press, 1967); David A. Shannon, *The Socialist Party of America: A History* (New York: Macmillan, 1955); Irving Howe, *Socialism and America* (New York: Harcourt, Brace,

Jovanovich, 1985); Paul Buhle, *Marxism in the United States: Remapping the History of the American Left* (London: Verso, 1987); Howard H. Quint, *The Forging of American Socialism: Origins of the Modern Movement* (New York: Bobbs-Merrill, 1964); Nathan Fine, *Labor and Farmer Parties in the United States, 1828–1928* (New York: Russell and Russell, 1961); Daniel Bell, "The Background and Development of Marxian Socialism in the United States," in *Socialism and American Life*, ed. Donald Drew Egbert and Stow Persons (Princeton, N.J.: Princeton University Press, 1952); John P. Diggins, *The Rise and Fall of the American Left* (New York: W. W. Norton, 1992); Albert Fried, ed., *Socialism in America: From the Shakers to the Third International* (Garden City, N.Y.: Doubleday, 1970); Ira Kipnis, *The American Socialist Movement, 1897–1912* (Westport, Conn.: Greenwood Press, 1952); John H. M. Laslett and Seymour Martin Lipset, eds., *Failure of a Dream: Essays in the History of American Socialism* (Berkeley and Los Angeles: University of California, 1984); and Michael Bassett, "The Socialist Party of America, 1912–1919: Years of Decline" (Ph.D. diss., Duke University, 1964). Morris Hillquit's *Loose Leaves From a Busy Life* (New York: Macmillan, 1934) is a helpful autobiographical account of an important party leader.

Other useful works which treat the Socialist Party of America in a less general manner are Mari Jo Buhl, *Women and American Socialism, 1870–1920* (Urbana: University of Illinois Press, 1981); Jerry W. Calvert, *The Gibraltar: Socialism and Labor in Butte, Montana, 1895–1920* (Helena: Montana Historical Society, 1988); Donald T. Critchlow, ed., *Socialism in the Heartland: The Midwestern Experience, 1900–1925* (Notre Dame, Ind.: University of Notre Dame Press, 1986); John Graham, ed., *"Yours for the Revolution": The Appeal to Reason, 1895–1922* (Lincoln: University of Nebraska, 1990); Richard W. Judd, *Socialist Cities: Municipal Politics and the Grass Roots of American Socialism* (Albany: State University of New York Press, 1989); Aileen S. Kraditor, *The Radical Persuasion, 1890–1917: Aspects of the Intellectual History and Historiography of Three American Radical*

Organizations (Baton Rouge: Louisiana State University, 1981); Kent Kreuter and Gretchen Kreuter, *An American Dissenter: The Life of Algie Martin Simons, 1870–1950* (Lexington: University of Kentucky, 1969); Sally M. Miller, *Victor Berger and the Promise of Constructive Socialism, 1910–1920* (Westport, Conn.: Greenwood, 1973) and *Race, Ethnicity, and Gender in Early Twentieth-Century American Socialism* (New York: Garland Press, 1996); Nick Salvatore, *Eugene V. Debs: Citizen and Socialist* (Urbana: University of Illinois Press, 1982); Elliott Shore, *Talkin' Socialism: J. A. Wayland and the Role of the Press in American Radicalism, 1890–1912* (Lawrence: University Press of Kansas, 1988); and Arthur Zipser and Pearl Zipser, *Fire and Grace: The Life of Rose Pastor Stokes* (Athens: University of Georgia Press, 1989).

It is interesting to note that a surprising amount of the scholarship on the Socialist Party of America emphasizes the relative absence of socialist influence in the United States. Indeed, since Werner Sombart's assertion in the early twentieth century that socialism failed in the United States because of the "embourgeoisiement" of the nation's workers, much of the historiography of American socialism has been dominated by theoretical discourses on the question of its "failure." Among the explanations offered are Louis Hartz's notion of the absence of a feudal tradition, Ira Kipnis's thesis that the socialist movement was killed by the rise to power of the "right wing" within the organization, Daniel Bell's argument that the Marxist ideology of the Socialist Party prevented it from taking the meaningful political stands necessary for the survival of political organizations in the United States, and James Weinstein's emphasis on governmental repression and the divisive effects of the Third International.

See the following works for more detail on such arguments. Werner Sombart, *Why is There No Socialism in the United States?*, trans. Patricia M. Hocking and C. T. Husbands (White Plains, N.Y.: International Arts and Sciences Press, 1976); Louis Hartz, *The Liberal Tradition in America: An Interpretation of American Political Thought Since the Revolution* (New York: Harcourt, Brace, 1955); Eric Foner, "Why is There No Socialism in the United

States?" *History Workshop* 17 (1984): 57–80; D. H. Leon, "Whatever Happened to an American Socialist Party? A Critical Survey of the Spectrum of Interpretations," *American Quarterly* 23 (1971): 236–58; Leonard B. Rosenberg, "The 'Failure' of the Socialist Party of America," *Review of Politics* 31 (1969): 329–52; and Robert A. Rosenstone, "Summing Up the Division of the Left," *Reviews in American History* 7 (1979): 439–44.

Finally, it is appropriate to single out two works that helped me to come to terms with aspects of Oklahoma socialism that seemed anomalous to the socialist tradition described in most of the books listed above. First, Lawrence Goodwyn's "The Cooperative Commonwealth and Other Abstractions: In Search of a Democratic Premise," *Marxist Perspectives* 3 (1980): 8–42, helped me make sense of Oklahoma socialists' positions on agrarian issues. Goodwyn demonstrates that agrarian activists called upon their own ideological heritage, rooted in past insurgent movements, in formulating their ideological positions—in much the same way that most socialists referred to Marxism. On agrarian issues, the positions taken by Oklahoma socialists were entirely consistent with their experience in past movements.

In "Americans as Radicals" (*Radical History Review* 24 [Fall 1980]: 142–52), Nick Salvatore makes much the same argument in terms of the adoption by Oklahoma socialists of such American cultural forms as fundamentalist Christianity, another aspect of the movement that seemed "unsocialistic" to some. Salvatore argues that this feature of Oklahoma socialism represents its contribution to a long and rich tradition of indigenous American radicalism. "We need not feel uncomfortable," he assures us, "with this commingling" of Marxist and American religious traditions.

II. AMERICAN AGRICULTURE

From the immense body of works on southern American agriculture, the following provide a most useful overview: Harold

Woodman, *King Cotton and His Retainers: Financing and Marketing the Cotton Crop of the South, 1800–1925* (Lexington: University of Kentucky, 1968); Pete Daniel, *Breaking the Land: The Transformation of Cotton, Tobacco, and Rice Cultures Since 1880* (Urbana: University of Illinois Press, 1985); Gilbert C. Fite, *Cotton Fields No More: Southern Agriculture, 1865–1890* (Lexington: University of Kentucky, 1984); and Steven Hahn and Jonathan Prude, *The Countryside in the Age of Capitalist Transformation: Essays in the Social History of Rural America* (Chapel Hill: University of North Carolina Press, 1985).

Of course, it is impossible to explore the history of agricultural America without considering the crisis on the land. A timely overview of this topic can be found in Osha Gray Davidson's *Broken Heartland: The Rise of America's Rural Ghetto* (New York: The Free Press, 1990). Among those works that deal explicitly with the late nineteenth- and early twentieth-century manifestations of the agricultural crisis, Roger L. Ransom and Richard Sutch, *One Kind of Freedom: The Economic Consequences of Emancipation* (Cambridge: Cambridge University Press, 1977) remains the most comprehensive. Also useful are Pete Daniel, *The Shadow of Slavery: Peonage in the South, 1901–1969* (New York: Oxford University Press, 1973); Jonathan Wiener, "Class Structure and Economic Development in the American South," *American Historical Review* 84 (1979): 970–1006. A different interpretation is provided by Stephen J. DeCanio in *Agriculture in the Postbellum South: The Economics of Production and Supply* (Cambridge: M.I.T. Press, 1974); and Gavin Wright, *Old South, New South: Revolutions in the Southern Economy Since the Civil War* (New York: Basic Books, 1986).

A series of studies published in Oklahoma as the *Agricultural Experiment Station Bulletin* (Stillwater, Oklahoma) deals specifically with agricultural problems in the Sooner State. The most relevant of these are O. D. Duncan and J. T. Sanders, "A Study of Certain Economic Factors in Relation to Social Life Among Oklahoma Cotton Farmers" (no. 211, 1933); Arthur N. Moore and J. T. Sanders,

"Credit Problems of Oklahoma Cotton Farmers" (no. 198, October 1930: 32–34); J. T. Sanders, "The Economic and Social Aspects of Mobility of Oklahoma Farmers" (no. 195, August 1929); and John H. Southern, "Farm Tenancy in Oklahoma" (no. 239, 1939).

Finally, a number of works chronicle the early twentieth-century movements sparked by the crisis on the land. The most important are Charles Simon Barrett, *The Mission, History and Times of the Farmers' Union* (Nashville, Tenn.: Marshall and Bruce Co., 1909); John A. Compton, *The National Farmers' Union: Ideology of a Pressure Group* (Lincoln: University of Nebraska, 1965); Lowell K. Dyson, *Farmers' Organizations* (Westport, Conn.: Greenwood Press, 1986); Commodore B. Fischer, *The Farmers' Union* (Lexington: University of Kentucky Press, 1920); Joseph G. Knapp, *The Rise of American Cooperative Enterprise, 1620–1920* (Danville, Ill.: Interstate Printers and Publishers, 1969); and Theodore Saloutos's *Agricultural Discontent in the Middle West, 1900–1939* (Madison: University of Wisconsin Press, 1951) and *Farmer Movements in the South, 1865–1933* (Berkeley and Los Angeles: University of California Press, 1960). For valuable statistical evidence, see Robert L. Tontz, "Memberships of General Farmers' Organizations, United States, 1874–1960," *Agricultural History* 38 (1964): 143–156.

The most valuable source concerning the rise of the Farmers' Union and its arrival in the Oklahoma and Indian Territories is Robert Lee Hunt's *A History of Farmer Movements in the Southwest, 1873–1925* (College Station: Agricultural and Mechanical College of Texas, 1935). John Thompson's *Closing the Frontier* offers commentary on the Indiahoma Farmers' Union, as does Danney Goble in *Progressive Oklahoma: The Making of a New Kind of State* (Norman: University of Oklahoma, 1980). For additional commentary on agrarian activism in Oklahoma during the first decade of the twentieth century, see Worth Robert Miller, "Building a Progressive Coalition in Texas: The Populist-Reform Democrat Rapprochement, 1900–1907," *Journal of Southern History* 52 (1986): 163–82.

III. RELIGION AND INSURGENCY

At the center of the relationship between fundamentalist Christianity and Oklahoma socialism is the notion that as an institution in society, religion plays a much more complex role than we as interpreters are generally willing to admit. Bruce Laurie's language from *Artisans Into Workers: Labor in Nineteenth-Century America* (New York: Noonday Press, 1989) is helpful here—while organized religion most often serves to confirm the status quo, it on occasion serves the opposite function. This idea was pioneered in E. P. Thompson's *The Making of the English Working* Class (New York: Pantheon Books, 1963), where Thompson portrays religion as both liberating (*Pilgrim's Progress* takes its place beside *The Rights of Man* as a "foundational text" of the working-class movement) and oppressive (as Methodism, in the hands of the enemies of workers, proved to be). Donald Mathews's *Religion in the Old South* (Chicago: University of Chicago Press, 1977) describes the same dynamic. Early American Evangelicalism briefly led to questions about the institution of slavery, yet within a generation, white evangelical Christians used their religious beliefs to defend the institution of slavery.

Presented with this enormous complexity, historians have most often tended to ignore religion's radical potential. Given this circumstance, Herbert G. Gutman's argument that Protestantism inspired workers to protest in the late nineteenth century (presented in "Protestantism and the American Labor Movement: The Christian Spirit in the Gilded Age," *American Historical Review* 72 [1966–1967], 74–101) becomes especially germane. Jean B. Quandt makes a similar argument in "Religion and Social Thought: The Secularization of Postmillennialism," *American Quarterly* 25 (1973): 390–409. Numerous historians have followed suit, several of which bear special mention. H. Richard Niebuhr pioneered the idea of class divisions contributing to denominationalism in *The Social Sources of Denominationalism* (New York: Henry Holt and Company, 1929). Robert C. McMath, in "Populist Base Communities: The Evangelical

Roots of Farm Protest in Texas" (*Locus* 1 [Fall 1988]: 53–63), points to religion's contribution to Populism. In "Pentecostal Politics in Kansas: Religion, the Farmers' Alliance, and the Gospel of Populism" (*Kansas Quarterly* 1 [1969]:24–35), Peter H. Argersinger argues persuasively that Populism "was not only a movement of religious people, but a religious movement of people." Both E. J. Hobsbawm, *Primitive Rebels* (New York: Praeger, 1963) and Liston Pope, *Millhands and Preachers: A Study of Gastonia* (New York: Oxford University Press, 1942) treat insurgent movements in a way that is respectful of religion's influence. Nathan O. Hatch's *The Democratization of American Christianity* (New Haven: Yale University Press, 1989) portrays the religious values of the Second Great Awakening as "profoundly democratic," and Mickey Crews in *The Church of God: A Social History* (Knoxville: University of Tennessee Press, 1990) emphasizes the social/class nature of the Church of God.

IV. WORLD WAR I AND ANTIRADICAL HYSTERIA

Several studies explore the phenomenon of antiradical hysteria in the United States during World War I. The best of these remains Horace C. Peterson and Gilbert C. Fite, *Opponents of War, 1917–1918* (Madison: University of Wisconsin Press, 1957). Also important are Julian F. Jaffe, *Crusade Against Radicalism: New York During the Red Scare, 1914–1924* (Port Washington, N.Y.: Kennikat Press, 1972); and Robert K. Murray, *Red Scare: A Study in National Hysteria, 1919–1920* (Minneapolis: University of Minnesota Press, 1955). David M. Kennedy's *Over Here: The First World War and American Society* (New York: Oxford University Press, 1980) and *Woodrow Wilson and World War I, 1917–1921*, by Robert H. Ferrell (New York: Harper and Row, 1985) examine the many ways America was changed by its experience in the European war. In addition, the following works explore the hysteria of the war years: William J. Breen, *Uncle Sam at Home: Civilian Mobilization,*

Wartime Federalism, and the Council of National Defense, 1917–1919 (Westport, Conn: Greenwood Press, 1984); Paul L. Murphy, *World War I and the Origin of Civil Liberties in the United States* (New York: W. W. Norton, 1979); and Stephen Vaughn, *Holding Fast the Inner Lines: Democracy, Nationalism, and the Committee on Public Information* (Chapel Hill: University of North Carolina Press, 1980). For additional detail on the Socialist Party of America's antiwar position, see Norman Bindler, "American Socialism and the First World War," (Ph.D. diss., New York University, 1970).

A series of articles published in Oklahoma concentrates on the hysteria engendered in the Sooner State during the war. Among these are James H. Fowler II, "Tar and Feather Patriotism: The Suppression of Dissent in Oklahoma During World War One," *Chronicles of Oklahoma* 56 (1978–1979): 409–30; O. A. Hilton, "The Oklahoma Council of Defense and the First World War," *Chronicles of Oklahoma* 20 (1942): 18–42; Michael Morton, "No Time to Quibble: The Jones Conspiracy Trial of 1917," *Chronicles of Oklahoma* 59 (1981–1982): 224–36; James Arthur Robinson, "Loyalty Investigations and Legislation in Oklahoma (master's thesis, University of Oklahoma, 1955); and Sherry Warrick, "Radical Labor in Oklahoma: The Working Class Union," *Chronicles of Oklahoma* 52 (1974): 180–95.

For more on the Green Corn Rebellion, see Charles C. Bush, "The Green Corn Rebellion" (master's thesis, University of Oklahoma, 1932); and Virginia Pope, "The Green Corn Rebellion: A Case Study in Newspaper Self-Censorship" (master's thesis, Oklahoma A and M University, 1940).

Several primary sources provide useful insight into the tumultuous events of 1917 and 1918 in the Sooner State. Most useful of these is the Sam Williams Collection in the Western History Collections, University of Oklahoma. Williams was a county chairman of the War Savings Stamp Committee during these years; his correspondence provides a wealth of information on the war at home. Also important is *Sooners in the War*, published by the Oklahoma

Council of Defense in 1919, and the reports of the Military Intelligence Division of the U.S. Army, compiled by University Publications of America as *U.S. Military Intelligence Reports: Surveillance of Radicals in the United States, 1917–1941.*

V. OKLAHOMA SOCIALIST AND FARMERS' UNION NEWSPAPERS

Agitator (Sayre, Beckham County)
Beckham County Advocate (Carter, Beckham County)
Berlin Herald (Berlin, Roger Mills County)
Boswell Submarine (Boswell, Choctaw County)
Constructive Socialist (Alva, Woods County)
Durant Independent Farmer (Durant, Bryan County)
Ellis County Socialist (Shattuck, Ellis County)
Farmers' Union Advocate
Grant County Socialist (Medford, Grant County)
Hammon Advocate (Hammon, Roger Mills County)
Indiahoma Union Signal (Shawnee, Pottowattomie County)
Industrial Democrat (Oklahoma City, Oklahoma County)
Johnston County Socialist (Tishomingo, Johnston County)
Kay County Populist (Newkirk, Kay County)
Kiowa Breeze (Kiowa County)
Musings of the Old Kuss (Sayre, Beckham County)
Newkirk Populist (Newkirk, Kay County)
Oklahoma Leader (Oklahoma City, Oklahoma County)
Oklahoma Pioneer (Oklahoma City, Oklahoma County)
Oklahoma Socialist (Newkirk, Oklahoma Territory)
Otter Valley Socialist (Snyder, Kiowa County)
Roger Mills Sentinel (Cheyenne, Roger Mills County)
Sayre Citizen (Sayre, Beckham County)
Sayre Social Democrat (Sayre, Beckham County)
Sledge Hammer (Okemah, Okfuskee County)
Social Democrat (Oklahoma City, Oklahoma County)

Socialist Herald (Madill, Marshall County)
Strong City Herald (Strong City, Roger Mills County)
Sulphur New Century (Sulphur, Murray County)
Sword of Truth (Sentinel, Washita County)
Tenant Farmer (Kingfisher, Kingfisher County)
Union Review (Ardmore, Carter County)
Woodrow's Monthly (Hobart, Kiowa County)

Index

Acreage reduction, 29–30, 32, 40
Agricultural crisis, 3, 9–16, 65;
   Democratic Party's response, 106;
   Oklahoma socialist response, 97–98,
   101–103, 106–109. *See also* Crop
   lien; Tenancy
Albert, Carl, 155–56
Allen, J. D., 153
American Indians: Five Civilized Tribes,
   17–18; white settlement of Indian
   lands, 9, 16–19
American Revolution, 66, 186, 196n.4
Ameringer, Oscar, 10–11, 68, 72–73, 83,
   106–107, 109, 170, 173, 175
Appeal to Reason, 63–64, 76, 78, 121
Armstrong, C. H., 73, 75, 83
Aydelotte, J. M., 157

"Baptism of the spirit," 99
Benson, Allan, 140
Berger, Victor, 71, 72, 78, 170, 184,
   207n.19. *See also* "Milwaukee
   Plan"
Blaylock, Ed, 153
Branstetter, Otto, 75, 82, 206n.8,
   208n.50, 209n.70
Brown, Marvin, 75, 83
Bryan, William Jennings, 21, 58

Carter, A. J., 24
Christianity: contributing to the success
   of the Socialist Party of Oklahoma,
7, 86–87, 94–95, 97–104, 185–86;
   used to communicate socialist ideals,
   6–7, 88–91, 185
Christian Socialist Fellowship, 94
"Churches of the disinherited," 98–99,
   215n.60
Clark, Stanley, 79–80, 83, 92–93, 109
Collective marketing. *See* Crop
   withholding
Communist Manifesto, 63, 196n.4
Congress for Progressive Political
   Action, 174
Connors, J. B., 26, 53
Cooperative stores, 34–35, 38, 180. *See
   also* Farmers Alliance
Corley, J. W. L., 53
Councils of defense, 157–65. *See also*
   European War (1914–1918)
Credit, 15. *See also* Usury
Crop lien, 14–15, 18, 197n.11
Crop prices: and crop withholding, 28,
   33, 36, 45–46, 187–91; decline in, 3,
   10, 13, 125, 145–46
Crop withholding, 28–29, 33–36, 40,
   45–46, 56, 85, 179, 187–91, 202n.18.
   See also Indiahoma Farmers' Union
Cruce, Lee, 56
Cumbie, J. Tad, 70, 79, 95, 153, 193
Currie, John A., 87, 101

Davis, G. W. (Pap), 75, 83
Dawes General Allotment Act, 18

Daws, S. O.: appointment as Oklahoma State Librarian, 59, 206n.4; controversy with Thomas B. Tobin, 52–54; cooperation with the Democratic Party in 1908, 59–60; editor of the *Indiahoma Union Signal*, 43, 52; president of the Indiahoma Farmers' Union, 22–23, 24–26, 34–38, 42, 48–49; removal by large landowners, 53–55, 184; "traveling lecturer" in the Farmers Alliance, 22
Debs, Eugene Victor, 88, 103, 121, 122, 172, 215n.61
Declaration of Independence, 8, 196n.4
DeLeon, Daniel, 62
Democratic Party, 85; anti-socialist New Election Law (1916), 133–41, 167; criticized by socialists, 96–97, 101; disfranchisement of blacks, 114–16, 132–33, 221n.94; and the Indiahoma Farmers' Union, 24–25, 55–58; the party of the agricultural and business elite, 56, 105–107, 217n.3; responses to the Socialist Party, 109–13, 129–31; "secret plan" of 1908, 58–60; use of wartime repression against the Socialist Party, 153–54, 166–67, 178
Durant, Okla., 88

Edge, J. C., 152
Enfield, O. E., 87, 95, 103–104, 164, 171, 193, 215n.57
Espionage and Sedition Acts, 161–62, 164
European War (1914–1918), 8, 141, 146–50; causing falling cotton prices, 125, 145–46; sparking hysteria in the United States, 154–68

Farmer-Labor Reconstruction League, 174–76
Farmers Alliance, 20–21, 40, 54, 197–98n.1, 198n.3, 212–13n.28;

contributing to the Indiahoma Farmers' Union, 22, 23, 25, 39, 179–80, 199n.12; contributing to the Socialist Party of Oklahoma, 4–5, 7, 179, 199n.12; cooperative stores, 34–35, 41–42; and the election of 1896, 20–21, 56, 204n.52; and the Great Southwestern Strike, 25; insight on agricultural issues, 5, 20; in the Oklahoma Territory, 23–24; Texas Exchange, 35, 42, 201n.44
Farmers' Educational and Cooperative Union. *See* National Farmers' Union
Farmers' Union. *See* Indiahoma Farmers' Union; National Farmers' Union
Farmers' Union clearing houses. *See* Indiahoma Farmers' Union, clearing house system
Fisk, O. A., 152
Fowler, George, 100–101, 102
Fundamentalism, 98–100, 215n.60
Furnishing merchant, 13–14, 29, 35, 38, 135, 180, 181

"Grafting" of Indian lands, 18
"Great American Desert," 17
Great Revival, 7, 212–13n.28
Green Corn Rebellion, 150–53, 170
Gresham, Newt, 21

Hagel, John, 175
Hamilton, George G., 95, 193
Hampton, Sam, 21–22, 23, 212n.25
Harlow, Victor, 129–30, 141, 152, 168
Harriman, Job, 65
Harrison, J. W., 24, 26, 202n.9
Haskell, Charles, 56
Hickey, Thomas A. ("Red Tom"), 82, 209n.69. *See also* "Texas Plan"
Hicks, William Madison, 164
Hillquit, Morris, 96
Hogan, Dan, 175
Holt, Fred W., 126–27
Homestead Act, 68

Houchin, J. W., 55
Hubbard, Wood, 219n.50
Hutton, George W., 95, 194

Indiahoma Farmers' Union: clearing house system, 36–39, 51, 56, 85, 179–80, 201n.51; coal purchasing plan, 41–43, 51; crop withholding, 28–36, 40, 45–46, 56, 144, 179, 187–91, 202n.18; Daws/Tobin controversy, 52–54; debate over aiding or participating in strikes, 25–26; decline in 1907, 57, 175; formation in Shawnee, Okla., 22; insight on agricultural issues, 39, 179–80; large landowner/working farmer split, 26–27, 29, 31, 39, 46–47, 52–57, 85; membership figures, 55, 57, 204–205n.56; migration of members into the Socialist Party of Oklahoma, 4, 57, 60–61, 64, 180, 205n.57; "overproduction debate," 29–33; participation in politics, 55–57; role in the rise of the Socialist Party of Oklahoma, 4–5, 7, 57, 60–61, 63–64, 72, 77, 83, 85, 175, 179–84, 209–10n.73; separate Indian Territory Union, 36, 47–51, 203n.28; Tishomingo Convention, 30–33, 51, 184
Indiahoma Union Signal, 43–45, 52–55, 77, 184
Indian Territory, 4, 17–19, 47–48
Indian Territory Farmers' Union, 36, 47–51, 184, 203nn.28,36
Industrial Democrat, 72–77, 83
Industrial Workers of the World, 26, 152, 156–57, 209n.73

Jefferson, Thomas, 58, 66, 70, 97, 183, 196n.4. *See also* Jeffersonian democracy
Jeffersonian democracy: and the Farmers' Alliance, 5, 20, 21; and the Farmers' Union, 5, 21, 22–23, 39, 179–80; and the Socialist Party of Oklahoma, 7, 67, 105, 196n.4; and yeoman farmers, 5, 12, 180–81
Jennings, Al, 223n.9
Jesus Christ, 8, 87, 100, 101, 196n.4; celebrated as a socialist hero, 89–90, 212n.25
Johnson, Leonard, 70, 95, 194

Keltner, J. H., 24
King, R. D., 21

Literacy test and grandfather clause, 114–16, 121, 131–32

Marx, Karl, 7, 8, 57, 70, 87, 90–91, 96, 97, 183, 196n.4; and religion, 211n.3
Marxism: anti-agrarian bias, 65, 180–81; class struggle, 88, 97–98, 101, 115, 120, 183; influence on the Indiahoma Farmers' Union, 23, 63; influence on the Socialist Party of Oklahoma, 7–8, 66, 97–98, 125, 148, 181–83, 186, 196n.4
McLemore, Thomas H., 95, 194
McNabb, L. C., 142–44, 223n.5
Merchant. *See* Furnishing merchant
Milner, H. Grady, 70, 97, 118
"Milwaukee Plan," 71–72, 76–78, 80. *See also* Berger, Victor
Moore, J. S., 24, 26–27, 30, 31
Mounts, N. S., 90, 97, 147–48, 156
Munson, H. H., 150, 224n.29
Murray, William H., 26, 30–33, 34, 40, 47–51, 55, 56, 203n.22, 205n.1, 224n.25

Nagle, Patrick S., 79, 108, 112, 170, 175, 224n.38
National Farmers' Union, 4–5, 7, 49, 203n.28; expansion to Oklahoma and Indian Territories, 21–22; formation in Texas, 21. *See also* Indiahoma Farmers' Union
Niebuhr, H. Richard, 98, 214–15n.56

O'Hare, Kate Richards, 228n.120
Oklahoma Pioneer, 73–77, 79–81, 83, 184
Oklahoma state constitution, 59, 72–73, 131, 177
Oklahoma State Federation of Labor, 60, 74
Oklahoma Territory, 4, 13, 17–19, 47
Owen, George E., 79, 153
Owen, Robert, 110, 127, 129–30

Panic of 1907, 45–46
Pentecostal-Holiness Church, Oklahoma Conference, 94–95
People's Party, 20–21, 23; in the Oklahoma Territory, 24
Populism. *See* Farmers Alliance

Ransom, Roger and Richard Sutch, 15
Religion. *See* Christianity
Renters' Union, 69–70, 95, 208nn.37,38
Republican Party, 85, 101, 167–68; and blacks, 115, 119–21; charges of fusion with the Socialist Party of Oklahoma, 120, 219–20n.56; electoral gains in 1908, 58, 114, 159; losing second–party status to the Socialist Party of Oklahoma, 122, 125
Rip Saw, 78, 131
Roll, Okla., 87, 91, 95, 171–72
Roosevelt, Theodore, 43
Russell, Campbell, 25, 26, 31–32, 34, 40, 53, 55, 56, 204n.55

Scientific farming, 30–33, 40, 200–201n.31
Sedition Act. *See* Espionage and Sedition Acts
Sermon on the Mount, 196n.4
Shawnee, Okla., 22, 43, 47, 50, 80–81, 109
Simons, Algie Martin, 65–66
Sinclair, H. M., 80–81, 82, 126, 151–52, 165, 222n.114, 224n.38, 228n.120, 229n.7

Social Gospel, 215n.61
Socialist encampments, 91, 104, 121–22, 148, 173
Socialist Labor Party, 62–63
Socialist Party campaign book, 1916, 107–108, 110–11
Socialist Party of America: position on agricultural issues, 65–66, 69, 207n.32; response to the European War (1914–1918), 146–47, 227n.102
Socialist Party of Oklahoma: attacked by the Democratic Party, 96, 109–12, 130–31; and blacks, 116–21, 219n.54; blamed for the Green Corn Rebellion, 151–53; commitment to Marxism, 7–8, 66, 97–98, 104, 119–20, 125, 148, 182–83, 229–30n.8; debate on agricultural issues, 5, 64–69, 180–83; decentralization of organizational authority, 70–83, 183–84; democratic nature of internal decision-making process, 5–6, 7, 183–84; and the Democratic New Election Law, 133–41; electoral success (1912–1914), 122–28; Fair Election Law, 131–32, 136–37, 139–41, 153, 167, 177–78; formation in the Oklahoma Territory, 62–63; opposition to the literacy test and grandfather clause, 115–16; religious nature of, 6–7, 86–104, 185–86; response to the agricultural crisis, 97–98, 101–103, 106–109; response to the European War (1914–1918), 147–49, 168–71; sophistication on agricultural issues, 5, 7, 70, 179–83, 184–85; victim of electoral fraud, 112–13, 137–40, 166–67, 177, 222nn.112,114, 229n.7; victim of wartime repression, 153–69, 172–74, 176, 178
Spence, J. Homer, 150, 224n.29
Stallard, H. H., 79, 117, 168, 171
Street buyers, 13, 37, 181
Sword of Truth, 88, 96

Tenancy, 10–12, 15, 18–19, 105, 134, 137, 140–41, 217n.2
Texas Exchange, 35, 42, 201n.44. *See also* Farmers Alliance
"Texas Plan," 82. *See also* Hickey, Thomas A. ("Red Tom")
Thurmond, J. C., 155
Tishomingo, Okla., 30–33, 51, 184, 201n.39
Tobin, Thomas B., 52–54

Usury, 101–102, 143. *See also* Agricultural crisis; Credit

Walton, Jack, 174–75
Ward, Robert J., 24–25
Williams, Robert L., 106–11, 132, 135, 152, 155, 218n.40
Wilson, Woodrow, 118, 146, 149, 151, 169, 215n.61
Wood, Jack, 109, 112
Woodrow, Thomas W., 94
Working Class Union, 142–45, 149, 150–52
World War I. *See* European War (1914–1918)

www.ingramcontent.com/pod-product-compliance
Lightning Source LLC
Chambersburg PA
CBHW020749160426
43192CB00006B/285